PG-II-186

PG-II-186

Geographical Perspectives and Urban Problems

A Symposium organized by the
Committee on Geography
of the Division of Earth Sciences
NATIONAL ACADEMY OF SCIENCES

September 20 and 21, 1971
Washington, D.C.

NATIONAL ACADEMY OF SCIENCES
Washington, D.C. 1973

NOTICE: The symposium at which these papers were read was sponsored by the Committee on Geography of the National Academy of Sciences and held on September 20 and 21, 1971, in Washington, D.C. The participants in the symposium were selected for their scholarly competence and for the particularly relevant specialty that enabled them to contribute to the exposition of the subject under discussion. The participants were responsible for their own papers, and the views expressed were their own.

Available from
Printing and Publishing Office
National Academy of Sciences
2101 Constitution Avenue
Washington, D.C. 20418

Library of Congress Cataloging in Publication Data

Main entry under title:

Geographical perspectives and urban problems.

"A symposium organized by the Committee on Geography of the Division of Earth Sciences, National Academy of Sciences, September 20 and 21, 1971, Washington, D.C."
  Includes bibliographies.
  1. Cities and towns—United States—Congresses.
I. National Research Council. Committee on Geography.
HT123.G44   301.36'3'0973   72-13487
ISBN 0-309-02106-5

Printed in the United States of America

Preface

The translation of basic research into usable material for public and private policy development and decision making is an important responsibility of the academic community. Although not all members of a particular discipline may feel inclined to perform this function, some should. A discipline that dwells primarily on its own internal problems to the exclusion of problems that are important to society as a whole will stagnate and become irrelevant to the current needs of society and the nation.

For many years, urban geographers have focused on major issues confronting metropolitan areas in this country and elsewhere. It is urgent that they now interact with federal and local agencies in an effort to define, evaluate, and help to overcome specific urban problems. It is important, too, that geographers receive feedback from such agencies on the utility of theoretical, methodological, and applied research currently being conducted or contemplated. With these aims in mind, the Committee on Geography of the National Academy of Sciences decided to hold a symposium centering on the research activities of urban geographers in an effort to initiate a dialogue between those geographers and the public agencies responsible for shaping and implementing urban policy and planning.

Through the efforts of Dr. John Borchert, Chairman of the Committee on Geography, and Dr. Arch Gerlach, a member of the Committee on Geography and Chief Geographer of the U.S. Geological Survey, planning for the proposed urban geography symposium was set in motion. An *ad hoc* committee, consisting of Drs. Borchert, Gerlach, Leslie King, and Frank Horton, defined the nature and content of the symposium, which was entitled "Geographical Perspectives and Urban Problems." One of the hardest tasks of this committee was to choose the participants from among the many excellent geographers who were interested in urban affairs. It was encouraging that all those contacted consented to participate, and the two-day symposium was interesting and informative. About 250 persons from federal and local agencies and representatives of a broad range of disciplines attended the symposium, which was held on September 20 and 21, 1971, in Washington, D.C.

The papers presented at the symposium form the text of this monograph. John R. Borchert and Frank E. Horton, in their paper, "Geography and Public Policy," illustrate several ways in which geographers interpret and conceptualize urban issues and processes. They identify the nature of some urban problems and the role geographers can play in planning and implementing practical solutions. After citing specific projects involving the fruitful collaboration of geographers with urban policy makers and administrators, the authors turn their attention to the general problem of urban-policy development and its application to specific cities.

Spatial analysis and its implications for urban-policy planning are the bases for Peter Gould's paper. He demonstrates the manner in which spatial analysis can provide insight useful in solving critical problems, for example, the relation of income level and severity of hunger, of housing purchases and differential flows of information about supply and demand, and the location of hospitals, schools, social-welfare-service offices, and other facilities to maximize services to the people.

Julian Wolpert's paper, prepared jointly with Anthony

Mumphrey and John Seley, examines changes in land use at the community level as a function of interplay among the community's residents, outsiders, and city administrators. Changes in the location of activities within the community result from the considered actions of these participants. It is Wolpert's contention that certain planning activities are most effectively addressed at the community level; these activities might include elimination of undesired activities, maintenance of existing properties, prevention of entry of noxious facilities, and attracting desired services. Conflict among the community's residents, outsiders, and administrators over land-use change involves a struggle for control over these activities.

The significance of knowledge concerning the relation of the physical environment to human settlement and culture is considered by M. Gordon Wolman. One of his major themes is that although much information about the natural world is relevant to the design of cities, we are only using a fraction of the useful information already available. Wolman skillfully illustrates the significance to planning of physical characteristics of the land and of the processes that take place on the land. He also discusses the interrelated problems of water and land, the climate of cities, and attributes of landscape.

Integrated regional planning is increasingly necessary because urbanization in America has produced an intricate web of economic and other interactions among cities. Leslie J. King finds that the state of our knowledge of the nature and significance of this interdependence, however, is at present inadequate for a totally integrated approach. He briefly reviews selected aspects of geography's contribution to understanding economic change in urban systems and describes work under way that seems likely to provide a better understanding of interurban processes and methods useful in their analysis.

Richard L. Morrill reviews the evolution of settlement polarization—metropolitan concentration and rural decline—and assesses the impact of this process on future population distributions. He compares alternatives to the continuation of present trends toward metropolitanization, such as rural economic growth, and the development of new intermediate-sized metropoles and discusses their advantages, disadvantages, and costs. Morrill concludes by outlining a mixed strategy that he thinks is the most effective and realistic.

The final paper, by Brian J. L. Berry, focuses on new and emerging forms of urbanization in the United States and on policy problems arising from changes in the nature of urbanization processes and the scale and pattern of urban life. In his discussion, Berry emphasizes the impact of new forms of communication and the needs for and consequences of different modes of private and public intervention. The paper discusses trends apparent from the analysis of the 1970 Census and earlier data.

These seven presentations should not be construed to be an exhaustive review of geographic contributions in urban research. Recent commercial and professional publications more adequately perform that function. Nor are these papers pointed as much toward the professional geographer as toward planners, policy makers, and decision makers. We who were involved in this effort hope that this short volume will encourage its readers to explore more thoroughly the substantive work of urban geographers.

I should like to thank all the participants for their contribution: the National Academy of Sciences and its Committee on Geography for its help and cooperation; the National Science Foundation and the Geographic Applications Program of the U.S. Geological Survey for their financial support; and Mr. Walter Bailey, Executive Secretary of the Committee on Geography, and his staff for their help in making the symposium a success and facilitating the publication of this monograph. Finally, I should like to thank Mrs. Muriel Duggan, Earth Sciences Division Editor for her help and cooperation during the publication effort.

FRANK E. HORTON
Symposium Chairman and Editor
University of Iowa
Iowa City
October 1971

COMMITTEE ON GEOGRAPHY

JOHN R. BORCHERT, *Chairman;* University of Minnesota

WALTER H. BAILEY, Executive Secretary

ROBERT DOLAN, University of Virginia

ARCH C. GERLACH, U.S. Geological Survey

PRESTON E. JAMES, Syracuse University

CLYDE P. PATTON, University of Oregon

EDWARD J. TAAFFE, The Ohio State University

ROBERT J. VOSKUIL, Central Intelligence Agency

We announce with regret the untimely passing of ARCH C. GERLACH, Chief Geographer of the U.S. Geological Survey, on May 20, 1972, at the age of 61. The architect and editor of the National Atlas of the United States, he was a member of the Committee on Geography of the National Academy of Sciences, which conceived and planned this symposium. We wish he had lived to see this volume completed.

Contents

GEOGRAPHY AND URBAN PUBLIC POLICY   1
   John R. Borchert and Frank E. Horton

GEOGRAPHIC EXPOSITION, INFORMATION, AND LOCATION   25
   Peter Gould

COMMUNITY DISCRETION OVER NEIGHBORHOOD CHANGE   41
   Julian Wolpert, Anthony Mumphrey, and John Seley

THE PHYSICAL ENVIRONMENT AND URBAN PLANNING   55
   M. Gordon Wolman

SPATIAL PERSPECTIVES ON ECONOMIC CHANGE AMONG AMERICAN CITIES   71
   Leslie J. King

FUNDAMENTAL ISSUES CONCERNING FUTURE SETTLEMENT IN AMERICA   81
   Richard L. Morrill

CONTEMPORARY URBANIZATION PROCESSES   94
   Brian J. L. Berry

Geography and Urban Public Policy

JOHN R. BORCHERT
University of Minnesota
FRANK E. HORTON
University of Iowa

For several decades, geographers in America have played a leading role in the study of the changing location of urban places and urban activities (Mayer, 1965; Berry, 1965; Ginsberg, 1965; Berry and Horton, 1971; Bourne, 1971). Although not all contemporary urban problems have dominant, or even significant, spatial components, many of them do, and a geographic perspective is often important in developing and evaluating alternative approaches to the problems and in helping to anticipate and avoid future difficulties.

GEOGRAPHIC CHANGE AND PROBLEMS OF URBANIZED SOCIETY

One of the principal reasons for geography's importance in urban studies is its traditional basic concern with the spatial system of human settlement (Taaffe, 1970; Bunge, 1962; Ackerman and others, 1965; MacKinnon, 1970, pp. 350–366). The structure of the settlement system includes aggregations of resources, of man and his works, and the web of connecting routes. The flows through this structure, the changes in it, and particularly the geographic variations in the rate and kind of change provide the raw material for the study of process. Geographical maps portray the system of human settlement; maps of distributions over time portray the process of evolution of that settlement.

Furthermore, regions, routes, nodes, and flows—in continuous process of change—are an aggregate expression of human decisions, technology, behavior, and values. They are one set of reflections of our aspirations for personal and general welfare, the division of labor and functional specialization, social inequality, unequal distribution of natural resources, and the technology of transportation and industry.

In a sense the structure and flows of the settlement system resemble a vast integrated machine whose purpose is to facilitate the human use of the earth. Our nation's cities are nodes in a circulation system that links all of America's diverse resource regions and many more across the world. On a map of a metropolis the circulation network links every kind of land use or activity center. Because our activities and the problems and issues associated with them are distributed throughout the settlement system, geography should play an important role in both the management of these activities and the formulation of public and private policy.

The human settlement system is open and constantly disturbed by changes in the resource base, in knowledge, and in custom. Perhaps the most important source of new energy is the frequent but irregular eruption of new knowledge and ideas within a system of any geographic scale. As the accumulation of man's knowledge grows in size and diversity, there is always the chance and the necessity for new combinations of data, for new and disruptive knowledge within the settlement system. As a result, new configurations keep emerging: new functional specialties, new transportation and industrial technologies, and new evaluations of resources (Berry and Neils, 1969). One has only to try to use the enormous array of existing data banks to see the endlessly unfolding problem of even classifying and describing these configurations.

The changes within these open systems have two especially important characteristics. They are localized in time and place, and they are essentially unpredictable in time and place, except at very short range.

Initiation and adoption of a change occurs in one element of the urban settlement system at a specific time and place (Brown, 1968), creating a sudden increase in the rate of obsolescence or change in aspirations in other parts of the system. Because change is not instantaneous throughout the spatial system, lags develop in certain countries, regions, or cities. Trends become inconsistent or conflicting, goals become confused, and problems and hardships, both real and imaginary, emerge.

Outstanding examples of these lags and the resulting problems in urban America today occur in matters of housing, waste management, local government organization, poverty, and racism.

MIDWEST CASE STUDY

In the Midwest, where we have done much of our work, illustrations abound of the nature of these lags, of some of the approaches that society has taken toward their correction, and of some of the potential contribution of geographic information. In the Midwest, as elsewhere in the nation, the nature of the region is changing rapidly.

Minnesota and its regional metropolis, Minneapolis-St. Paul, are dealt with in one case study. They have attracted national attention for their innovative approaches to the control of piecemeal municipal incorporation through the Minnesota Municipal Commission, and to guidance of metropolitan development through the Twin Cities Metropolitan Council (*City,* 1971; *National Civic Review,* 1969; *HUD Challenge,* 1971; Beckman, 1970). These accomplishments have been the chief manifestations of a much wider array of actions directed toward reforming both governmental organization and public policy during a period of revolutionary urbanization. We review here the nature of recent geographical changes in the settlement pattern, the insights that the community has gained from the study of these changes, and subsequent community actions.

THE MINNEAPOLIS-ST. PAUL AREA

The maps in Figures 1 and 2 show the main outlines of the Twin Cities settlement pattern on the eve of the post-World War II era (Borchert, 1961, pp. 47-70). Four distinct density classes existed in the residential regions. The highest-density core areas were dominated by multiple dwellings. Population per square mile in the four density zones averages approximately 400, 2,000, 5,500, and 9,000 respectively.

Major railway-industrial belts appear in Figure 2. An intercity corridor joined the two central business districts at the historic river port at St. Paul and at the water-power site at Minneapolis (Borchert and Yaeger, 1969, p. 197, and supplementary land-use map of Twin Cities). Additional radial corridors, following belts of flatland either along the Mississippi or tributary to it, radiated toward the northern Great Plains and Pacific Northwest, Chicago, and the mid-continent.

The principal blue-collar residential districts adjoined the rail-industrial corridors, and commuter-residential spokes pointed away from the central business districts and trackage-industrial zones. Major variables explaining the directional growth of these white-collar residential spokes were flatland and extension of the streetcar network for middle-income, high-density areas and wooded rolling lakeshore land near commuter rail lines for low-density areas (Borchert and Yaeger, 1969, pp. 202-204).

THE POST-WORLD WAR II BUILDING BOOM— CONSERVATION OF DIRECTIONAL BIAS

In the unprecedented residential building boom that followed World War II, roughly between 1946 and 1958 (Figure 3), the locational decisions of developers and new residents were essentially extrapolated from the trends and the thinking of the streetcar and flatland constraints of preceding eras. In fact, an analysis showed that the aggregate behavior of these developers and settlers was highly predictable from 1900-1940 trends, with the necessary adjustment for larger numbers and larger average lot size. A simple graphic procedure could have correctly predicted the location of 81 percent of the actual new square miles of high-density development, and 95 percent of the new square miles forecast actually developed (Borchert, 1961; Borchert and Carroll, 1961; Morrill, 1965b; Harvey, 1967; Tobler, 1970). Comparable percentage scores in the medium- and low-density classes were 86 and 88, 71 and 78, respectively. The postwar boom brought a massive extension of the flatland spokes of residential development and expansion of low-density development near already well-known lakes and within the historic city-to-lake corridors where early rail and trolley-car commuter service had operated (Figure 4) (Adams, 1969). Although more than two thirds of the high-density expansion remained on flatland, low-density growth was attracted mainly to rough or rolling land. Industry also expanded mainly in the traditional railway belts that included the

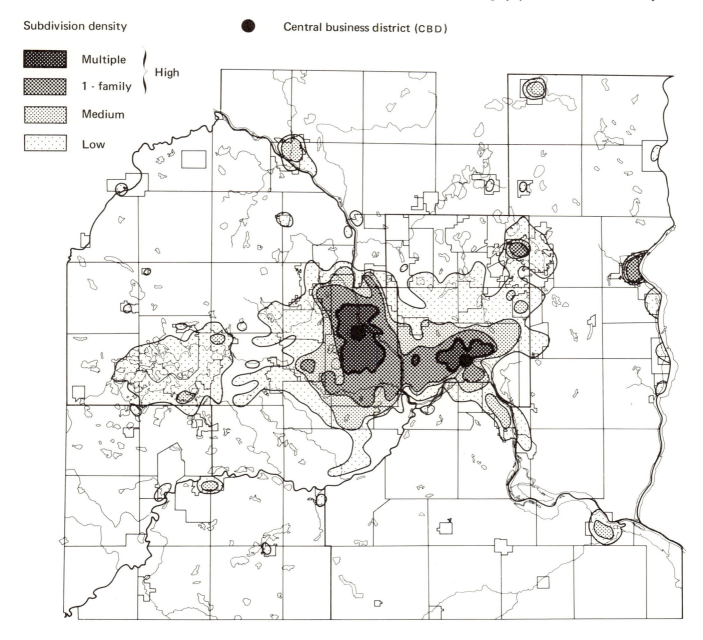

FIGURE 1 Subdivided area, 1940. The two densely settled areas adjoin the central business districts of Minneapolis (west) and St. Paul (east). The Mississippi River crosses the map area from northwest to southeast. The Minnesota River enters the metropolitan area from the southwest. The large isolated low-density area west of Minneapolis surrounds Lake Minnetonka, with roughly 200 mi of shore. Distance from southwest corner to southeast corner of map is 50 mi. (From Borchert, 1961.)

land around the fringes of the central business districts.

The net result of these growth patterns was to exaggerate the historic pattern of spokes and interstices that was a legacy from the railroad and streetcar era and to lead to a crisis in the congestion of historic arterial streets and roads that formed the spines of the major development sectors. An exaggeration of the historic bias toward suburban growth on the Minneapolis side of the metropolis was also a legacy from the railroad era, when the more westerly of the two centers had an advantage in commercial dealings with the metropolitan hinterland in the northern plains and northern Rockies.

In short, the localization of the postwar building boom tended to be inconsistent with some major contemporary

4 GEOGRAPHICAL PERSPECTIVES AND URBAN PROBLEMS

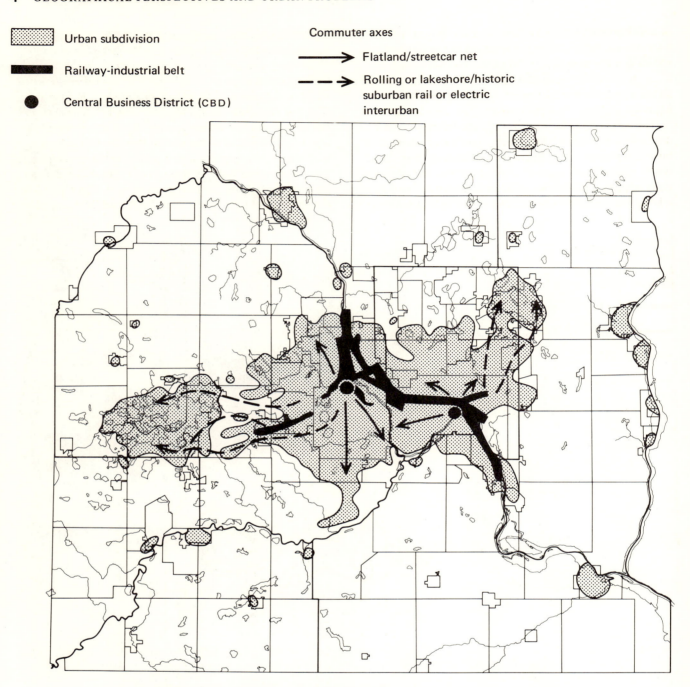

FIGURE 2 Industrial districts and residential spokes, 1940. (From Bochert, 1961.)

realities. It reflected streetcar technology in the era of the automobile and flatland technology in the era of the bulldozer and latent explosive demand for site amenities. It also continued to ignore large areas of undeveloped relatively accessible site amenities on the St. Paul side of the metropolitan fringe.

THE FREEWAY ERA—RESTRUCTURING THE METROPOLIS

The freeway epoch, from 1958 to the present time, has brought the first full impact of automotive transportation and modern earth-moving equipment on the spatial pattern of development (Figure 5) (Horwood and Boyce, 1959; Garrison and others, 1966). Reduction of the flatland constraint and the ubiquity of the paved-road network led to deemphasis of the spoke-like pattern of growth. It also led to the well-known reduction of residential density and the highway- and amenity-orientation of new developments.

The circumferential expressways and freeways created multiple new nodes in the metropolitan fringe where they intersected major radial highways and railway lines. As a result, new major centers of commercial and industrial activity appeared in outlying areas to drastically alter the relative locations and comparative advantages of both the historic central business districts and, more drastically still, the old suburban retail centers and the strips along the former streetcar arterials.

A geography research team made a detailed comparative study of the oldest of these belt expressways and the parallel, but more remote, route of the new belt freeway on the western side of the metropolis (Borchert, 1960; Fielding, 1968). The study emphasized that the new freeway was only one among five major factors in the developmental process, along with the developers of residential and nonresidential projects, the local governments, which put down the network of streets, sewer, and water utilities, and the

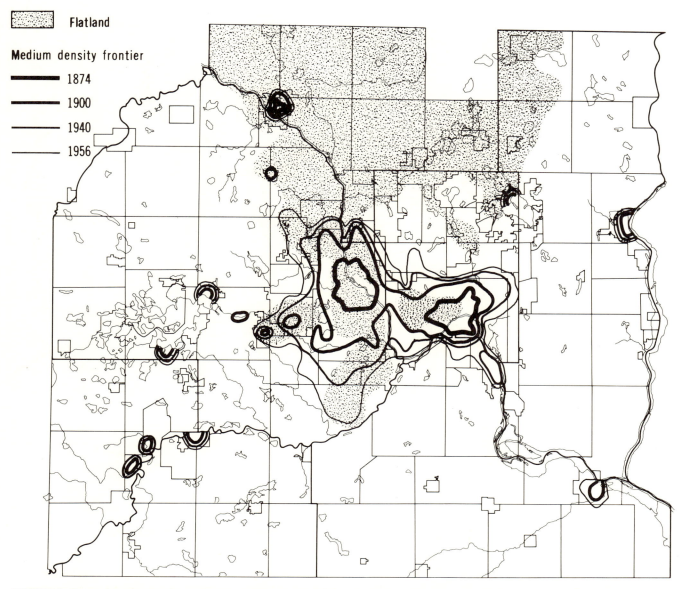

FIGURE 3 Expansion of medium-density subdivision, 1874–1956. Persistence of distinctive rates and directions of growth in different sectors of the metropolitan area is evident. (From Borchert, 1961.)

railroads. The researchers pointed out the distinctly different planning and development problems that had accompanied different chronological and geographical relations between the highway department and these other development agents in different segments along the older expressway; it then projected those experiences to the new freeway as the basis for policy. The analysis demonstrated numerous points of lasting importance; Borchert remarks, for example (1960, pp. 4–5):

If the highway comes late in the developmental sequence, it is impossible to avoid disruption of an established urban land-use pattern. Then planning . . . must be directed toward retention of values, adjustment, and redevelopment. If the highway comes early in the sequence, municipal and private planning may be directed toward reservation of vacant land and provision of facilities for the highest-value, most desirable, or most essential uses in the most probable locations.

These variations in sequence and timing stem in large part from the fact that various agents in the development process are operating with basically different geographical ideas. The concern of residential developers, municipalities, and their residents has been local. Their task has been the expansion of the metropolis along one small segment of the frontier. Their geographical frame of reference has been

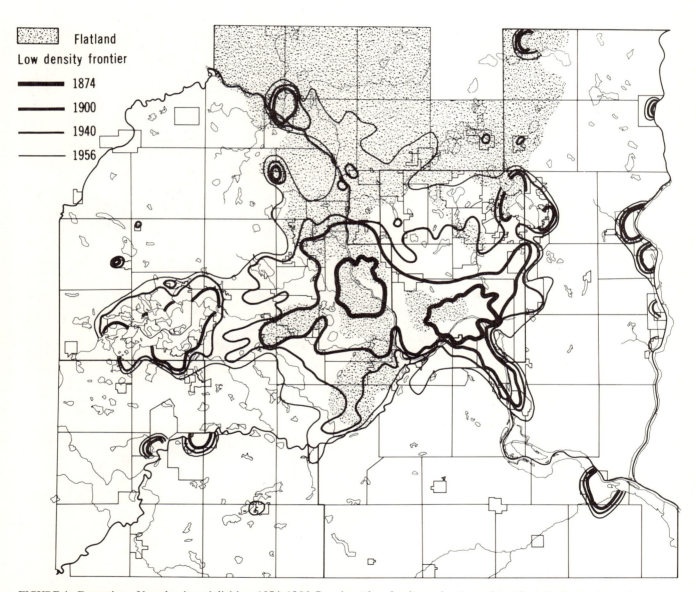

FIGURE 4 Expansion of low-density subdivision, 1874–1956. Prominent low-density spokes to northeast from St. Paul and west from Minneapolis reflect the pull of major lakes. (From Borchert, 1961.)

the neighborhood or the municipality. The major objective of the railway or highway builder has been interstate or intercity movement.

To the municipality and the developers the city has been the "universe." To railway and highway builders the city has often been a large "place" to be connected with many other distant and equally important "places." Each group represents an important point of view held by a large segment of the public. Each group must understand the geographical frame of reference and point of view of the other if there is to be an agreed plan of development in any community bordering a major highway.

The report pointed out that the new freeway would be introduced at an early stage in the developmental process, and it made consequent policy recommendations for both the highway department and the bordering municipalities.

The study opened by establishing analogies between the new freeway and the older parallel expressway in terms of intersecting radial corridors and position relative to the low- and medium-density frontiers. Within that framework, it presented an inventory of development along the older expressway at several points in time, using aerial photographs

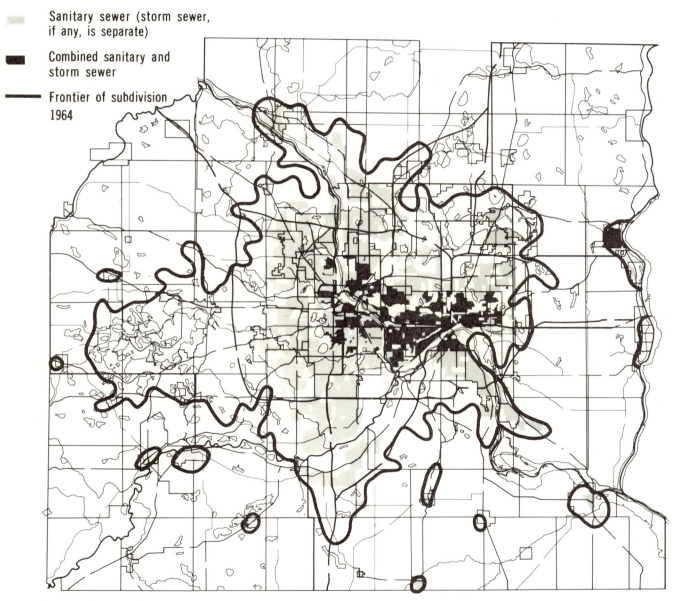

FIGURE 5 Central sewerage systems, 1966, and outer boundary of low-density subdivision, 1964. Comparison of the low-density frontier position in 1964 with 1940 (Figure 4) shows deemphasis of spokes of growth and fill-in of interstitial open land in the 1960s. Map also shows lag of sewer extension behind subdivision expansion. (From Borchert and Yaeger, 1969.)

and fieldwork; projected further development against the ceiling of available land and thus estimated "surplus" pressure for growth along the older route; and then transferred the surplus to the newer freeway route.

On this basis, a forecast of nonresidential land development was prepared for the freeway corridor 1 mi wide, and acreages were allocated to specific grids according to an order of location and site desirability. A verification study was made by students 10 years later, in 1970, nearly 5 years after the opening of the new circumferential freeway. Actual developed acres equalled 90 percent of the forecast amount for that date for commercial purposes and 76 percent for industrial purposes; developments were within the parts of the strip that had been indicated as most likely target areas.

THE LOCAL-GOVERNMENT PUZZLE

As they did in other urban areas, many public institutions remained static while the metropolis changed so drastically in size and structure. The major set of problems arose because the functional metropolis expanded across the boundaries of more than 100 independent units of general local government. Many of these units were unprepared to manage their affairs when the wave of urban expansion reached them. Particularly stubborn management difficulties arose because most local officials could not easily think of various problems on different geographical scales—regional, metropolitan, local—and act as metropolitan citizens where metropolitan decisions were needed. The officials reflected the perceptions and fears of their constituents, and they were frustrated by the lack of any metropolitan organization.

One major result of these difficulties was fragmentation of management responsibility for government services among many different political-geographic units (Mayer and Kohn, 1959; Berry, 1965; Mayer, 1965; Murphy, 1966; Yeates and Garner, 1971). This meant that land was often zoned incompatibly on opposite sides of a street or of a thin line that separated two municipalities. There were a few long-standing classic cases of this problem along the Minneapolis–St. Paul boundary, but the cases increased and spread quickly during the 1950s. Vast unsewered populations and development areas appeared on the map (Figure 5). Some municipalities did not have the management or the public understanding of the problem to get the facilities built, and neighboring municipalities that already had sewer services were reluctant or ill-equipped to serve their neighbors. There was also minimal and uncoordinated preservation of open space (Figure 6). The map indicates that for more than half a century the urban frontier had expanded with no significant addition to public open space until the first county park board was organized. A study then called attention to the existing and future geography of parks in the area as it had evolved by the mid-1950s and as it could be by 1980 if appropriate action were taken (Doell and Daihnin, 1958).

A second major result of the lag in local-government reorganization was increasing inequity in the property-tax base. Municipalities varied by a factor as large as 10 in their assessed valuation per school pupil. Equally great differences existed in ability to finance public services and improvements of all kinds between one local unit and another. These inequities were widely publicized and were compared with the maps of residential and industrial expansion to bring wider understanding of the cause of the problem and to help indicate that the development pattern did not and could not match the pattern of local need for tax-supported services.

There has consequently been a gradual increase in the proportion of the voters who see that geographically spreading industrial and commercial development is not a feasible solution to the problems of fiscal inequities, that only a change in the tax distribution scheme or consolidation of local governments will meet the fiscal need. Meanwhile, there is also increased awareness of the need for smaller political entities that recognize the coherence of neighborhood groups in terms of income, occupations, or social-cultural interests. In other words, just as a need emerged for a widely available geographic description and interpretation of the metropolitan settlement pattern, now a need is emerging for a dynamic description and understanding of the internal cultural regionalization of the metropolis [Palm (in preparation)].

Meanwhile, measures have been taken to compensate for these lags of institutional change behind physical and technologic change. In the late 1950s the state legislature created the Metropolitan Planning Commission and the Hennepin County Park Reserve District in its first formal recognition of the need for coordinated action (Altschuler, 1965), and the Minneapolis–St. Paul Sanitary Sewer District made its first large-scale study of metropolitan sewerage needs and plans for meeting them (Schroepfer, 1960). A decade later, in the late 1960s, the legislature converted the Planning Commission to the Metropolitan Council. The Council had broad review and regulatory powers over special districts and agencies operating services that included transportation and health facilities for the whole metropolitan area. The legislature also created a Metropolitan Sewer Board with planning, financing, and operating powers. During the years that followed, community councils and the Metropolitan Federation have organized in the private sector to coordinate and articulate the work and the interests of neighborhood groups in the central-city and metropolitan-governmental arena. The 1971 legislature also passed a landmark bill that takes 40 percent of all new nonresidential, property-

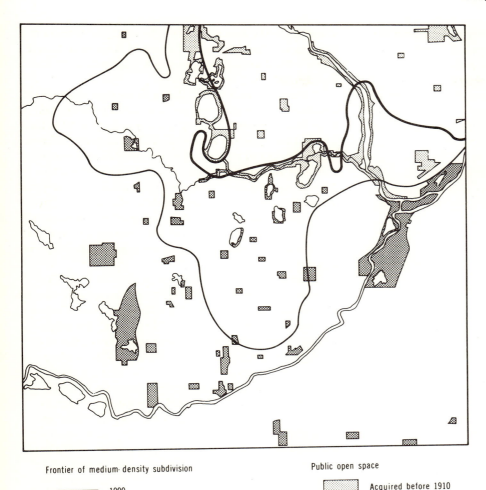

FIGURE 6 Public open-space acquisition. Map covers west and south Minneapolis, roughly inside the 1900 frontier line, and neighboring suburban areas. Most public open space was acquired either when the frontier of development approached the city limits early in this century or near the end of the post–World War II building boom in the late 1950s. Periods of rapid development and relative neglect of public land acquisition preceded both occasions. Distance across map, east to west, is 15 mi. (From Borchert, 1961; Borchert and Yaeger, 1969. Timing of acquisitions taken from records in local government offices.)

tax revenue from all municipalities in the seven-county metropolitan area and redistributes it to those same municipalities on the basis of population.

There has thus been significant public action on the problems that have come with metropolitan growth and change. Knowledge of geographic structure and change has been an important part of the growing body of information to which public officials and citizen groups have responded (Pred and Kibel, 1970).

THE FUTURE SHAPE OF THE METROPOLIS

New questions on the possible future pattern of metropolitan settlement are arising now. A recent geographic study for the Minnesota State Planning Agency included a review of the possible allocation of growth from 1970 to 1985 among three different zones of the metropolis (Borchert and Carroll, 1971).

Forecasts of overall population and housing increases (Table 1) were based on five assumptions (Borchert and Carroll, 1971, p. 21; Birch, 1971):

Population-retention power in the Midwestern states will be somewhat higher than that which now prevails, but not as high as Minnesota and Twin Cities rates would be if the federal government renewed the spending patterns that characterized either the Vietnam escalation or the heyday of the manned-space program, or carried out some equivalent fiscal program to "arrest the drift of people from the American Heartland" to milder climates or more glamorous places.

Five main classes of residential building will comprise virtually all new construction: high-rise tower apartments; two- or three-story walk-up flats or garden apartments; two-story town houses in cluster developments; mass-produced one-family dwellings (mobile and other preassembled, precut, or other systems); and traditional custom-built one-family homes.

New apartments will continue to be occupied by . . . couples with relatively few children.

TABLE 1 Two Postulated Mixes of New Housing Construction

Type of Dwelling Unit	Density Classes		Percentage of Dwelling Units	
	Gross Population per Acre	Persons per Dwelling Unit	Mix I[a]	Mix II[b]
24-story towers	320	2.5	8	8
2-3-story garden apartments	48	2.8	25	13
2-story townhouses	20	3.0	30	13
1-family, mass produced	11	3.5	31	48
1-family, custom built	3	3.5	6	18

[a]Mix I: 37 percent of families occupy one-family units.
[b]Mix II: 66 percent of families occupy one-family units.
Source: Borchert and Carroll, 1971 (Table 10).

Either the present high rate of apartment construction will continue or the proportion of one-family homes will increase toward the long-term level for this century, as the wave of young married couples begin to have children.

Continuation of current trends toward more town houses and mass-produced housing, proportionately fewer custom-built units; continuation of trends toward large, clustered, planned developments on the one hand, and individual units on scattered acreages on the other hand. In other words, the 90 percent of us who normally depend on an organization to provide housing will become dependent on fewer and larger developers; meanwhile the regulatory system will remain open enough to permit the 10 percent who are normally "frontiersmen" to continue to scatter independently along the outer "frontier" of the metropolitan area.

These seem to be eminently plausible assumptions (Janis, 1971). If they hold, the seven-county metropolitan area will develop between 115 and 260 sq mi of new residential areas during the period 1960-1985. One-family houses, most of them mass-produced, would account for three fourths to nine tenths of the total new area.

Where will this new housing be? To answer that question, the postulated new housing was allocated among three zones outside the central business districts (Figure 7):

The zone of redevelopment—platted and mostly built up before 1900. Consists mainly of obsolescent and poorly maintained dwelling units; it is the most likely locus of clearance and redevelopment, both privately and publicly financed. Residential redevelopment will be mainly apartments.

The zone of traditional maintenance—mostly built up in the 1920s and during the period from 1946 to the mid-1960s. Likely to continue in owner occupancy with accompanying traditional maintenance by the occupant family. Scattered prime sites will be redeveloped, and scattered bypassed areas newly developed in apartments or town houses. Widespread resident resistance to apartment invasion will continue in this zone.

The zone of new growth—most platting and building will be done in the next 15 years. Most land is now undeveloped.

Tables 2 and 3 summarize the results of the allocation. The new-growth zone accounts for 80-95 percent of new square miles of development, 50-80 percent of all newly built units; the traditional-maintenance zone, 1-3 percent of new square miles, 5-8 percent of new units; and the redevelopment zone, 4-17 percent of new square miles, 15-40 percent of new units (much depends on the rate of demolition and clearance). To attain the highest assumed apartment-dwelling and replacement rates, roughly 20 sq mi would have to be rebuilt in the redevelopment zone. That rate is far higher than the current rate of clearance and redevelopment. At most, one third to one eighth of the redevelopment zone will be rebuilt; at least two thirds of the present housing stock there will still be standing in 1985, either remodeled or just older and more worn. The new-growth zone could expand by as many square miles as it did during the post-World War II building boom, although the pattern will be very different. The report summarizes the situation in 1985 in this way:

New high-rise towers will produce major changes in the skylines of the central cities.

The physical problem of aging and deteriorating inner-city areas will be only partly solved because most of the work will remain unfinished.

Major new growth will continue on the surrounding open land, much more clustered and comprehensively planned than in the past.

The Twin Cities will remain one of the two lowest-density metropolitan areas in the million-or-more population class in the nation, with the development pattern continuing to reflect the presence of nearly 1000 lakes and ponds within the seven-county area.

This particular study gives only a glimpse of one facet of the geography of the Twin Cities in the near future; its impact cannot yet be assessed. The report reinforces the argu-

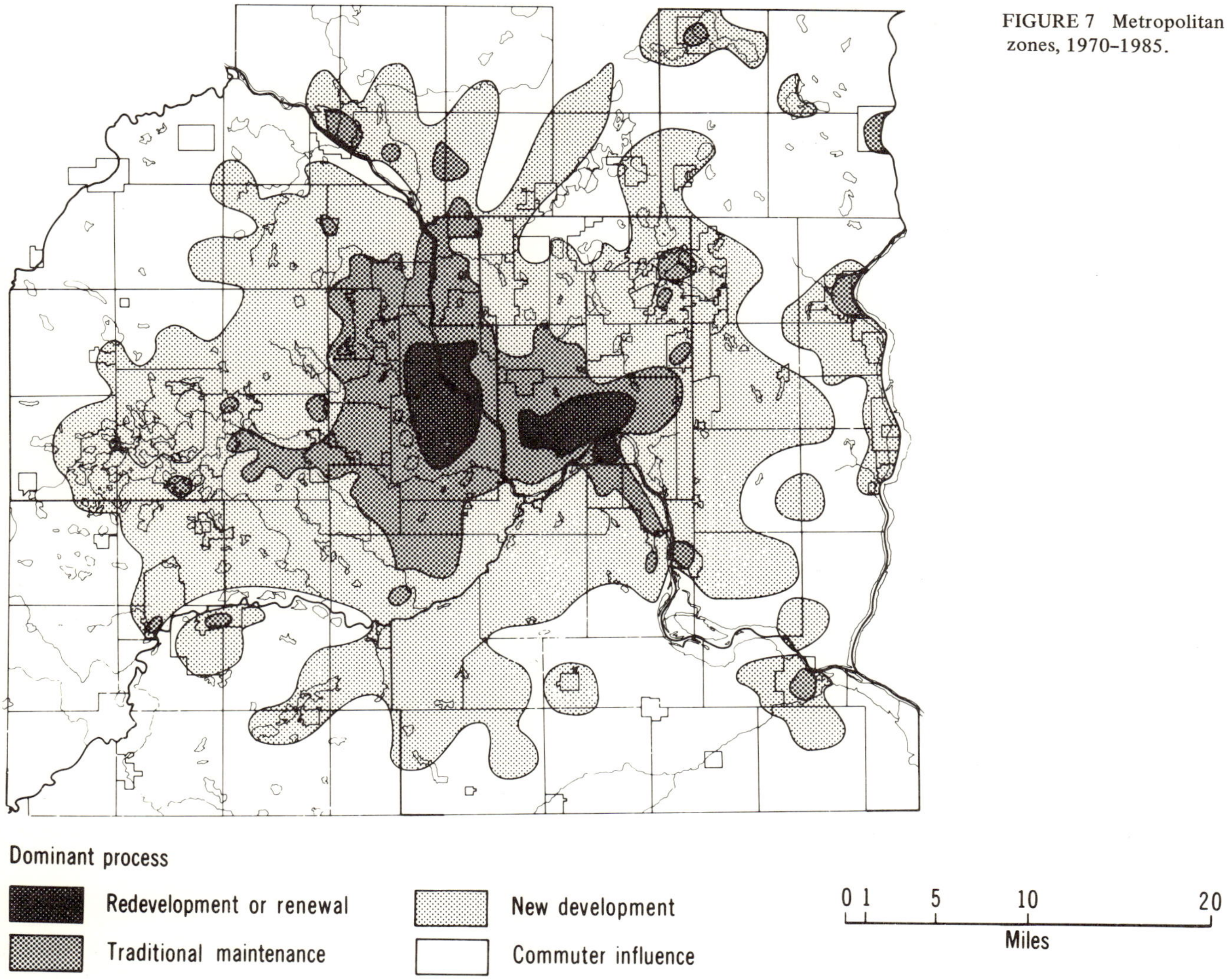

FIGURE 7 Metropolitan zones, 1970–1985.

Dominant process

- ■ Redevelopment or renewal
- ▨ Traditional maintenance
- ░ New development
- ☐ Commuter influence

0 1 5 10 20 Miles

ment against a traditional rail-transit approach in the current public-transportation debate, and it supports those who question the likelihood of revolutionary short-run changes in the urban-settlement pattern to accompany currently perceived revolutionary changes in life-style. The study indicates, however, that within two generations the regions both inside and outside the present zone of traditional maintenance will have been essentially transformed. It also suggests that a highly plausible and direct way to improve housing in the short run for the great mass of low-income people in that urban area would be a major expansion and simplification of grant and educational programs for remodeling and home improvement in those parts of the redevelopment zone that will not soon be rebuilt.

THE METROPOLITAN FIELD

Other geographic studies prepared for state agencies help to evaluate current suggestions that the Twin Cities growth rate should be reduced, the metropolis dispersed, and a modular experimental city for about one quarter million inhabitants erected in a remote area. Advocacy of legislation to accomplish those goals proceeds from the notion that the way to solve problems in the city is to disperse the city throughout the state and that just the opposite trends are being demonstrated.

In fact, it appears that the Twin Cities metropolis has to some extent already dispersed over a large part of both southeastern Minnesota and western Wisconsin. Since 1920,

TABLE 2 Distribution of New Residential Construction among Development Zones under Two Postulated Housing Mixes and Two Replacement Rates, Minneapolis–St. Paul Metropolitan Area, 1970–1985

	Distribution			
	With a 10% Replacement Rate, 100 High Rises per Decade		With a 4% Replacement Rate, 80 High Rises per Decade	
Type of Dwelling Unit	Mix I[a]	Mix II[b]	Mix I[a]	Mix II[b]
In the redevelopment zone				
towers	70	70	70	70
apartments	60	90	80	80
town houses	50	90	13	63
1-family, mass produced	10	10	0	0
1-family, custom built	0	0	0	0
In the traditional-maintenance zone				
towers	30	30	30	30
apartments	10	10	10	10
town houses	10	10	10	10
1-family, mass produced	0	0	0	0
1-family, custom built	0	0	0	0
In the new-growth zone				
towers	0	0	0	0
apartments	30	0	10	10
town houses	40	0	77	27
1-family, mass produced	90	90	100	100
1-family, custom built	100	100	100	100

[a]Mix I: 37 percent of families occupy one-family units.
[b]Mix II: 66 percent of families occupy one-family units.
Source: Borchert and Carroll, 1971 (Table 11).

in the automobile era, the area encompassed by the continuous frontier of subdivision (Figures 4 and 5) has increased from 250 to 700 sq mi whereas the population of the Standard Metropolitan Statistical Area (SMSA) has grown from about 750,000 to 1.8 million. Beyond the edge of that traditional zone of urban expansion, however, lies a vast zone of metropolitan assimilation. The assimilation zone has urbanized as a result of sharply increased interaction both internally and with the expansion zone that it surrounds. The area has urbanized largely through the transformation of its indigenous population and not by an invasion of suburbanites moving outward from the central cities. If one includes the zone of assimilation, the population of the Twin Cities metropolis has grown from 750,000 to 2.7 million in the automobile era; it has expanded from 250 sq mi to 15,000 sq mi. The percentage of the total population living at traditional central-city densities, therefore, has dropped from 58 to 32 (Berry and Horton, 1971).

TABLE 3 Acres of Land Required for Housing, 1970–1985, under Two Assumed Replacement Rates and Two Postulated Housing Mixes

	Acreage Required							
	With a 10% Replacement Rate				With a 4% Replacement Rate			
	Mix I[a]		Mix II[b]		Mix I[a]		Mix II[b]	
Zone	Cleared	Newly Built	Cleared	Newly Built	Cleared	Newly Built	Cleared	Newly Built
In the redevelopment zone	23.0	23.0	22.2	22.2	8.8	8.7	8.8	8.8
In the traditional-maintenance zone	1.0	3.4	1.0	1.6	1.0	2.9	1.0	1.4
In the new-growth zone	0.0	110.3	0.0	232.9	0.0	104.0	0.0	198.6
TOTAL	24.0	136.7	23.2	256.7	9.8	115.6	9.8	208.8

[a]Mix I: 37 percent of families occupy one-family units.
[b]Mix II: 66 percent of families occupy one-family units.
Source: Borchert and Carroll, 1971 (Table 13).

Numerous measures of the extent of the zone of assimilation are available. Figure 8 shows how potential accessibility to the total population of Minnesota, the eastern Dakotas, and western Wisconsin has changed in the past four decades (Borchert, 1963). Within that regional system the potential accessibility value that enclosed the subdivided area of the two cities and their adjacent suburbs in 1930 now encloses all or the most populous parts of 33 counties in the two states (Lukermann and Porter, 1960; Brown and Horton, 1970; Olsson, 1970).

These latent changes in accessibility have been realized to a great extent during the past two decades. The traffic density that characterized the state highways in the periphery of the traditional urbanized area in 1950 is now exceeded throughout almost all of the zone of assimilation. The outer limit of daily work trips into the SMSA counties approximates the area of expanded potential accessibility.

Throughout this zone, rural townships and municipalities of all sizes have gained population for two decades. Younger people are remaining and making homes. Small towns, farmsteads, and new houses clustered in wooded or lakeshore

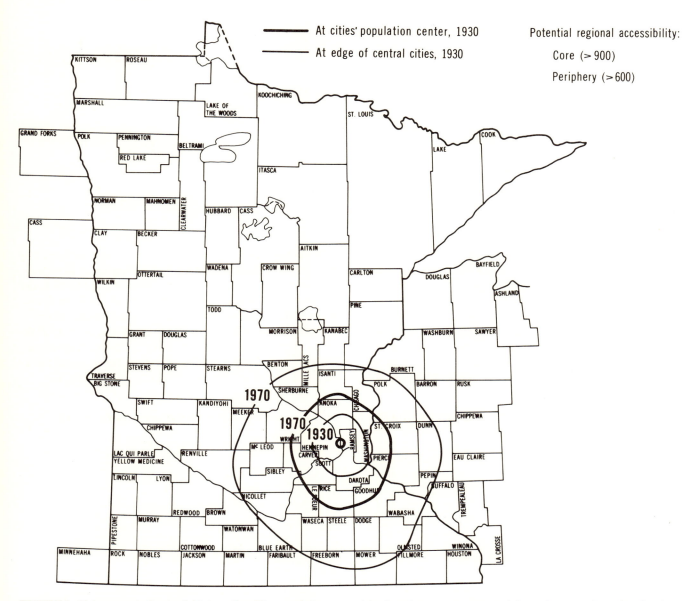

FIGURE 8 Enlargement of potential interaction. The population-potential values shown were computed for each county from data for the individual counties shown on the map. The study from which the map is taken covered the years 1870–1970. Peak value of population potential has been located at the Twin Cities in all census years during that period. (From Borchert, 1963.)

sites function as dormitory suburbs (Borchert, 1964; Hart and others, 1968).

Approximately the same region has a distinctive kind of intensification and suburbanization of its agriculture (Figure 9). Farmland productivity per acre is among the highest in the Upper Midwest, despite widespread soil and terrain disadvantages, whereas the proportion of part-time farmers has increased to well above the Minnesota average. Tractor headlights pierce the darkness of an early spring evening as a commuting machinist puts in his crop of soybeans, or a young dairy farmer does the milking after returning from a day's work at an office desk, factory bench, or service-station grease rack.

Home offices of major corporations are dispersed widely through the zone of assimilation (Figure 10). These tend to be home-grown industries or financial institutions based historically on accessibility to the regional market and resources of labor, management, and financing. All of them within the assimilation zone are no farther in time from the Twin Cities air terminal than Westchester and Fairfield counties are from Kennedy Airport in New York (Krumme, 1969; Barker, 1970). Branch plants (Figure 11) are concentrated mainly in the zone of assimilation, although the importance of the farm market for machinery tends to pull the pattern outward toward the rich agricultural area to the southwest, and a copious supply of underemployed farm labor tends to stretch the pattern toward the northwest (Borchert, 1968). The establishment of branch plants coincides with the major area of manufacturing-job growth. Not all the plants are branches of Twin Cities firms; some are Twin Cities area branches of national firms; others are branches of firms headquartered elsewhere within the zone of assimilation. All comprise an interacting network extending over the whole zone and reaching its highest intensity at and inside the circumferential freeway.

The Twin Cities urban field, defined by the permanent residential and work locations of its population, includes not only the traditional zone of urban expansion, which covers parts of seven counties, but also a much more extensive zone of assimilation.

In addition, however, a "part-time" zone of urban expansion extends far out across the lake regions of Minnesota

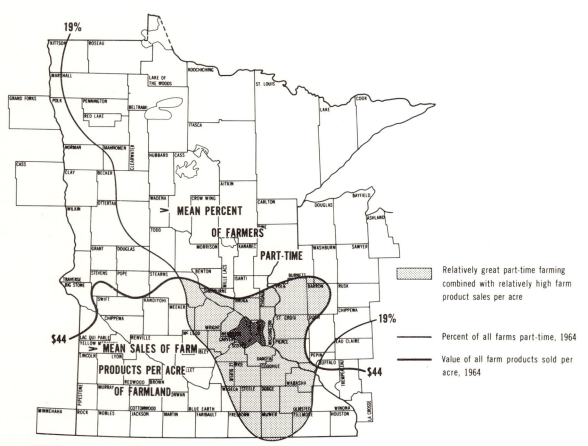

FIGURE 9 Region of above-average part-time farming, combined with above-average productivity of farmland. Isolines on the map represent mean values for the state. (From Borchert and Yaeger, 1969.)

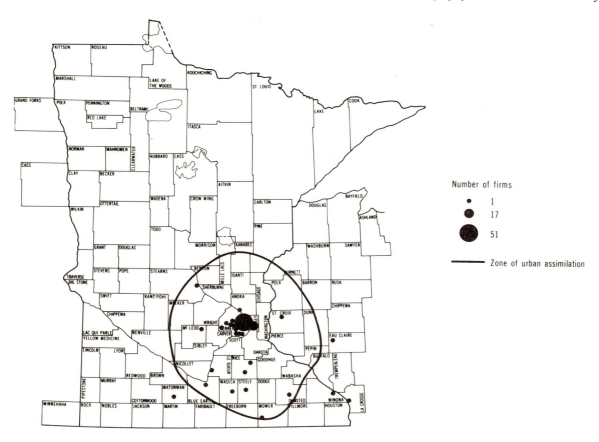

FIGURE 10 Headquarters of major corporations. Corporations are Minnesota- or Wisconsin-based firms included in the regular listing of 100 local-interest stocks by the *St. Paul Pioneer Press*. Firms are included in the New York or American Stock Exchange or national over-the-counter listings.

and northwestern Wisconsin. Figure 12 indicates the extent of development of lakeshore leisure and retirement homes largely for permanent residents of the Twin Cities and the neighboring urban areas. These are suburban residences for families during the summer months, during increasingly extended periods of winter, and year-round or seasonally in retirement. A dozen of these homes means as much in added basic income to the local community as new industrial work. And there are more than 60,000 of them.

The largest, highest-quality, most accessible lake districts have become extended part-time cities with familiar management problems associated with changing and increasing settlement. They have problems of development planning. For example, the traditional section-line road grid today serves thousands of miles of lakeshore (Figure 13). A few large-scale lakeshore real-estate promoters are platting at densities like those of the streetcar-era central city but providing no sewerage (Figure 14). Consumers from city areas are purchasing land that is on lakeshore during the current epoch of high rainfall and high lake levels without the knowledge that they will be far removed from lakeshore in future times of drought, or under water in future very wet years.

A recent statewide geographic study of lakeshore settlement was a major factor in the adoption of a comprehensive shorelands regulation act by the state legislature, and it provided the basis for applying the law to specific lakes throughout the state (Borchert and others, 1970).

Thus the residential urban field of Minneapolis–St. Paul can be conceived in two main parts (Figure 15): the permanent residential field, which includes not only the zone of traditional urban expansion but also the zone of urban assimilation, and the intermittent residential field, which is a part-time extension of the permanent field (Wolf, 1969; Berry and Horton, 1971).

Most of the metropolis is a very low-density system, but it is highly interactive internally and closely connected with other regions and nodes in the national economy. Furthermore, at its outer edges it overlaps other sets of urban clusters that cover more remote parts of the state and region (Figure 15). These clusters of major retail and employment centers constitute a family of lower-order, low-density

16 GEOGRAPHICAL PERSPECTIVES AND URBAN PROBLEMS

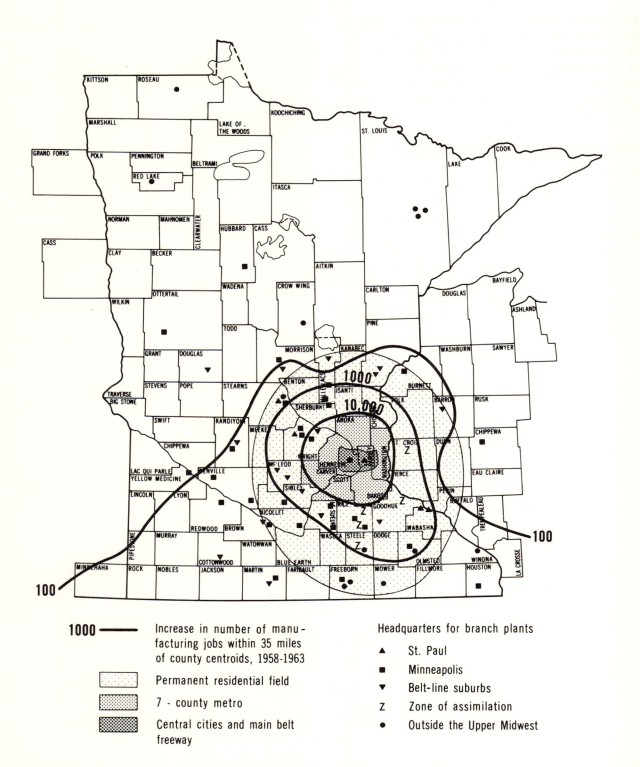

FIGURE 11 Branch plant locations compared with the Twin Cities permanent residential field. (From Minnesota Department of Economic Development, 1971.)

metropolitan systems, each with 200,000 to 250,000 inhabitants (Borchert and Carroll, 1971, pp. 14-15). The clusters will provide the framework for increasing multicounty planning and development under a 1969 act of the legislature; a series of urban geographic studies of the Upper Midwest provided much of the basic documentation of need for that act.

NONWHITE MINORITIES IN THE METROPOLITAN FIELD

Every year, thousands of new families and individuals migrate into this Twin Cities system. We wonder how they attach themselves to it. What are their patterns of circulation and interaction, their evolving personal geographic pattern of settlement? How do those finally relate to the aggregate? We still have no answers to those questions; hence, we cannot interpret with certainty the shifting pattern of the nonwhite populations who have migrated to this metropolitan area. This group, two-thirds black and one-third American Indian, totaled about 29,000 in 1960 and about 53,000 in 1970.

Table 4 indicates the percentages of the total nonwhite population residing in each of four zones in 1970 and the net shift among those zones during the preceding decade. The long-established ghettos lie within the zone of redevelopment. The nonwhite population within that zone has increased absolutely in the past decade (Table 5), although the share of the metropolitan nonwhite population total declined significantly. Table 4 also shows how the nonwhite population would be shared among the four zones if the income structure of the nonwhite population remained unchanged, but if there were complete freedom of housing location. The final column in Table 4 indicates the difference there would be in the geographic distribution of nonwhites if there were complete equality of both income and housing opportunity.

It is apparent from Table 4 that the past decade has seen an important, though small, move toward the goal of equal housing opportunity, and the gains in this respect have been relatively greater in the suburbs than in the central-city areas outside the nonwhite ghettos.

Tables 4 and 5 also show the further changes that could

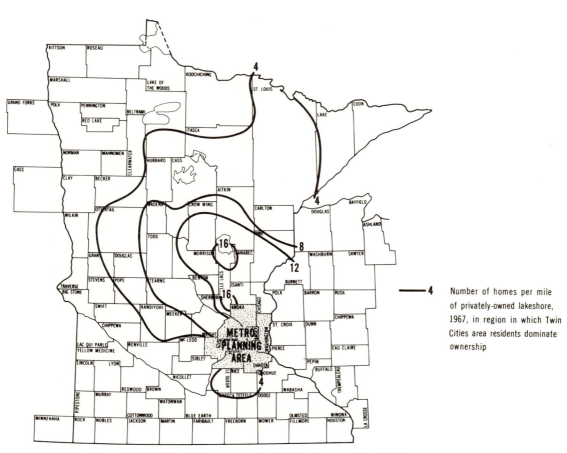

FIGURE 12 Lakeshore homes in the Twin Cities permanent and intermittent residential field. (From Borchert and others, 1970.)

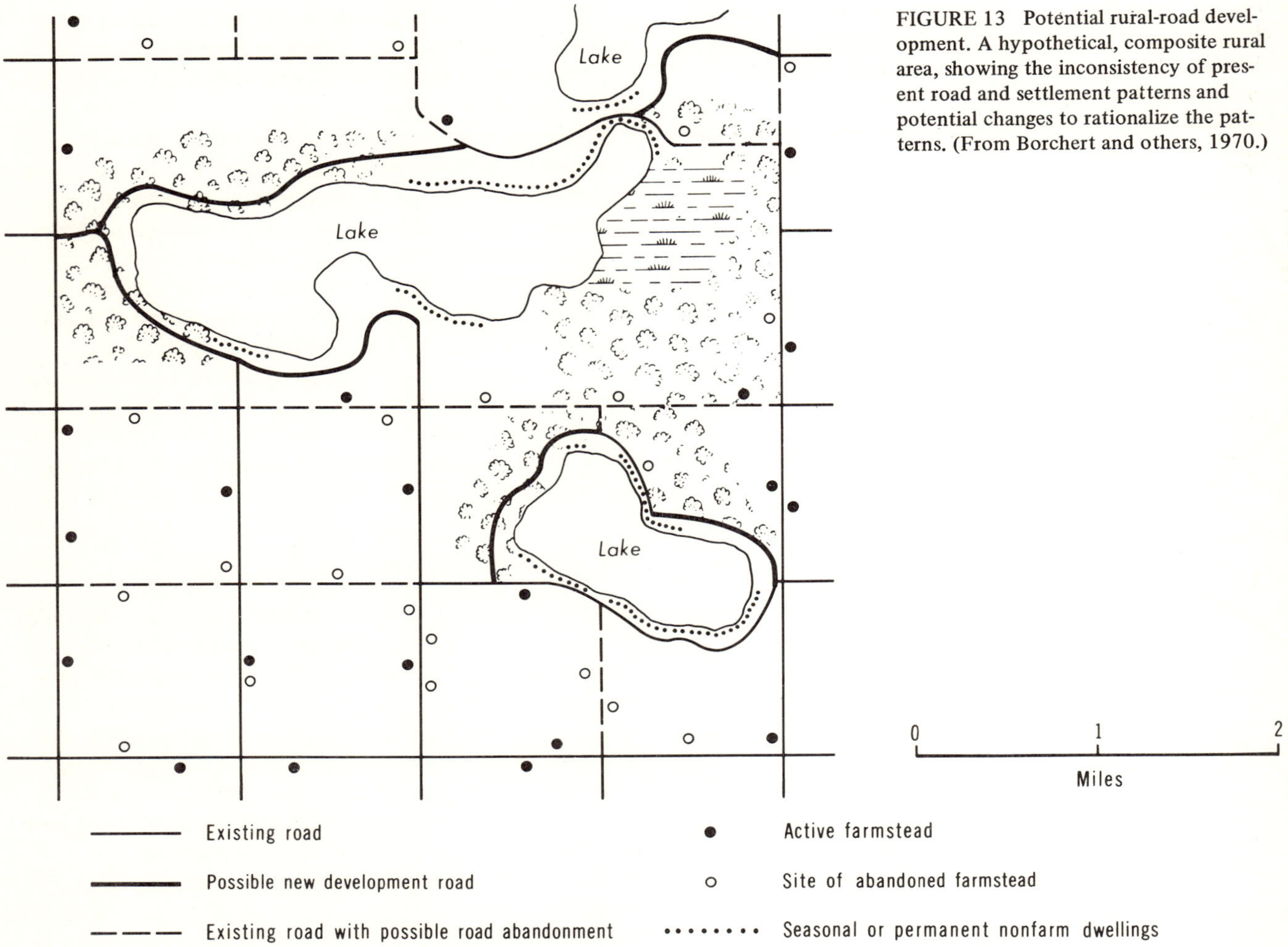

FIGURE 13 Potential rural-road development. A hypothetical, composite rural area, showing the inconsistency of present road and settlement patterns and potential changes to rationalize the patterns. (From Borchert and others, 1970.)

——— Existing road
━━━ Possible new development road
– – – Existing road with possible road abandonment
● Active farmstead
○ Site of abandoned farmstead
······· Seasonal or permanent nonfarm dwellings

take place in the spatial distribution of the nonwhite population over the next three decades. The tables rely on three important assumptions.

1. The nonwhite population will have a relatively high, but gradually declining, natural-increase rate.
2. The net migration of nonwhites to the Twin Cities will remain a constant share of the national nonwhite population and will therefore grow in direct proportion to the growth of the national total.
3. The same relative net shift of nonwhite population away from the ghettos and into the rest of the central cities, the seven-county suburbs, and the assimilation zone, will continue in subsequent decades at least until the end of the century.

The results indicate the plausibility by the end of this century of nonwhite population distributed 36 percent in the redevelopment zone, 23 percent in the rest of the central cities, 32 percent in the seven-county suburbs, and 9 percent in the present zone of assimilation. The share in the redevelopment zone might well remain highly segregated, as it is now; other shares might well be highly integrated, as they are now, although there is a likelihood that some suburban and small-town or rural segregated areas will emerge in the early stages of this process as they have in the peripheral regions of most other large metropolitan areas.

The diffusion of nonwhites into the assimilation zone, which is the domain of a largely indigenous, white, and—until the present generation—rural population is especially interesting. Those counties with major corporate headquarters or branch plants of a major national corporation increased their nonwhite population by 182 percent. Those counties with colleges gained 89 percent; the others gained 66 percent.

The following tentative inferences could be made:

1. The nonwhite population that settles in the Twin

Cities can be expected to diffuse throughout the urban field as its members become increasingly a part of the circulation and information network (Morrill, 1965a; *Economic Geography*, 1970).

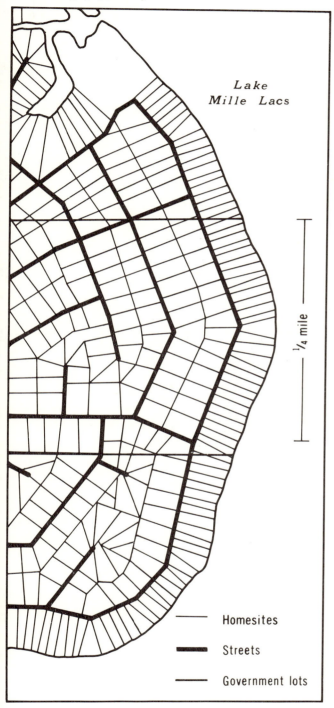

FIGURE 14 Lake Mille Lacs area. Note very small lots, high density, and chaotic pattern of subdivision. (From Borchert and others, 1970.)

2. The traditional ghettos will house a declining share of the total nonwhite population, and by the last decade of this century the absolute numbers of residents may also begin to decline.

3. In the outer zone of the urban field, one can judge that major institutions and corporations, acting in response to national and organized social pressures, will probably continue to be the chief advance agents of integration.

4. The goals of equal housing opportunity will probably be reached before the goals of equal employment and income opportunity. And progress toward income equalization will speed progress toward housing equalization.

5. Pressures that have resulted in the significant net shifts of the past decade must have their effective equivalents sustained over the next four decades if racially equal housing opportunity throughout the metropolitan field is to become a reality.

THE EXPERIMENTAL CITY

From these few examples it is apparent that the Twin Cities are a productive and social system spreading over an area much larger than the SMSA or even the metropolitan planning area. Its current density patterns are unstable. The latent redistribution of population and major-activity centers resulting from automotive technology, either current or future versions, are far short of equilibrium; and the same can be said for the latent redistribution resulting from modern concepts of racial and social integration.

The present metropolis is, for all practical purposes, a new city. Except for the residual areas of the zone of redevelopment, all of it has been built in the automotive era, most since 1946. By 1985 at least one third and possibly 40 percent of all its dwelling units will have been built since 1970, with or without government programs. The population residing in the present redevelopment zone will comprise only about one eighth of the metropolitan field, about one sixth of the metropolitan planning area.

The urban clusters farther out in the rural areas of the state (Figure 15) are also new cities in the sense that they are new multicentered interacting systems. Within their regions they embrace all the management problems of older cities—waste management, deteriorating old business and residential districts, open-space preservation, location and service of new developments. In addition, they provide opportunities for organization of local government and finance along wholly new lines and demonstrate clear needs for completely new technologies of transportation, utilities, and waste handling.

An experimental city has been proposed in Minnesota, but in fact a major experiment is already going on (University of Minnesota, 1969). The goal is to determine whether a population on farms, in farm-trade centers, and

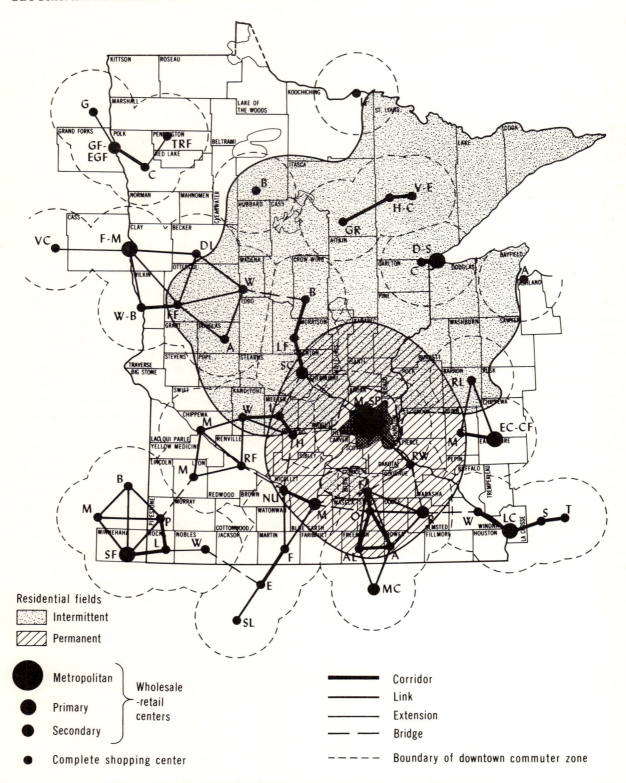

FIGURE 15 Twin Cities residential field and regional urban clusters. The map shows not only the Twin Cities residential field but also the low-density urban interaction systems that are emerging in the rural areas. Major rural trade centers, which are linked on the map, are less than 50 mi apart and have overlapping commuter zones. Those with corridor connections have mutual commuter zones and are less than 25 mi apart. (From Borchert and others 1970; Borchert and Carroll, 1971.)

TABLE 4 Relative Diffusion of Nonwhite Populations

Zone	Relative Net Shift[a] 1960-1970	Percentage Share of Nonwhite Residents					1960 with Equal Opportunity	
		1960	1970	1980	1990	2000	Housing[b]	Income[c]
Traditional expansion								
Redevelopment	-11	80	69	58	47	36	32	19
Other central city	4	7	11	15	19	23	54	19
Suburbs	6	8	14	20	26	32	14	62
Assimilation	1	5	6	7	8	9	–	–

[a] Change in percentage of total metropolitan nonwhite population residing within each of the zones. Percentages in the following columns (1960-2000) assume that the 1960-1970 relative shift rate will persist in each of the subsequent decades.
[b] Percentages under conditions of equal housing opportunity assume that income distribution in the nonwhite population remains unchanged, but the fraction of nonwhite population below and above $6,000 annual income (1965) in each zone would be identical to the fraction of the total white population in the same income groups in the same zones.
[c] Percentages under conditions of equal income opportunity assume equal housing opportunity and identical income distributions within both the white and nonwhite populations.

in a regional metropolitan center can integrate itself into the national urban economy in a period of prolonged and profound decline in farm employment without abandoning its cherished rolling, lake-studded surroundings and without contaminating those surroundings in the process of urbanization. A similar process is or could be going on in much of urban America. Monitoring and evaluation are the main missing elements.

THE WIDER CHALLENGE

Geographic research and information have played a small but important role in policy formation and organization in the projects mentioned in this paper and in many others. They have provided documentation that helped to stimulate and support the creation of new public attitudes, innovative management agencies, and new patterns of organization. More important, interaction with public groups and leaders was an important stimulus to teaching and research.

These studies were designed to fit the needs of officials and private citizens who needed information on their specific region, with its own distinctive history, geography, and contemporary personalities and institutions. Yet the methods and concepts have rested on a growing body of generalized and theoretical work. That combination characterizes the stream of geographical literature over the years—local, regional, or topical studies that are increasingly applied to policy questions, beside general studies that synthesize and conceptualize with increasing rigor.

There is much more to be done, and two challenges that deserve special emphasis are geographical information systems and methods of designing and evaluating alternative spatial structures and urban environments.

INFORMATION SYSTEMS

Much of the geographic work that has contributed to public-policy formation has essentially monitored and reported the state of the urban spatial system or some part of it. Although this work has been valuable, in general it has been

TABLE 5 Absolute Diffusion of Nonwhite Population

Zone	Nonwhite Population (in thousands)				
	1960	1970	1980	1990	2000
Redevelopment	22.8	36.3	47	44	37
Other central city	2.1	5.9	12	18	24
Suburbs	2.3	7.2	16	24	33
Outer region	1.5	3.1	6	7	8
TOTAL[a]	28.7	52.5	81	93	102

[a] Projections assume (1) natural-increase rates in the nonwhite population of 17, 12, and 8, respectively, in the decades ending in 1980, 1990, and 2000; and (2) a rate of increase in the net immigration of nonwhites to the Twin Cities equal to the growth rate of the national nonwhite population. Population numbers in each zone are derived by applying the shares from Table 4 to the totals projected for Table 5.

very crude, because it depends on census data gathered at 5- or 10-year intervals, or on other data series with noncomparable categories, discordant or once-only reporting times, gaps in coverage, and often difficult access.

The routine reporting systems of public agencies and private firms have a very large undeveloped potential for providing geographical information about the content, structure, and dynamics of the settlement system. Geography and geographers have an important role to play together with these agencies or firms, in the planning and development of management information systems for resources, settlements, routes, or flows at the geographic scale.

A relatively well-developed example is the Minnesota Land Management Information System, which has evolved from the detailed study of lakeshore development previously cited (Borchert and others, 1970). The system began with a card for every lakeshore "forty" or government lot in the U.S. Land Survey. Each card contains a large amount of quantitative data on land use, value, ownership, resources, and accessibility. More recently, the system has been extended to cover every 40-acre parcel in the state, and it has been linked with another system to add data on tax revenue and expenditures.

The data can be aggregated either by geographic reference units such as counties, townships, municipalities, or drainage basins, or by topical classes such as land use, ownership classes, value, or accessibility. All data are quantified on objective scales and will be used in analysis of trends, description of systems, and projections.

Output from any part of the data bank can be in map form. The maps range from simple numerical printouts for research or management decisions to copy for direct production of lithographic plates for printing conventional-looking multicolor maps of land use. Although input to the system now comes entirely from courthouse archives, agency reporting systems, field surveys, and air-photo interpretation, data could also come from satellite-borne sensors.

The initial assembly of the data and its regular updating is a very large undertaking, requiring the cooperation of a number of state, federal, and university departments. The system will, however, increase enormously the capacity to monitor the changing cultural and economic geography of the state and will facilitate much more informed public policies and decisions.

Similar systems are in various stages of development in other states and metropolitan areas and include a wide range of topics (U.S. Department of Housing and Urban Development, 1968). Geographers have made substantial contributions to the development of information systems relevant to geographical science and to the conceptualization of geographical information systems that utilize data from orbiting satellites and aircraft (Garrison and others, 1966; Dueker and Horton, 1971).

Thus far these studies and experiences lead to the conclusion that geographic concepts are needed, perhaps crucially, in the design and organization of these systems; geography will use them often and profitably; both the development and the use of the systems will involve geographers in broadly interdisciplinary efforts.

DESIGN AND EVALUATION OF SETTLEMENT PATTERNS

For the long-range redevelopment of our older cities and the construction and maintenance of new cities, a difficult and dynamic planning strategy is necessary. A review of the current planning strategy in many of our cities shows that planning can easily be placed under the general rubric of responsive planning—or attempting to forecast changes in the urban environment and to make capital-investment decisions on the basis of those forecasts. Too often all the implications of capital expenditures within the urban system as a whole are not considered in the light of their ultimate impact on the quality of urban life. The models used in the forecasting procedures contain too few control and policy variables by which decision makers can change the course of urban growth and development (Horton and Hultquist, 1971).

Although these models have been very useful and could become even more useful if their primary utilization would focus on the impact of alternative public policies, little innovative work concerning new forms of urban areas has so far been completed. Under existing technology and approaches, we have generally developed an orientation whereby planners and decision makers have placed primary emphasis on responding to, and formulating plans on the basis of, past behavior of decision-making entities in cities. Subsequently, the objectives of the current planning strategies often are to evaluate current patterns and trends under minimum-constraint situations and plan for the forecasted development. This obviously results in a tautology that allows or increases the likelihood of forecast becoming reality. This procedure often results in the entrenchment of such current problems as urban sprawl and traffic congestion.

An alternative approach is to develop criteria for optimal or, more probably, suboptimal urban growth and development and policy-evaluation models that will assess the value of alternative facilities and technologies in creating an environment to which we aspire.

We are at present woefully lacking in new approaches and methods for evaluating activity locations and the arrangement of cities. No experiments have been undertaken with alternative modes and configurations of transportation systems that could be used to facilitate designed activity arrangements and population densities that would improve the quality of urban environment rather than detract from it. Whether these new technological and morphological urban entities would be successful remains to be determined. The careful monitoring of these experimental urban environments, morphologies, and spatial structures would at least provide an empirical basis for the design of appropriate new communities. Large-scale experimentation in institutional and spatial organizational aspects of cities is equally desirable.

It is as though a diabolical plot precludes the introduction of totally new technologies by architects, planners, and social engineers of our cities. Although new cities and suburbs are planned, they are generally based on similar technology and differ only in street patterns. Outmoded construction regulations, zoning, the failure of the federal government to supply funds or absorb some of the risk of truly new urban development are all impeding progress at present.

The development of new communities will not necessarily provide for a better total environment. Many of the problems of our cities are not related to the physical structure but to institutional and societal problems outside the influence of the spatial organization of the physical city. Further, new communities can only be considered as experimental because of the lack of experience in such endeavors.

Decisions must be made on the characteristics that the society wishes to see in its cities. Instead of a plethora of inefficient, stopgap action programs, long-range planning requires firm policies on the desirable characteristics of the future urban environment. Who will establish such a policy? Who will evaluate these characteristics? How will they be evaluated? In 1968 a Presidential commission recommended housing goals aimed at the needs of the poor and suggested programs that would produce 500,000 housing units annually in the nation for low- and moderate-income families; 60 percent of these would be for those with income under $4,500 per year (National Commission on Urban Problems, 1968). In addition, steps to encourage home ownership were recommended, such as a reduction in the general level of interest rates. A national commitment to these recommendations reflects the preference for single-family detached housing, town houses, or condominiums. Might the implications of this policy be at odds with environmental planning and other social goals? This is only one situation that shows the intermingling and interaction of the various urban components.

How we want our cities to be arranged and what types of institutional structures can best supply public services adequately and efficiently are dealt with in much of the geographic research completed and in progress.

With the new surge of activity in urban geography related to behavioral research, we are moving closer to the development and integration of knowledge that will make possible even greater utilization of existing models for alternative urban-planning policies. If we are to be able to derive the difficult and complex answer to the question of what we want our cities to be, we must have models that will allow us to evaluate the impact of the implementation of policies. In this way, we shall be able to judge whether our policies are shaping cities in such a manner as to improve and maintain the quality of urban life. As individuals, we have little impact on the spatial structure and form of our cities; we respond mainly to alternative opportunities that ultimately define the success or failure of public and private investments. Models with integrated behavioral elements should allow us to assess individual response to alternative urban spatial structures and enable us ultimately to evaluate whether the urban environments that we are creating are appropriate for our long-term goals.

Geographers are naturally in the forefront of these research endeavors. They should also lead in informing others of the importance of spatial considerations in our society and in the world. They should be involved in developing, implementing, and managing programs designed to improve the quality of life. In many other countries geographers now hold relatively high policy positions at national, regional, and local levels. In this country geographers have, for some reason, been generally timid in seeking out these positions and in using their training and research as a springboard to the introduction of better and more appropriate environmental, activity location, and social policy formulation and implementation. As responsible citizens of both the scientific community and the United States, American geographers can and should perform these tasks.

REFERENCES

Ackerman, Edward A., Brian J. L. Berry, R. A. Bryson, S. B. Cohen, E. J. Taaffe, W. L. Thomas, Jr., and M. G. Wolman, 1965. The science of geography. Washington: National Academy of Sciences–National Research Council. 88 pp.

Adams, John S., 1969. Directional bias in intra-urban migration. Economic Geography, 45 (1969), 302-323.

Altschuler, Alan, 1965. The city planning process: A political analysis. Ithaca: Cornell University Press. 476 pp.

Barker, Diana E., 1970. Offices: An element of urban geography. The case of Minneapolis, Minnesota. M. A. Thesis, University of Minnesota. 142 pp.

Beckman, Norman, 1970. Legislative review: Planning and urban development, 1968-1969. Journal of the American Institute of Planners, 36 (1970), 345-346.

Berry, Brian J. L., 1965. Research frontiers in urban geography. In Philip M. Hauser and Leo F. Schnore, Eds., The Study of Urbanization. New York: John Wiley and Sons.

Berry, Brian J. L., and Frank E. Horton, 1971. Geographic perspectives on urban systems: With integrated readings. Englewood Cliffs, N.J.: Prentice Hall. 576 pp.

Berry, Brian J. L., and Elaine Neils, 1969. Location, size, and shape of cities as influenced by environmental factors. . . . In Harvey S. Perloff, Ed., The Quality of the Urban Environment. Baltimore: The Johns Hopkins Press for Resources for the Future. 322 pp.

Birch, David L., 1971. Toward a stage theory of urban growth. Journal of the American Institute of Planners, 37 (1971), 78-87.

Borchert, John R., 1960. Belt line commercial-industrial development: A case study in the Minneapolis–St. Paul metropolitan area. Minneapolis: University of Minnesota Highway Research Project, Departments of Geography and Agricultural Economics. 87 pp.

Borchert, John R., 1961. The Twin Cities urbanized area: Past, present, future. Geographical Review, 51 (1961), 47–70.

Borchert, John R., 1963. Population and highway traffic in Minnesota. Minneapolis: University of Minnesota Highway Research Project, Departments of Geography and Agricultural Economics. 53 pp.

Borchert, John R., 1964. Urbanization of the upper Midwest 1930–1960; Urban dispersal in the upper Midwest. Urban Reports 2 and 7. Minneapolis: Upper Midwest Council. 56 pp. and 24 pp.

Borchert, John R., 1968. Upper Midwest urban change in the 1960's. Minneapolis: Upper Midwest Council. 50 pp.

Borchert, John R., George Orning, Joseph Stinchfield, and Les Maki, 1970. Minnesota's Lakeshore. Parts I and II. Minneapolis: University of Minnesota Lakeshore Development Study for the Resources Commission of the Minnesota Legislature. 119 pp.

Borchert, John R., and Donald D. Carroll, 1971. Minnesota land use and settlement 1985. Minneapolis: University of Minnesota Center for Urban and Regional Affairs. 43 pp.

Borchert, John R., and D. P. Yaeger, 1969. Atlas of Minnesota resources and settlement. Minneapolis: University of Minnesota and Minnesota State Planning Agency. 261 pp. and supplementary land-use map of Twin Cities.

Bourne, Larry S., 1971. Internal structure of the city. New York: Oxford University Press. 536 pp.

Brown, Larry A., 1968. Diffusion dynamics: A review and revision of the quantitative theory of the spatial diffusion of innovation. Lund Studies in Geography, Series B, No. 29. 94 pp.

Brown, Larry A., and Frank E. Horton, 1970. Functional distance: An operational approach. Geographical Analysis, 2 (1970), 76–83.

Bunge, William, 1962. Theoretical geography. Lund Studies in Geography, Series C, Vol. 1. 306 pp.

City, 1971. Twin Cities. City, 5 (1971), 29–32.

Doell, Charles, and Felix Daihnin, 1958. A system of parks for Hennepin County, Minnesota. Minneapolis: Hennepin County Park Reserve Board. 16 pp.

Dueker, Kenneth J., and Frank E. Horton, 1971. Urban change detection systems: Status and prospects. Proceedings, Seventh International Symposium on Remote Sensing of the Environment, 2 (1971), 1523–1536. Ann Arbor, Michigan: Center for Remote Sensing Information and Analysis, University of Michigan.

Economic Geography, 1970. The shape of diffusion in space and time. Economic Geography (supplement), 46 (1969), 259–268.

Fielding, Gordon J., 1968. Locating urban freeways: A method for resolving conflict. In Frank E. Horton, Ed., Geographic Studies of Urban Transportation and Network Analysis. Evanston: Northwestern University Studies in Geography, No. 16.

Garrison, William L., Brian J. L. Berry, D. F. Marble, J. D. Nystuen, and Richard L. Morrill, 1959. Studies of highway development and geographic change. Seattle: University of Washington Press. 307 pp.

Garrison, William L., R. Alexander, W. Bailey, M. F. Dacey, and D. F. Marble, 1966. Data systems for geographical research. Evanston: Northwestern University Department of Geography.

Ginsberg, Norton, S., 1965. Urban geography in "nonwestern" areas. In Philip M. Hauser and Leo F. Schnore, Eds., The Study of Urbanization. New York: John Wiley and Sons.

Hart, J. F., N. E. Salisbury, and E. G. Smith, 1968. The dying village and some notions about urban growth. Economic Geography, 44 (1968), 343–349.

Harvey, David, 1967. Models of the evolution of spatial patterns in human geography. In Richard J. Chorley and Peter Haggett, Eds., Models in Geography. London: Methuen and Co.

Horwood, Edgar M., and Ronald R. Boyce, 1959. Studies of the central business district and urban freeway development. Seattle: University of Washington Press. 197 pp.

HUD Challenge, 1971. New regionalism—The Minnesota experience. HUD Challenge, pp. 25–28.

Horton, Frank E., and John F. Hultquist, 1971. Urban growth and development models: Transition and prospect. Journal of Geography, 70 (1971), 73–78.

Janis, Jay, 1971. Meeting the national housing goals. Urban Land, 30 (1971), 9–15.

Krumme, Gunther, 1969. Toward a geography of enterprise. Economic Geography, 45 (1969), 30–40.

Lukermann, F. E., and P. W. Porter, 1960. Gravity and potential models in economic geography. Annals of the Association of American Geographers, 50 (1960), 493–504.

MacKinnon, Ross D., 1970. Dynamic programming and geographical systems. Economic Geography (supplement), 46 (1970), 350–366.

Mayer, Harold M., 1965. A survey of urban geography. In Philip M. Hauser and Leo F. Schnore, Eds., The Study of Urbanization. New York: John Wiley and Sons.

Mayer, Harold M., and Clyde F. Kohn, 1959. Readings in urban geography. Chicago: The University of Chicago Press. 630 pp.

Minnesota Department of Economic Development, 1971. Directory of Minnesota Manufacturers, St. Paul, Minnesota.

Morrill, Richard L. 1965a. The Negro ghetto: Problems and alternatives. Geographical Review, 55 (1965), 339–361.

Morrill, Richard L. 1965b. Expansion of the urban fringe. Papers and Proceedings of the Regional Science Association, 15 (1965), 185–199.

Murphy, Raymond E., 1966. The American City. New York: McGraw Hill. 473 pp.

National Civic Review, 1969. Strength in unity. National Civic Review, 55 (1969), 154.

National Commission on Urban Problems, 1968. Building the American city. Washington, D.C.: Government Printing Office. 515 pp.

Olsson, Gunnar, 1970. Explanation, prediction, and meaning variance: An assessment of distance interaction models. Economic Geography (supplement), 46 (1970), 222–233.

Palm, Risa, (in preparation). Geographical perspectives on community: The idea of social space. Ph.D. dissertation. University of Minnesota.

Pred, Alan R., and Barry M. Kibel, 1970. An application of gaming simulation to a general model of economic location processes. Economic Geography, 46 (1970), 136–156.

Schroepfer, George J., 1960. Report on the expansion of sewage works in the Minneapolis–St. Paul metropolitan area. St. Paul: Minneapolis–St. Paul Sanitary Sewer District. 672 pp.

Taaffe, Edward J., Ed., 1970. Geography. Englewood Cliffs, N.J.: Prentice-Hall. 153 pp.

Tobler, Waldo, 1970. A computer movie simulating urban growth in the Detroit region. Economic Geography (supplement), 46 (1970), 234–239.

University of Minnesota, 1969. The Minnesota Experimental City progress report. Minneapolis: University of Minnesota Experimental City Project. 79 pp. and appendices.

U.S. Department of Housing and Urban Development, 1968. Urban and regional information systems: Support for planning in metropolitan areas. Washington: U.S. Department of Housing and Urban Development. 482 pp.

Wolf, Laurence G., 1969. The metropolitan tidal wave in Ohio, 1900–2000. Economic Geography, 45 (1969), 133–154.

Yeates, Maurice H., and Barry N. Garner, 1971. The North American city. New York: Harper and Row. 554 pp.

Geographic Exposition, Information, and Location

PETER GOULD
The Pennsylvania State University

The word "spatial" permeates geographic writing and analysis, but because all the sciences investigate things in space and time, many nongeographers are puzzled at the ubiquity of the word in contemporary geographic discussion and at the possessiveness that many geographers feel about it. The word appears frequently in geographic discourse for two simple reasons (Taaffe and others, 1970). With every other social and behavioral science, human geography shares a concern for man's social organization and behavior. Any discipline in the human sciences that tries to carve out a particular set of topics for itself alone, does so at the peril of its own intellectual vitality. Economics fades into a political science strongly linked to sociology, which is rooted in psychology. Anthropologists, without a flicker of diffidence, record and investigate all these aspects of human culture. Any discipline that pointedly cultivates a core for too long ultimately wakes up to find most of the important and interesting questions far away at frontiers that are rapidly being invaded by other sciences. Social scientists are never truly classified by the phenomena they investigate. What distinctiveness we have and nurture is characterized by a particular viewpoint more than anything else, and for the geographer the word "spatial" signifies the essence of his concern. He is possessed by an intellectual passion for spatial structure, pattern, and process—in brief, by questions of human spatial organization (Abler and others, 1971).

The second reason for the geographer's concern is that he sees in all the other viewpoints of the human sciences a distressing lack of awareness for these crucial dimensions of society. Economic systems have never existed at points; the division of geographic space is at the heart of many political questions; we can speak of human cultures in the plural precisely because they are separated and protected by distances that take time, effort, and money to overcome. The sheer friction of distance prevents human homogenization, or has until recently in human history. In many developing countries, as well as our own, questions of "where" are often more important in the long run than questions of "when"; yet five- and seven-year *plans*, fiscal *years*, next year's *budget*, long- and short-term planning *horizons* all attest that questions are constantly considered in the temporal dimension of man's existence. Only now are we slowly turning our thoughts to metropolitan *regions*, ghetto *areas*, political *redivisions*, *realignments*, and *reapportionments*—indications that we are finally considering problems of society in terms of the specific "where" questions of the geographer. I would contend that the most important contribution of the geographer comes precisely from his own particular bias—namely, his spatial viewpoint and the locational questions he brings to bear on human problems (Haggett, 1965).

Many of these human problems today lie in our burgeoning cities whose difficulties are being carefully monitored by other societies in the hope that they can gain some lead time in which to alleviate the most pathological aspects of rapid and barely controlled urbanization. Rightly, or wrongly, we feel we are the most economically advanced nation on earth, but we realize that we are paying a terrible human price for such a simplistic and, in important aspects, such a meaningless index as median income per capita. Every day our newspapers record the further breakdown of our cities and illustrate the unpalatable truth that in human and social terms we are an underdeveloped country with a lot of catching up to do. It is a hard salt to rub in, and on occasion it stings some of us into such resentfulness that we are unwilling to learn from more advanced countries, and we react to the daily indictments with further despair, if not downright apathy.

But despair and apathy are not going to last long. Our history shows that we are sometimes slow to move, and that on occasion we have been late on the scene. But it also tells us that we have an ability to solve problems of numbing complexity with enormous skill, imagination, and dispatch once we are willing to make the effort. Nevertheless, the problems are complex, and their solution will take all the intellectual and *political* skills we can muster. No geographer will pretend that his perspective on the human condition in America's cities holds the key. But he will declare that his spatial perspective is a fundamental and crucial one that can make a vital contribution to the difficult and patiently constructed solutions that we must all seek. With this in mind, I shall attempt, with a series of geographic vignettes in map form, to show how the geographer thinks about urban problems. Maps are used exclusively to illustrate the three major themes of spatial exposition, spatial information, and spatial location.

SPATIAL EXPOSITION

Even to define, let alone to solve many problems, we need facts. Many questions can barely be raised without the basic factual information that can lead us to them, and many controversies of social policy and planning are already halfway to solution once the relevant and pertinent facts are available for all to examine and evaluate. The way facts are presented also makes an enormous difference to our perception, understanding, and evaluation. For example (Figure 1), many of us think of our northern neighbor Canada as a country of vast stretches of farmland and northern wilderness; yet the map shows Canada to be quite different, for it can be transformed into demographic space, with all the areas shown in proportion to their populations (School of Community and Regional Planning, 1971). Canada, in one reality at least, is a nation consisting almost exclusively of cities, with little in between. The transformation is not a unique one, of course, but it can be made easily in a matter of hours by hand, or in seconds by geographic computer programs (Tobler, 1971). For the presentation of most social and planning facts, this may be by far the most pertinent base map, because it presents the information in the spatial context most relevant to human problems—namely, people. Similarly, in conventional space (Figure 2, left), Detroit has a very varied family-income surface, with a few small pockets of poor families in the core and perhaps some considerable poverty problems around the rural fringe of the area (Hunter, 1968). Transformed to demographic space, however, with each area proportional to the number of people living there (Figure 2, right), poverty literally explodes into view as the core of the central city expands, while the problems of the rural fringe shrink and, in some cases, virtually disappear from sight.

The geographer, with nagging persistence, insists that the presentation of facts torn from their spatial context may so

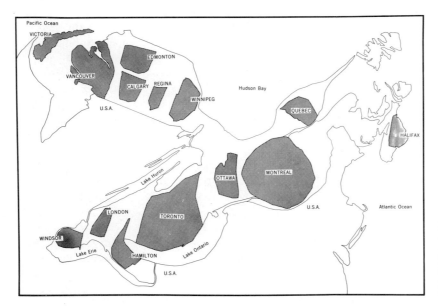

FIGURE 1 Canada in isodemographic space, with county units drawn in proportion to the population they contain. (Adapted from a map prepared by the School of Community and Regional Planning, University of British Columbia, 1971. Reprinted by permission.)

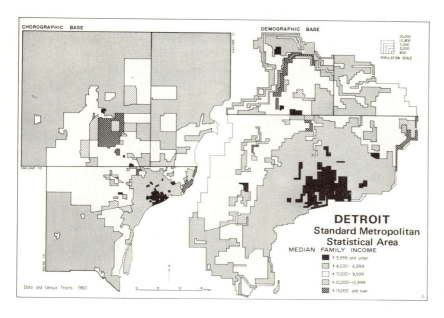

FIGURE 2   The population of Detroit in conventional geographic space (chorographic base) and in demographic space. (Courtesy of John Hunter.)

distort them that the crucial information is lost. Tables and appendixes in reports cannot substitute for presentation in the relevant space. We do not, however, always need such transformations of geographic space to present relevant facts about our society and its cities (Figure 3). Sometimes a conventional map records with proper intensity a shame of our rich society that no table, or simple listing in an appendix, could convey (Peet, 1970). It is not enough to know that children are suffering from malnutrition; if help is to be given, we must know where the major pockets of hunger are. We must also seek the underlying reasons for such distinct clusters and alignments, and consider a sequence of other variables that might go hand in hand with hunger (Figure 4). The almost perfect visual match between hunger and poverty immediately suggests the strong relation between the two and leads the viewer to consider possible short-term measures until long-term solutions can be found (Peet, 1970). After all, we have just considered two maps that many other nations would find incomprehensible in view of our resources.

Within the urban areas themselves, simple facts shown in their spatial context acquire an immediacy that no other presentation can convey. Traffic statistics are so familiar to us all that the mere figures for a particular time now have

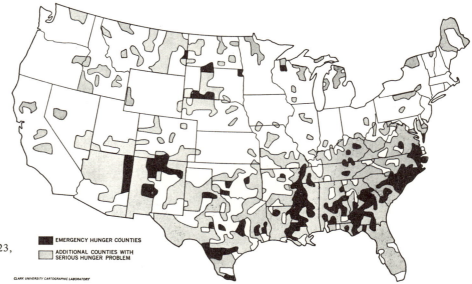

FIGURE 3   Areas with emergency or serious hunger problems in the 1960's. (Reproduced by permission from *The Professional Geographer* of the Association of American Geographers, Volume 23, 1971, and from Richard Peet.)

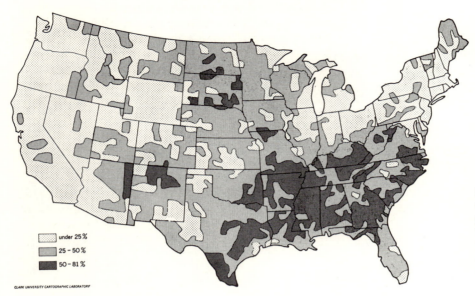

FIGURE 4 The percentage of families with incomes below the approximate poverty level of $3,000. (Reproduced by permission from *The Professional Geographer* of the Association of American Geographers, Volume 23, 1971, and from Richard Peet.)

hardly any impact. Torn from their setting in geographic space, they are incapable of producing any reaction, because they are unable to raise the explicit "where" question of the geographer (Figure 5). Consider the map of a black area in Detroit that lies between commuter origins in the white suburbs and destinations in the downtown business district (Warren, 1971). The area straddles the main commuter line through which tens of thousands of automobiles pass daily. Here, on the map, the appalling slaughter of young children is not only presented in stark form, but clear alignments and clumps, in brief spatial patterns of infanticide, immediately suggest a series of traffic-safety policies that could be put into effect to bring down the continuing death toll. At the moment, white suburbia appears to use the black areas of Detroit as a freeway. In marked contrast is the situation in Sweden, where attempts are being made to model and simulate both children's spatial behavior and patterns of urban traffic. Then schools, playgrounds, and parks can be located, and traffic routes set and directed to minimize the joint probability of collision between the two spatial systems (Nordbeck, 1967).

Facts on maps can sometimes be embarrassing. In some cities, zoning violations are either not known, or are tolerated for years without any action. In one New England town (Figure 6), land use that was inconsistent with the current zoning regulations was plotted to reveal hundreds of nonconforming uses, variances, and illegal uses of the land (Nash, 1956). The map was on public display in the town for a brief period, but the geographer who constructed it was told by the city solicitor and manager to remove it—otherwise the city would be responsible for prosecuting all the violations.

Some facts can be more than embarrassing, and when they are mapped, they sometimes suggest hypotheses in areas where all previous leads have run dry. Many examples come from the field of medicine, and some of the most dramatic advances in diagnosis and public health have resulted from plotting raw statistical information to examine basic spatial patterns, alignments, and relations (Stamp, 1958). In the United States, for example, there are between 15,000 and 25,000 crib deaths each year. An infant is put to bed at night in an apparently healthy condition and is found dead in the morning for no apparent reason. *Post mortems* disclose nothing, and the "sudden infant death syndrome" is now one of the leading causes of infant death in countries where child mortality is generally at very low levels. None of the many hypotheses on the cause of death

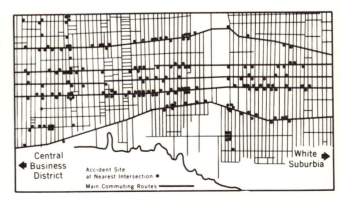

FIGURE 5 Where white commuters run over black children in Detroit. (Adapted from Warren, 1971. Reprinted by courtesy of Robert Colenutt.)

FIGURE 6 Land use inconsistent with zoning in a New England town. (Adapted from Nash, 1956).

appears valid to date, and there is widespread disagreement about the cause of crib death.

In Philadelphia, crib deaths for a 2-year period were plotted on a map (Figure 7) by Dr. Marie Valdés-Dapena of St. Christopher's Hospital for Children (Valdés-Dapena, 1963). Concentrations of infant deaths formed three very distinct clusters with a random scattering elsewhere. When compared with socioeconomic measures (Figure 8), the pattern coincided almost perfectly with that of dilapidated housing units in the city. In England, too, research workers have recently discovered distinct clusters in the older working-class areas left over from Victorian days (Teare and Knight, 1971). These maps have suggested the new hypothesis of extreme chilling of young children as the cause of death. With a window open, a small infant kicking the covers off, poor heating in old housing, and a sudden drop in temperature in the early morning hours, the hypothesis gains considerable credibility. The marked seasonality in the crib deaths, with a much higher incidence in the winter, reinforces the chilling hypothesis. Our concern here is simply that two maps, with some basic facts, have created fresh leads in an area of medical investigation where every trail had run dry.

SPATIAL INFORMATION

When we look at a modern city with its overburdened systems of transportation carrying vast quantities of goods and people, we are apt to forget that the most important flows may be less visible. The major functions of many of our major cities today are the handling and exchange of information, which is the most important commodity in the urban marketplace. Many of the more traditional flows of material goods and people only exist to sustain and serve the function of information processing. Despite the growth

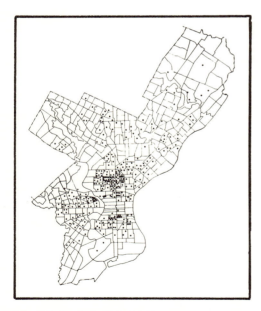

FIGURE 7 Crib deaths in Philadelphia, 1960–62. (From Valdés-Dapena, 1963. Reprinted by permission.)

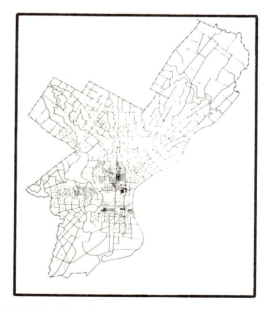

FIGURE 8 Dilapidated housing units in Philadelphia, 1960. (From Valdés-Dapena, 1963. Reprinted by permission.)

of electronic communications media, much information is still passed on a face-to-face basis, and there are many who feel that electronic means of communication can never supersede these older, and perhaps subtler forms of information processing and exchange.

Information is frequently considered in a temporal context: The value of certain kinds of information decays over time, as the stockbroker and newspaper reporter know only too well, but too often we forget that information has a spatial component. The perception we have of our immediate environment, the information we store away about it, varies over the local space, and much of the information we hold may be predictable from fundamental geographic theory. Even the social and political attitudes of people can be shown to vary in a regular way with the degree of accessibility to the larger system of urban nodes and their linkages. For example, in a recent study of 29 Pennsylvanian towns of under 15,000 people (Figure 9), measures of social conservatism were derived from attitudes to atheism, flag-burning, clergy at nonviolent demonstrations, marijuana, long hair on schoolboys, welfare, interracial marriage, and parental authority (Marsh, 1971). These indices were clearly related to measures of accessibility or isolation and also to the degree of immigration. Social conservatism seems to be perpetuated by a lack of opportunities to encounter diverse cultures and other people.

Within our urban centers, children living in the same neighborhood may emphasize completely different sets of information about the local space, and the maps they draw may reveal much about their lives (Ladd, 1967). In the Mission Hill area of Boston, for example, the white children live in the Mission Hill housing project (Figure 10). One black youth, living across the street, only 50 ft away, simply records this as the largest area on his cognitive map without any detail whatsoever. For him it is a totally alien territory, and a tape-recorded conversation indicates that he is physically afraid of it and has never dared to explore this local *terra incognita*. The location and intensity of most of his information is shown by the considerable detail immediately around his home and school. Another black child (Figure 11) places great emphasis on Parker Street and uses nearly a quarter of his map to illustrate, quite unconsciously, the width of the psychological and physical barrier between his home and the adjacent white area. Finally (Figure 12), a third black boy, who happens to be a student at the Boston Latin, rather than a local school in a black neighborhood, reduces the size of the white housing project and emphasizes five institutions of education in the immediate area. His tape-recorded conversation reveals that he has a sister who attends college, and that he is well aware of education as an escape route from the segregated life of his neighborhood. Sampling the information content of these children's cognitive maps con-

firms in a direct and dramatic way that housing desegregation is essential to a healthy urban psychology in our cities.

Many of the neighborhoods and areas in our cities are no longer places for relaxed and healthy living, but regions of extreme physical danger and sometimes overburdening psychological stress (Figure 13). Residents in a northern portion of Philadelphia, for example, have an aggregate view that can be mapped as an environmental stress surface in the geographic space. Here the hills are places of highly perceived stress, to be avoided at all costs, while the valleys are possible channels of relative safety. Negotiating one's way through this area demands a knowledge of an invisible topography that is acquired very early in life, and a lack of information can sometimes be fatal. Children select, from all the visual and verbal information they obtain, that portion that permits them to survive, and the spatial location of the stress peaks is perhaps the most important piece of information they can acquire.

All human beings are information seekers, and people in our cities are no exception. Every family moving from one house to another has been involved in an intensive search of the urban space for new residential opportunities, sampling locations for new houses at the right price, in pleasant neighborhoods, with access to schools and shop-

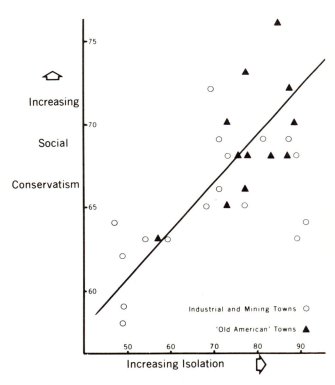

FIGURE 9 The relationship between social conservatism and geographical isolation of Pennsylvania towns. (From Marsh, 1971. Reprinted by permission.)

Geographic Exposition, Information, and Location   31

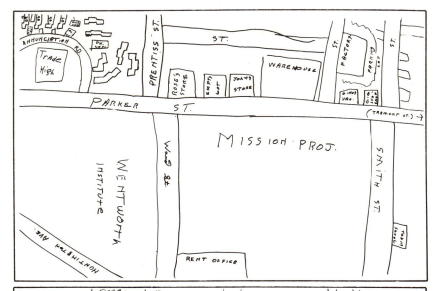

FIGURE 10 Dave's map of his neighborhood in Boston, showing the white area (Mission Hill housing project) as *terra incognita*. (From Ladd, 1967. Reprinted by permission.)

FIGURE 11 Ernest's map, exaggerating Parker Street, the boundary between the black and white neighborhoods. (From Ladd, 1967. Reprinted by permission.)

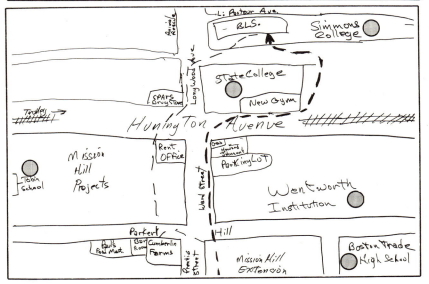

FIGURE 12 Ralph's map, with shaded circles added to locate five institutions of education. (Adapted from Ladd, 1967. Reprinted by permission.)

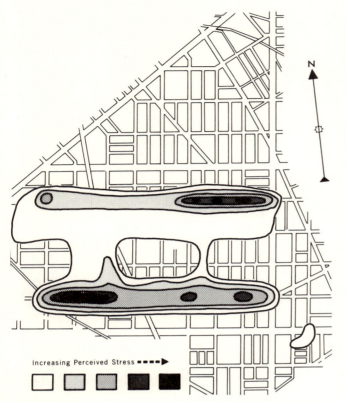

FIGURE 13 Perceived environmental stress surface for residents living in a part of the inner city of Philadelphia. (From Ley, 1972. Reprinted by permission.)

mation levels of those seeking new houses (Miller, 1970). Many people in the center of the city, for example, are simply unaware that medium-cost housing is available in pleasant areas around the nation's capital. Without such a source of information, many might never bother to search these areas.

The geographer is not only concerned with flows of information within the city. The most dramatic movements of population, with crucial implications for public policy at metropolitan, state, and national levels, have been the vast tides of interurban and rural-to-urban migration. These flows have swollen our cities to the point that many public services can no longer handle the demands made on them. New cities are already being considered to handle the migration streams and the overspills from our largest and most congested metropolitan areas (Morrison, 1970). Underlying these vast streams of people, each of which are the aggregate result of millions of individual human decisions, are countercurrents of information that guide and inform each individual decision to to move. We know almost nothing about the way in which people acquire spatial information, the way in which it is related, in turn, to people's perception and evaluation of places, and the manner in which images of residential desirability are related to migrational decisions and the urbanization process itself. What little evidence we have at the moment comes from Sweden (Figure 15), where we can construct a series of "information surfaces" for chil-

ping facilities. Geographic research has recently shown that there are distinct orientational biases to housing moves (Figure 14). We can measure the angles between old and new housing locations from an axis drawn from the old location to the downtown area (Adams, 1969). If there were no orientational bias, we would expect an even, or rectangular distribution of angles between 0 and 180°. A move in any direction would be equally likely. There are, however, significant departures from such an expected distribution, with higher frequencies at the extreme values, indicating a distinct bias to move into or away from the city core, rather than laterally at 90° from the old location. It has been suggested that the bias reflects uneven spatial sampling to acquire housing information. Most people are more familiar with the wedge-shaped region of the city from downtown to their homes, and their spatial behavior reflects their information bias. Increasing information about housing opportunities in the region would not only articulate demands and supplies of housing more effectively, but would have distinctly positive social consequences. For example, in the region around Washington, D.C., a carefully color-coded map has been prepared to increase the infor-

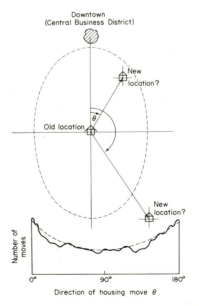

FIGURE 14 Directional bias when searching for new housing in a city. (Adapted from Abler and others, 1971. Reprinted courtesy of Prentice-Hall.)

FIGURE 15 An information surface for 7½-year-old children in the town of Jönköping, Sweden. Notice the geometric interval between the contour lines here and on subsequent maps. (From Gould, 1970. Reprinted by permission of *Geografisker Notiser*.)

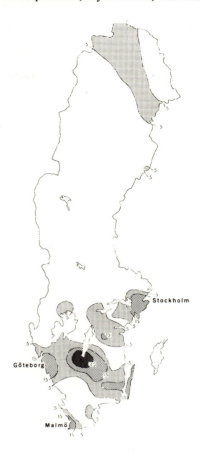

FIGURE 16 An information surface for 9½-year-old children in Jönköping. (From Gould, 1970. Reprinted by permission of *Geografisker Notiser*.)

dren in the town of Jönköping (Gould, 1970). When they are only 7½ years old, the surface is almost a flat desert of information with a major peak immediately around the home area, and subsidiary peaks at the three major cities of Sweden—Stockholm, Göteborg, and Malmö. The urban areas are already large information generators, even for these very young children. Spatial images are locked in at an early age. Two years later (Figure 16), the local peak has risen considerably, and some information is being acquired by 9½-year-olds of the interstitial areas, particularly where second-order urban centers are located. At 11½ years old (Figure 17), the whole information surface has been uplifted, and 2 years later (Figure 18), the children have obviously acquired considerable information about their country.

It is possible to forge links in two directions from this last map. In the first place, we can go back to more fundamental variables, because all the information surfaces are highly predictable from simple geographic theory of a gravity-model nature. Spatial information in children's minds can be predicted quite accurately when we know the size of the information-generating source and its distance from the perception point. We can also move in the opposite direction and link these expressions of spatial information to measures of perceived desirability of places for residential purposes (Figure 19). It is possible to construct a mental map, or residential-desirability surface for people, where the high areas on the surface are greatly desired and the low areas are shunned. What is important here is that there is a close relationship between the information and perception surfaces, and there is some evidence that for adults the perception surfaces, or mental maps, are also related to the aggregate migration flows. Thus, as we consider the growing problem of urbanization in the western world, including our own country, and try to devise public policies to alleviate existing congestion and to plan for the future, we must consider the information–perception–migration chain. The images of urban places are related to the information people acquire, which depends on variables such as size and distance. These geographic variables are influenced over time by migrational decisions and changing transport and communication technology. We have a circular causal chain here that must be understood in considerably greater detail if we wish to base our plans and policies for the future on knowledge, rather than on ignorance of the very process we are trying to guide and control.

SPATIAL LOCATION

The third theme focuses explicitly on one of the geographer's most fundamental problems, the question of location. Where things are is often vital to the physical and mental health of our people, as well as the political health of our nation. Hospitals that maximize accessibility to the people save lives in emergencies and increase the probability of remedial treatment (Eriksson, 1970). Schools that maximize accessibility to young children may well have more alert and well-adjusted pupils (Lee, 1957); voting stations that maximize accessibility to the people have positive consequences for the democratic process itself (Abler and others, 1971). Yet too seldom are questions of the best location raised, and, more important, seldom are the answers acted upon.

In more advanced countries, where access of the people to social services is a national concern, geographers play an integral part in the planning process. In Sweden, for example (Figure 20), surfaces showing the spatial variations in welfare and social services have been constructed to indicate the accessibility of all the Swedish people to such things as dentists, doctors, large public libraries, and facilities for adult education (Hägerstrand, 1970). As a result, most Swedish members of parliament and the interested public can obtain fairly clear ideas about national and regional priorities. The map can summarize an enormous amount of pertinent information that can be easily digested by men and women in public life who despair of the increasing information overload.

Facilities in Sweden are often located for maximum accessibility based on the notion of a day-return trip by public transportation. For example (Figure 21), when Sweden

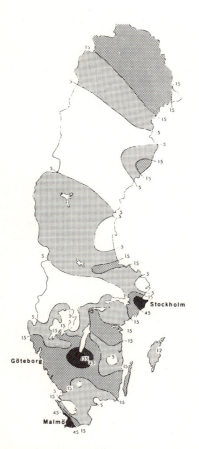

FIGURE 17 An information surface for 11½-year-old children in Jönköping. (From Gould, 1970. Reprinted by permission of *Geografisker Notiser*.)

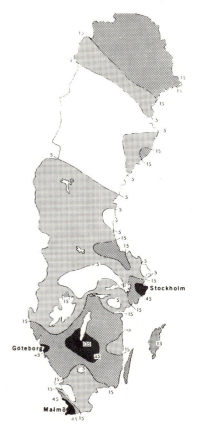

FIGURE 18 An information surface for 13½-year-old children in Jönköping. (From Gould, 1970. Reprinted by permission of *Geografisker Notiser*.)

decided to increase very specialized hospital facilities, a number of possible locations were available (Godlund, 1961). The question was: Which two possible locations would increase the accessibility of all the people to these public facilities the most? The problem was insoluble mathematically, because the tortuous population-density surface was incapable of even being approximated by a tractable function. However, geographers (Figure 22), by patient cartographic analyses, established the optimum solution, and new hospitals at Örebro and Linköping minimized the aggregate travel distance to these facilities. Of course, we assume here that a nation's health is a national concern and that we have a national health service. Perhaps we shall catch up one day with more advanced countries.

The problem of locating multiple facilities in geographic space to serve an unevenly distributed population is a problem that has never been solved mathematically. Geographers have devised, however, heuristic computer algorithms to help them to solve these difficult problems that are so immediately relevant to human well-being (Törnqvist, 1963).

Consider the hypothetical city New America (Figure 23), which might be the capital of a new national region formed from pieces of old political units that were devised nearly two centuries ago for other purposes. These archaic divisions are usually referred to as "states." Suppose we wish to locate three schools to maximize the access of the children to them. Using the Törnqvist algorithm, devised and used in Sweden for solving this kind of problem, the facilities start a process of iterative search by computer (Nordbeck and Rystedt, 1972). After millions of computations three locations are found (Figure 24), and these automatically determine the capacity of the facilities and the umlands or areas they will serve. If these capacities are impractical, it is a clear indication that more facilities are required to serve the children adequately.

Sometimes new facilities have to be located where older ones are already in existence. This problem raises important spatial questions of sequencing locations to maximize access over the long term, rather than simply the immediate planning horizon. Suppose that in New America (Figure 25)

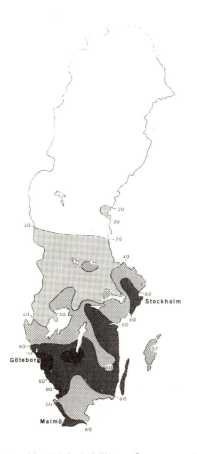

FIGURE 19 A residential desirability surface, or mental map, for 13½-year-old children in Jönköping. (From Gould, 1970. Reprinted by permission of *Geografisker Notiser*.)

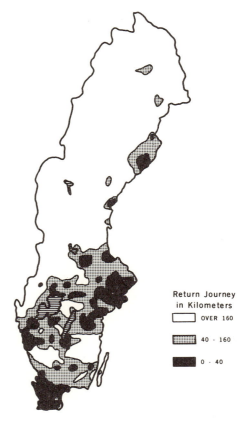

FIGURE 20 The social-welfare landscape of Sweden, showing access to such welfare goods as dentists, doctors, large public libraries, and adult education facilities, measured in terms of the aggregate distance of a return journey to these goods. (From Hägerstrand, 1970. Reprinted by permission.)

FIGURE 21 Possible locations for two new hospitals with specialized facilities. (Adapted from Godlund, 1961.)

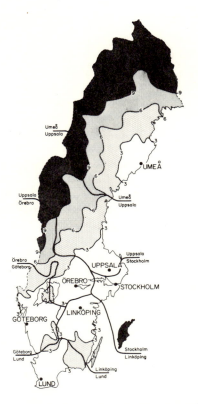

FIGURE 22 The optimal assignment of the two new hospitals, maximizing the accessibility of the hospitals to the Swedish people. (Adapted from Godlund, 1961.)

we have two overcrowded high schools, and we wish to locate three more facilities. Our geographic algorithm can easily be adapted to hold the existing schools in their present locations, and to allow only the three new facilities to search out the locations of maximum accessibility (Figure 26). Starting at random locations, the three new schools find new locations that maximize the accessibility of the children to them. Note, however, that this is not the same solution (or same overall cost) that we should get if all five schools were allowed to locate simultaneously. Had we been able to take into account the current configurations of population in the urban region earlier, perhaps we would have been willing to tolerate suboptimal locations for two schools over the short run to gain ultimate accessibility over the longer period. As we are rapidly finding out all over America, the optimal patterns of one era are not necessarily those of another.

Sometimes the question of school locations and their districts is not only a matter of optimizing an accessibility function; other factors may enter that are also shaped by explicit spatial considerations. In Detroit the 21 existing school districts were to be amalgamated into 7–11 new school regions of 25,000–50,000 students each (Figure 27).

The new areas were to have much greater local authority and control, and the question of combining existing districts brought deep anxieties to the surface (Shepard and Jenkins, 1972). Many black people felt that it was essential to have their children under what was termed "sympathetic authority," and the way the redivision took place could clearly alter the percentage of black children in districts under black control. Reaction to any plan proposed by the authorities was difficult, however, as there were no immediate alternatives to offer as solutions. Nor were such proposals easy to determine. There were 7,311 ways to recombine the districts that would conform to contiguity and enrollment-limitation constraints, and interest centered on the degree of black-white splits in these. Using computer algorithms, geographers determined that with 8 new regions, 4,967 of the combination possibilities would result in white dominance, 876 would result in black control, and 1,468 would have a 4–4 split. With even worse possibilities for gerrymandering in only 7 regions, 84 solutions meeting the constraints would result in a 6–1 white-dominance split, whereas in 8 regions, 28 solutions created a 6–2 black-dominance division.

We can consider four possibilities. The first school-board

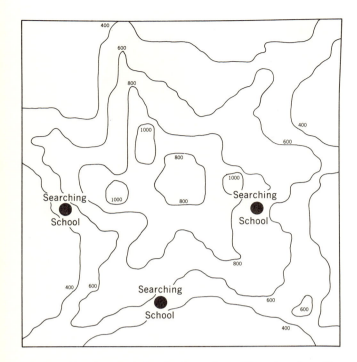

FIGURE 23 The population-density surface of New America with three new schools at random coordinates before their search for optimal locations. The underlying population grid of over 1,000 cells has been removed for clarity.

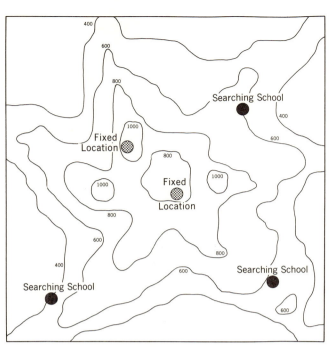

FIGURE 25 Two old high schools at fixed locations and three new ones at random locations in New America, waiting to start their search.

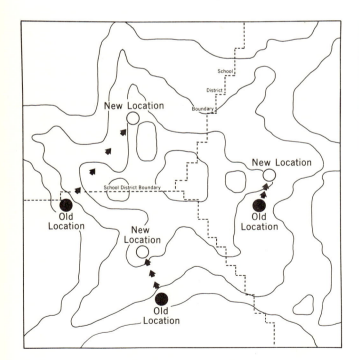

FIGURE 24 The optimal locations and school-district boundaries of New America, maximizing the accessibility of the schools to the children in the city.

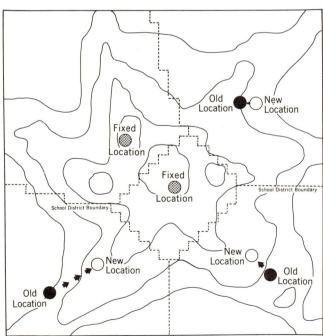

FIGURE 26 The optimal locations and school-district boundaries for the five high schools—two old and three new—in New America.

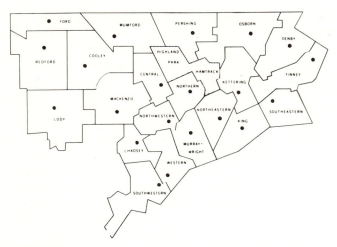

FIGURE 27 The present high-school districts in Detroit. (Adapted from Shepard and Jenkins, 1972.)

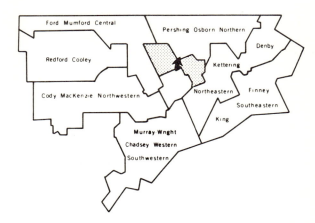

FIGURE 28 The Detroit school board's consolidation plan. Note the discontiguity across the park to achieve white dominance of a district. (Adapted from Shepard and Jenkins, 1972.)

plan (Figure 28) incorporated a spatial discontiguity to take a 99 percent black district into a new region that would be white dominated. Another plan maximizing integration drew very different boundaries (Figure 29) but was in marked contrast to the plan maximizing community control (Figure 30). Finally, a compromise solution (Figure 31) was offered from the set of 4-4 splits, which shared community control with the idea of integration under the Supreme Court ruling. Although gerrymandering is an old political game in geographic space, geographers have done much to provide a fair and equitable solution to a potentially explosive problem by bringing possible alternatives to public attention.

THE JUSTNESS OF CONTEMPORARY SPATIAL SYSTEMS

A paucity of fair and equitable solutions characterizes many of America's urban centers today. What few and halting measures we are taking are basically directed at alleviating social injustices that have exploded with the very cities in which they are embedded (Harvey, 1971). The causes are wearyingly familiar: archaic political forms that divide a metropolitan region such as New York into over 1,000 often antagonistic decision-making units; rapacious commercial values that drive all nonmonetary considerations out of court; gross inequities in schooling, educational opportunities, and medical care, and so on. We must recognize that we have lost our ability to lead in this crucial area of human social organization. Indeed, the situation is even worse than this: We are being monitored by others to give them sufficient lead time to avoid our mistakes. Our cities are too often bell-weathers of social and spatial decay in a modern industrial nation.

But if we have forfeited our chance to set an example, we can at least learn from others. We do not have to continue to conduct our urban affairs in the present way, and we could well examine some of the directions pioneered and constantly being explored by others. The political redivision of geographic space in America is a crucial problem that we must examine if the decision-making power to solve urban problems is to be properly allocated. Other nations with more deeply entrenched spatial divisions have already shown what can be done by converting a myriad of medieval units into a few functional regions that articulate major nodes with their umlands (Johnson, 1970). Land speculation can also be controlled, as it has been in Sweden since the 1930s. If the automobile changes a desirable human urban habitat into a lead-polluted atmospheric swill, the machine can be removed—as the city of Lund in Sweden has recently demonstrated. Today, in a fresh and quiet atmosphere, pedestrians and cyclists, dodging the occasional

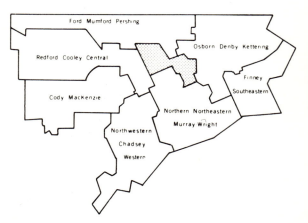

FIGURE 29 A plan maximizing school integration in Detroit. (Adapted from Shepard and Jenkins, 1972.)

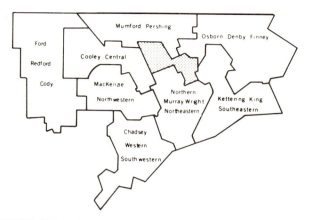

FIGURE 30 A plan maximizing community control of schools in Detroit. (Adapted from Shepard and Jenkins, 1972.)

public-transport bus, move in an area that has been restored to an acceptable habitat.

To solve urban problems we need two things: The first has already been alluded to—a political will, guided by a sense of humane social values, to divert energy and resources to our cities so that they become rewarding environments for all men, women, and especially children. But as we approach the difficult problems and attempt to formulate specific policy recommendations, we shall also need information, both to diagnose properly and to monitor progress toward the goals we set (Suchman, 1967). Information needed to diagnose problems is often difficult to obtain, but the geographer and other social and behavioral scientists cannot solve urban problems if that basic information is suppressed. And since problems, almost by definition, mean that something has gone wrong, the information that will expose and help to alleviate them is

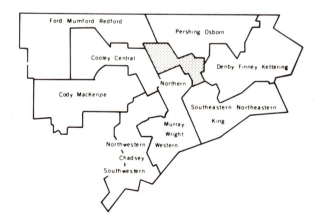

FIGURE 31 A compromise plan for Detroit from the numerous 4-4 splits combining community control of schools with integration. (Adapted from Shepard and Jenkins, 1972.)

frequently suppressed. Even a congressional committee, appointed to investigate such matters as hunger and malnutrition in America, will not release basic factual information gathered at the expense of the taxpayer, and the further one moves down toward the local scale, the more difficult it is to get certain types of information that should be made public. Too often, our municipal, state, and national bureaucracies seem to be finely tuned organizations for channeling legitimate and concerned enquiries into pillow-like areas where the final smothering decision can be ascribed to no one in particular. We also sometimes appear possessed by a mania for security classifications. Much of the vital information we need in our cities could be obtained by remote-sensing (National Academy of Sciences–National Research Council, 1966; Dueker and Horton, 1971). But military and intelligence classifications result in remotely sensed imagery for the public that can only be described as pathetic because it is so antiquated. Some people in the academic world who could bring such sensing to bear on spatial problems have given up in disgust. For example, high-resolution radar imagery is needed for moving-target traffic studies in all kinds of weather, particularly bad weather, when traffic behavior alters drastically in congested urban areas. We have the technical capability, but not the cooperation and interest of the Department of Defense.

Finally, even though immediate problems force their attention on us, we must somehow get out of the habit of bumping from one crisis to another and try to take longer-range views. We need thoughtful and informed investigations of properly posed and sharply defined questions about the future health of our urban society. Here again we could learn from Sweden and examine closely the tradition of the Parliamentary Seminar. When a problem appears imminent, and that may mean any time before the year 2000, a parliamentary committee is set up to examine the present state of knowledge, gather additional pertinent information, bring the best analytical minds to bear on the subject, and present the findings in a well-written public document. Geographers are currently involved in parliamentary and allied investigations of the urbanization process (Expertgruppen för Regional Utredningsverksamhet, 1970), the future of daily commercial activity in urban areas, and possible ways of consolidating and automating much of it. They are also concerned with studies of information exchange linked to the basic question of spatial accessibility and the closer articulation and extension of various modes of public transportation (Törnqvist, 1972).

The seminar reports, now constituting many volumes, form a most impressive set of sharply focused social commentary, and they form a crucial backdrop to many of the advanced social and political decisions made in Sweden. Their very presence is an indication that one democratic society, at least, can think about alternative futures and move toward an organization of geographic space that will help to meet the humane goals of all the people.

ACKNOWLEDGMENTS

I wish to acknowledge with grateful thanks the help of the following people who aided me with graphic materials and suggestions: John Hunter of Michigan State University, Michael Jenkins of Queen's University, Florence Ladd of the Radcliffe Institute, David Ley of The Pennsylvania State University, Elizabeth Marsh of Stockton State College, Edward Murray of George Washington University, Peter Nash of Waterloo University, Richard Peet of Clark University, John Shepard of Queen's University, Marie Valdés-Dapena of St. Christopher's Hospital, Philadelphia, and Barry Weller of Kansas University.

REFERENCES

Abler, R., J. S. Adams, and P. R. Gould, 1971. Spatial organization: The geographer's view of the world. Englewood Cliffs, N.J.: Prentice Hall Inc. 587 pp.

Adams, J. S., 1969. Directional bias in intra-urban migration. Economic Geography, 55 (1969), 302–323.

Dueker, Kenneth J., and Frank E. Horton, 1971. Urban change detection systems: Status and prospects. Proceedings of the Seventh International Symposium on Remote Sensing of the Environment, Vol. 2. Ann Arbor, Michigan: Center for Remote Sensing Information and Analysis, University of Michigan, pp. 1523–1536.

Eriksson, R., 1970. The spatial behavior of hospital patients. Chicago: University of Chicago, Department of Geography Research Paper 125.

Expertgruppen för Regional Utredningsverksamhet, 1970. Urbaniseringen i Sverige. Stockholm: Inrikesdepartementet. 467 pp.

Godlund, S., 1961. Population, regional hospitals, transport facilities, and regions: Planning the locations of regional hospitals in Sweden. Lund, Sweden: C. W. K. Gleerup. 32 pp.

Gould, Peter R., 1970. Var skulle du vilja bo? Geografisker Notiser, 3 (1970), 99–108.

Hägerstrand, T., 1970. Tidsanvändning och omgivningsstruktur. In Urbaniseringen i Sverige. Stockholm: Inrikesdepartementet. Pp. 4.1–4.146.

Haggett, P., 1965. Locational analysis in human geography. London: Edward Arnold. 338 pp.

Harvey, D., 1971. Social justice in spatial systems. Paper presented at the meeting of the Association of American Geographers, Boston, April 20, 1971.

Hunter, J. M., 1968. A technique for the construction of quantitative cartograms by physical accretion models. Professional Geographer, 20 (1968), 402–407.

Johnson, E. A. J., 1970. The organization of space in developing countries. Cambridge, Mass.: Harvard University Press. 452 pp.

Ladd, F., 1967. A note on the world across the street. Harvard Graduate School of Education Association Bulletin, 12 (1967), 47–48.

Lee, T., 1957. On the relations between the school journey and social and emotional adjustment in rural infant children. The British Journal of Educational Psychology, 27 (1957), 101–114.

Ley, D., 1972. The black inner city as a frontier outpost: Images and behavior of a North Philadelphia neighborhood. Ph.D. dissertation, The Pennsylvania State University. 324 pp.

Marsh, E., 1971. Geographical isolation and social conservatism in Pennsylvania's small towns. Ph.D. dissertation, The Pennsylvania State University. 151 pp.

Miller, J. C., 1970. Homeseeker's guide to Fairfax County. Washington, D.C.: The Washington Center for Metropolitan Studies and the Housing Opportunities Council of Metropolitan Washington.

Morrison, P., 1970. Urban growth, new cities, and the population problem. Paper presented at the annual meeting of the American Association for the Advancement of Science, Chicago.

Nash, P., 1956. The responsibilities and limitations of the planning director in a council-manager form of city government. Ph.D. dissertation, Harvard University.

National Academy of Sciences–National Research Council, 1966. Spacecraft in geographic research. Washington, D.C.: National Academy of Sciences. 107 pp.

Nordbeck, S., 1967. Barnens Skolvägar och trafikvanor. Lund, Sweden: Institutionen för Byggnadsfunktionslära. 98 pp.

Nordbeck, S., and B. Rystedt, 1972. NORLOC: A computer program for locating multiple facilities. In G. Törnqvist, P. Gould, S. Nordbeck and B. Rystedt, Eds., Locating Multiple Facilities, Part II. Lund, Sweden: C. W. K. Gleerup.

Peet, R., 1970. Outline for a second-year course on the socioeconomic geography of American poverty. The Geography of American Poverty, Antipode, 2 (1970), 5, 6.

School of Community and Regional Planning, 1971. Isodemographic map of Canada. Ottawa: Department of Energy, Mines, and Resources.

Shepard, J. W., and M. A. Jenkins, 1972. Decentralizing high school administration in Detroit: An evaluation of alternative strategies of political control. Economic Geography.

Stamp, D., 1958. A geography of life and death. Harmondsworth: Penquin Books, Ltd. 154 pp.

Suchman, E. A., 1967. Evaluative research: Principles and practice in public service and social action programs. New York: Russell Sage Foundation. 186 pp.

Taaffe, E. J., I. Burton, N. Ginsberg, P. Gould, F. Lukermann, and P. Wagner, 1970. Geography. Englewood Cliffs, N.J.: Prentice Hall Inc. 143 pp.

Teare, D., and B. Knight, 1971. Death in the cot. Science Journal, 7 (1971), 72–73.

Tobler, W., 1971. Cart I: A computer program for map transformations. Ann Arbor: University of Michigan, Department of Geography. 8 pp. (Mimeo)

Törnqvist, G., 1963. Studier i industrilokalisering. Stockholm: Geografiska Institutionen vid Stockholms Universitet. 392 pp.

Törnqvist, G., 1972. Manufacturing goods, servicing people, and processing information at multiple locations. In G. Törnqvist, P. Gould, S. Nordbeck and B. Rystedt. Eds., Locating Multiple Facilities, Part I. Lund, Sweden: C. W. K. Gleerup.

Valdés-Dapena, M., 1963. Sudden and unexpected deaths in infants: The scope of our ignorance. The pediatric clinics of North America. Philadelphia: W. B. Saunders and Co. 369 pp.

Warren, G., 1971. About the work in Detroit. Detroit Geographical Expedition Field Notes. Discussion Paper No. 3: The continents and islands of mankind. 54 pp.

Community Discretion over Neighborhood Change

JULIAN WOLPERT, ANTHONY MUMPHREY, and JOHN SELEY
University of Pennsylvania

INTRODUCTION

The neighborhoods that constitute our metropolitan areas have inherited a substantial residual from the past, and only modest incremental changes are possible (Natoli, 1971). Yet the changes that are taking place are significant, because they may reveal shifts in the complex resolution of forces from those that have shaped present neighborhood patterns.

The neighborhood is part of the package that an individual acquires when renting or purchasing a home or any other establishment within a metropolitan area. The price of rental or purchase includes neighborhood effects. Because this implies that market value will be affected by neighborhood changes, it is reasonable to assume that residents would prefer at least to maintain, and possibly improve, the external environment that lies beyond their own immediate territory or property rights. In observing the variety of neighborhood development, however, we find that highly differential patterns are clearly visible. Some neighborhoods, according to the point of view of their residents, are actively deteriorating, others remain stable, and others are improving. The most significant determinants of this process are probably external to the neighborhood, such as national economic forces or social and economic stratification and its associated syndromes at the lower level: unemployment, poor health, crime, and family instability. Control of the physical neighborhood and its land-use functions and activities is thus only a localized symptom of stratification and the institutions through which it is maintained and cycled. The neighborhood unit is a localized vantage point from which to observe not only the consequences of stratification but also the innovating exceptions in community activities that are to become even more prominent in the future.

The neighborhood has a population, a set of land-use types, architectural styles, and a set of functional and nonfunctional activities that link the people with each other and with the physical setting. The population can be stable or highly fluid as can the land use. Population change and land-use change can result in variations of neighborhood satisfaction.

The physical artifacts of a neighborhood are parallel to its population. Some new activities, functions, and artifacts enter periodically; others are restructured or adapted *in situ* to contemporary influences; and still others depart permanently or shift to other neighborhoods. Three categories of activities are available for the neighborhood or community to function as a collectivity: inducement, maintenance, and prevention. The community can induce entry into the neighborhood of people, activities, functions, institutions, and artifacts that will have beneficial neighborhood effects. The community can promote the maintenance of the present stock through minimizing negative neighborhood effects. The community can act to prevent the entry of activities that will have net negative neighborhood effects. Elimination of unwanted facilities is a fourth possible community activity.

Who has control over such changes? How is such discretion distributed? What are the legitimate and *ad hoc* institutions that determine such discretion and its relevant sanctions? What are the limits of such control when considering the mammoth social and economic problems that swamp some neighborhoods?

The community as a constituency is only one of the relevant actors with a right to exercise such discretion. Individual residents, property owners, and entrepreneurs from within and without the neighborhood may exercise their own discretion. The political unit within which the neighborhood is located may also participate on the basis of its own set of aggregate objectives and goals. Government at the county, state, and federal levels may also have established the right to participate. The objectives of these participants are likely to be in severe conflict, and the outcome of such contention is neither easily predictable nor so patterned through precedent as to enforce its tradition through any simplified causal analysis.

Our objectives here are to attempt to structure the resolution of discretion at neighborhood or community levels. We begin with several scenarios of the present, followed by a discussion of what is meant by noxious facilities, with taverns as an example. In addition, a set of suburban strategies, both formal and informal, is outlined for its relevance to inner-city neighborhoods. A number of activities that have been suggested or tried in ghetto neighborhoods of Philadelphia, such as community planning efforts, technical services, and remapping, are then discussed briefly. A number of scenarios are presented to abstract a range of community experiences with land-use change. In conclusion, we offer some policy recommendations that are suggested by the processes we have observed.

PRESENT SCENARIOS

Land-use changes in a community are the result of at least four contributing factors: individual resident action, individual nonresident action, community attitude and action, and city policy. These factors interact in such a way that any community may seem to be upgraded, downgraded, or remain the same according to the perspective used by the observer. A community may thus define its own utility differently from the way the city or an individual defines it. Any community, in turn, may have a definition of utility that differs from that of other communities. The process of community land-use change, with the available options, can thus be represented in diagrammatic form as in Figure 1. At each stage, a community has several options open to it. (Three has been arbitrarily chosen as the number of options here.) Depending on the discretion of the community, these options are more or less constrained by individual and city actions or failures to act. Each step in the life cycle of the community leads to further possibilities for change, either upgrading or downgrading.

The interactions of the forces listed as affecting a community's life cycle can be represented in a series of scenarios of existing conditions. The scenarios indicate the importance of active community groups, which effectively promote their own discretionary powers at the cost of the short-run profits of insiders and outsiders and which can compete with more affluent communities in the larger urban arena to attract positive facilities and to bar negative ones. Such community efforts can benefit from a number of specific activities while participating in them. The first three scenarios represent more or less current short-run processes of neighborhood threat and response.

SCENARIO 1

Community A is a low-income black community with a number of empty lots and vacant houses. There is little community mobilization and no resident organization. Almost all residents rent their homes. A private developer decides that an abandoned commercial strip in the area would be a good location for a hamburger take-out and short-order restaurant. The restaurant would need adequate parking as well as entrance and exit driveways. The devel-

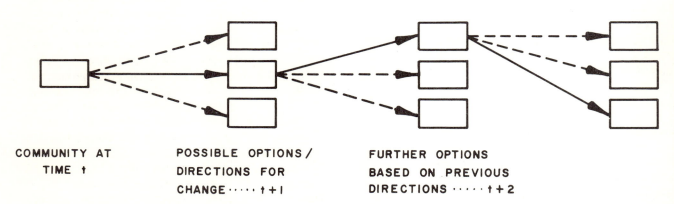

FIGURE 1 Process of community land-use change, with available options.

oper anticipates good business from maintaining late hours (until 2 a.m.) for the restaurant.

Although the required zoning notices are posted in the area, they are generally ignored and subsequently torn down. The residents don't really become aware of the impending installation of the restaurant until construction begins. By questioning construction workers, they are able to find out the proposed use of the site. They become concerned over the traffic problems (several of the adjacent families have small children) and the late hours. Representatives go to the local ward politicians and eventually to their councilman. He informs them that the change in zoning to allow construction of the restaurant is handled by the City Zoning Board of Adjustment, which approved a variance for the site well in advance of the planned construction. Hadn't they seen the notices of a public hearing? The residents are urged to give up the fight.

SCENARIO 2

Community B is also a low-income community. Although there are several vacant lots and empty houses, the residents have developed a certain amount of community pride. Several of them have been able to purchase their own homes and have begun to renovate them. A neighborhood civic association has conducted a campaign to clean up the empty lots to make areas suitable for play, and they have petitioned the city to do something about the empty houses.

The same developer wishes to install his restaurant in the area. This time, however, the public-hearing notice for a zoning change is not ignored. The residents organize a busload of people to attend the hearing and to register their sentiments. They inform their councilman of their intentions and their strength. They also notify the City Planning Commission and ask for assistance in understanding and fighting the zoning change. They go into the public hearing armed with numbers, facts, and alternative proposals for development.

At the public hearing the Board of Adjustment is overwhelmed by the community presentation. The developer decides that it is not worthwhile to fight, and he withdraws his petition for a variance. The community has won, and it is now in a position to develop and rezone as it wishes.

SCENARIO 3

Community C is a low-middle-income ethnic community situated close to center city. The location is ideal for a residential area with access to an expanding downtown, but the neighborhood has traditionally avoided encroachment because of its high stability. An enterprising young architect decides that he likes the character and location of the neighborhood and decides to purchase an old shell to renovate. Other young professionals learn of his successful renovation, and he forms a company to repair and sell old empty houses. Still others, encouraged by the upgrading, the location, and the relatively low price of the houses, start buying homes. The residents are quick to grab what seem to them to be immediate and substantial profits from selling their homes. As more young affluents move in and long-time residents move out, the character of the neighborhood changes. Pockets of ethnicity remain, but the community can no longer be classified as ethnic. Although only a few minor zoning changes were made, the community has been transformed.

NOXIOUS FACILITIES

Tavern location may be a good predictor of community discretion or its absence; where taverns are highly concentrated, community discretion is generally low. By examining the locational clusterings of such services and facilities, we may be able to find indicators of community discretion.

Within the city limits of Philadelphia, 2,961 establishments have liquor licenses (one for every 600 residents), whereas a 1951 Pennsylvania State law permits only one license for every 1,500 persons, which would mean 1,285 establishments. Because new licenses may not be issued, and there have been none since 1939, new tavern locations can be based only on transfers from existing sites, and liquor licenses are bought and sold. As a result of the transfers, taverns have a tendency to shift in their concentration and to form clusters in areas in which there is little community discretion. In one section of the city, a ninth bar is being added to a two-block zone in the immediate vicinity of an elementary school and other public facilities. In one fourth of Philadelphia's wards, one license exists for every 360 residents; in some of the newer sections of the city, there is only one tavern for more than 8,000 residents.

The neighborhood bar may serve as a beneficial social focus for a community; it may provide employment for community residents and an economic base for the local businessmen with only modest spillover effects on surrounding properties. As the market price of such licenses rises, however, ownership is becoming increasingly controlled by outsiders, and tavern clusters in low-income neighborhoods are beginning to replace the neighborhood bar. Such clusters are becoming more frequently the scene of drug traffic, prostitution, and violent crime in the city. They escalate the downgrading of neighboring land use and promote out-migration of those who can afford to leave.

The Liquor Control Board may refuse a location transfer if the proposed site is within 200 ft of another tavern; within 300 ft of a restrictive institution, such as a school or church; or can be proved to be harmful to the health, welfare, peace, and morals of the residents living within a 500 ft radius.

Use of the site as a tavern may be prevented only by the actions of well-organized indigenous community groups who can act quickly to investigate the proposal, assemble evidence and petitions, voice their objections to the city solicitor and the police, and produce a mass showing at the public hearing. Recent tavern sitings can be explained by an insufficient community awareness or response.

Taverns are not the only kind of establishment that can have negative neighborhood effects. Other examples are gas stations, used-furniture stores, pawnshops, and public housing. Facilities such as these are overwhelmingly concentrated in the older and poorer sections of the metropolitan area where their clustered existence exceeds the local demand.

On the basis of data derived from two disparate population groups, we have attempted to determine preferences with respect to a set of 50 facilities that might be located in residential neighborhoods. The control group consisted of university students whose responses indicated preference for two alternative patterns: a suburban neighborhood consisting only of housing within a narrow price category and with convenient stores collected into a shopping center, or a center-city location of housing intermixed with high-amenity facilities and with other needed facilities, such as hospitals or repair shops, confined to neighboring communities.

The other population group that was sampled consisted of residents of a low-income blue-collar white area of Philadelphia. The residents in this area were mainly homeowners of two-story row houses with a value of $7,000–$9,000. They seemed proud to own their homes, often given to them by their parents, and had positive feelings toward their community, even though most recognized that it was a poor or a tough neighborhood. Often they were resigned to annoying problems in their immediate neighborhood and thought they were incapable of changing things themselves. There were strong feelings about the threat from outsiders (especially the "colored"), but no sense of strategy about responding to such threats.

Many noxious facilities were in the neighborhood, but these posed little threat in comparison to such invasions as an expressway, public housing for blacks, or other facilities that might be used by black children. The overriding factor was wariness of any change, because they were sure that it would bring about downgrading; the city (the outsiders) would not help the area, and they would be powerless to prevent the intrusion. Residents wanted more police stations, libraries, day-care centers, and schools, but no other facilities, because these would attract black residents.

SUBURBAN STRATEGIES

Why are suburban areas not subject to this kind of problem in land use? Perhaps they have been able to develop better ways to control their communities.

The strategies employed by suburbs to control land use within their areas seem to fall into two general categories: formal strategies, or those that utilize existing codes to justify exclusionary policies; and informal strategies, or those that fall outside the realm of existing codes and regulations. Both sets are aided by existing laws that are either too loosely defined or too loosely enforced, or some combination of both. The informal strategies are aided, specifically, by a decision-making process that allows for traditional political pressures. In reality, the strategies work well enough for the suburban resident to maintain and perpetuate his homogeneous community with very little effort. We shall examine here some of the formal and informal strategies used by suburban communities to control land use and discuss the value of these strategies to the city dweller for control of his community.

FORMAL STRATEGIES

Formal strategies of exclusionary zoning are used to determine the supply, desirability, mix, and specific nature of housing permitted in an area (U.S. Commission on Civil Rights, 1970; Trubeck, 1970). Following is a list of the most commonly used strategies, employed generally in conjunction with each other to standardize and enforce the exclusion involved. This exclusion is justified for vague reasons of health, safety, public services, finance, land values, and aesthetics (Sager, 1969).

Large-lot zoning (U.S. National Commission on Urban Problems, 1968) specifies a minimum area per dwelling unit. Its effect is to reduce the total amount of housing available for an area.

Exclusion of multiple dwellings effectively excludes apartment houses. This is now successful, except in some token areas (National Commission on Urban Problems, 1968).

Establishment of minimum floor areas for houses was meant originally to ward off overcrowding and density problems.

High subdivision requirements determine minimum house size and cost, the costs of improvements of land, and the amount of land within each subdivision that can be specifically devoted to housing. This requirement is used to maintain the rural character of suburban communities.

INFORMAL STRATEGIES

Informal strategies are possible under zoning regulations because those regulations are set up in a manner conducive to community pressure (Williams and Norman, c. 1970; Weiner, 1971). As Allen Muglia (1961) points out, a board of adjustment for a suburban community generally equates the spirit of the community with the spirit of the law. In the absence of clear definitions of the public interest, local boards of adjustment rely on vocal pressures to determine the community attitude.

In other ways, too, the nature of suburban communities allows for more direct citizen control over zoning. The small size of the community generally makes control easier, and size and homogeneity imply that problems of suburbs are not as complex as for cities. This, in turn, means that citizens can more easily comprehend town problems and politics and can devote more energy to problems, such as zoning, that are considered to be important. Citizens don't have to apply much pressure because of the self-perpetuating nature of the political process in suburban communities and because of more direct control over that process. The citizens of a suburban community elect commissioners who are generally known to them. These commissioners then appoint the zoning board of adjustment for that community. The commissioners reappoint the board of adjustment members only if they maintain the "community spirit" (as interpreted by the commissioners). In addition, the zoning board members are subject to pressures (informal strategies) from local neighborhood and civic associations. The circular, ingrown nature of the process (community elects commissioners, who appoint zoning board, which is pressured by the community, which elects commissioners, and so forth) creates "tight little exclusionary islands" (Sager, 1969) that perpetuate their homogeneity by utilizing the loose enforcement of zoning codes on a regional level and strict enforcement on a local level.

Thus, informal strategies are related not so much to a specific political system as to the general makeup of suburban communities, including their politics (Babcock, 1966). In a very homogeneous suburb, the resident may have to do little or nothing to maintain and perpetuate his suburb. In a less homogeneous suburb, a resident may join a civic association to lobby for his zoning rights, but this seems more of a preventive safeguard than a necessary offensive. Unless his community is subject to a major change of form, the suburban resident can rest assured that the homogeneity of his area will, almost without aid, perpetuate itself.

The informal strategies noted above are those common to many activist groups. Sometimes a controversy splits a suburb; for instance, when businessmen propose expansion of the commercial district and are opposed by residents. In this case, strategies are aimed more at responding indirectly to specific opponents and less at directly influencing the formal decision makers. The deliberate mix of strategies, important though it may be to the ultimate outcome, does not generally affect the kinds of strategy available to suburban groups. A tentative list of informal strategies includes public hearing—speakers, petition, letters of support; picket; boycott; national advocate group support; legal threats or lawsuit; sit-in; local neighborhood groups referenda; general influence.

Zoning, as it is used in the suburbs, is a middle-class phenomenon. It is used to protect exclusivity, which is the backbone of homogeneity or compatibility. In low-income urban neighborhoods, homogeneity is not at such a premium, because restrictions on land use mean restraints on possibilities for change. If a resident wants to add a store or apartments to his dwelling or a store or a factory wishes to expand, it is more convenient not to have to fight strict zoning ordinances that prohibit such changes. The opportunity to enhance property for monetary advantage may be much more important in the low-income neighborhood than maintaining a homogeneous community. Middle- and upper-class communities see neighborhood value as crucial to house value; the pure value of a house is supplemented by a neighborhood value to make up the market value. In the ghetto, neighborhood value is less crucial to property value, and it is possible to alter the pure value of a property by simply changing its use. Conversion of individual properties becomes the road to optimal market value.

One can only ignore neighborhood value for a limited time when attempting to raise the market value of a property, which makes a certain amount of stability desirable in the long run. The short-run individualistic approach demands flexibility, but the long-run neighborhood approach demands stability. In the short run the low-income property owner can raise market value by adding to his property directly; in the long run, his property can only be enhanced by a general upgrading of his neighborhood (Fagin, 1955).

POLICY IMPLICATIONS

Flexibility, permitted by loose zoning restrictions, is more of a fringe benefit and is gained at the expense of discretion over the kinds of land use in a neighborhood. This becomes evident when the low-income resident tries to make the transition from flexibility to stability, or from individual property enhancement to neighborhood upgrading. At that point, he finds that he has no control over neighborhood change and that more often than not he cannot change the flexible character of zoning for his community.

What seems to happen is that the low-income resident finds that not only is he unable to affect neighborhood value, but his neighborhood is subject to an influx of outsiders who take advantage of the short-run flexibility and profit to build whatever they want. In a community striving for some kind of long-term stability, this creates a negative effect. In an efficient situation, the benefits that an outsider receives from installing a noxious land use in a neighborhood (such as a take-out hamburger house) are transferred as loss to the neighborhood. With no discretionary powers, the low-income community remains in the short-run position of flexibility. Middle-class communities, on the other hand, have developed discretionary powers, so that noxious facilities are placed in low-income communities both for traditional (i.e., economic) and practical (i.e., political) reasons. The ratio of pure and total or market (i.e., pure plus neighborhood enhancement) value (P_v/T_v) of property to discretion is defined as in Figure 2, with middle-class and low-income communities in the indicated places.

In some sense, too, the forced flexibility in low-income communities forms part of a vicious circle. Because of existing flexibility, the property owner finds that he can control his own property use and expects that others can control theirs. Mainly because of naïveté and existing practices, he does not try to control neighborhood value as a whole by an orderly pattern of land uses. This lack of neighborhood control is emphasized by outsiders, who take advantage of the flexibility not to upgrade but to ensure continued short-run advantages. The resident, perhaps later desirous of the advantages of increasing neighborhood value, must now face a great number and variety of land uses. His naïveté turns into defeatism when he tries to challenge outside forces that are better organized and have more political clout than himself. Whereas, initially, flexibility meant that he could easily enhance his own property, its exploitation soon indicates that it is a mixed blessing. The cycle is complete.

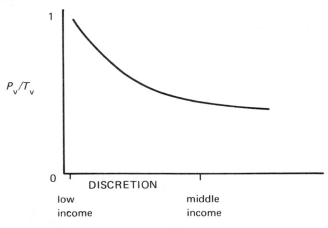

FIGURE 2 Ratio of pure and total value of property to discretion.

SUGGESTED COMMUNITY ALTERNATIVES FOR INCREASED DISCRETION

The suburban strategies previously discussed are not operative in low-income urban neighborhoods because of a number of factors that can only be outlined briefly here. Such areas have essentially inherited most of their physical stock from the prezoning period and therefore frequently contain mixed residential, commercial, and industrial activities that attract few entrants who have any degree of choice; there is little potential for enticing high-amenity land use into the areas. Existing stock is difficult to maintain because of the more pressing and immediate community problems of unemployment, crime, poor health, and education that occupy community leaders.

Community residents are relatively powerless to prevent further downgrading of their neighborhoods through the entry of noxious facilities. Mobilization and active participation in community organizations cannot be expected to develop and sustain themselves in the same degree as in other types of community, although the need for vigilance and pressure is much greater. Despair and defeatism because of the community's inability to stand up against city hall or a major gasoline company discourages such activism.

The recent movement to make ghetto communities more self-contained, with a mix of housing, services, and jobs, tends to perpetuate the negative externalities of a mixed land-use pattern. City government, so badly in need of revenue and simultaneously unable politically to offend remaining middle-income neighborhoods, is highly motivated to maintain and even to reinforce existing patterns of facilities with their positive and negative spillover effects. A low level of indigenous ownership of housing and establishments implies a higher level of outside discretion in land-use change.

These situations imply that low-income communities need different formal (and informal) structures to give them increased discretion over land-use changes. A number of such structures are discussed here, followed by several scenarios of actual land-use cases.

COMMUNITY TECHNICAL SERVICES

As matters stand, a community without resources has few alternatives to direct protest (Reiner and others, 1971). This is unfortunate. Events in citizen-opposition cases suggest that affected communities can indeed raise important planning and engineering questions. Effective and intelligent community participation can be made an integral part of the planning process, with significant gains in efficiency and a fallout of benefits to other parties. Therefore, to achieve more effective and productive planning, we offer the following proposal for a Community Technical Services (CTS) unit.

The Need for a New Institution

In the course of a controversy, affected parties are repeatedly asked for quick, carefully thought out, and detailed responses. Unfortunately, the public hearing, as it is now organized, is only an arena for contest, a therapeutic device for letting off steam; it is not a vehicle for deliberation. Current highway-planning procedures do not take into consideration that the region as a whole benefits when various entities have the capacity to contribute during the design process.

A locally based and operating planning and analysis unit, with specific operating functions and a qualified technical staff, seems to be the best way to respond to these needs. This idea is an outgrowth of precedents in the provision of legal services. It also draws inspiration from the continuing need to interpret the increasingly complex technical material of plans (Michael, 1968). As we elaborate on the possible tasks for a CTS unit, we shall further explain the justification for such a unit.

Tasks of the Community Technical Services Unit

We see a number of possible functions for a CTS operation. The unit could respond to the proposals presented by public agencies and develop alternatives to such proposals. A CTS unit could also play a role in the surveys of community characteristics that underlie many planning efforts. Also important is the rendering of assistance to the community in the gradual articulation of its objectives and standards, so that the previous tasks can be more effectively handled (Boyce and others, 1971). Finally, such an organization could serve as a training ground for more effective participation and development of certain skills by concerned citizens.

Response to Public-Agency Proposals. Perhaps the most visible of the tasks that a CTS unit might perform would be to respond to public-agency proposals. On the simplest level, this would include review of plans in terms of their internal structure and consistency. Are the avowed objectives met? Are accepted engineering standards satisfied? Are the various parts in harmony with each other, and are the constraints set by other projects recognized?

A more sophisticated version of this job is to question, when necessary, the validity of the standards and criteria that are used; these are not immutable statements or propositions that have unquestioned truth value. Thus, for example, in the controversy over the Crosstown Expressway in Philadelphia, it would have been reasonable to question early in the controversy whether a road with a design speed in the 40–50-mph range should be built, as well as to study whether traffic would indeed move at that speed. Further, it would have been appropriate to analyze the implications of alternative speed combinations. What effect would different road speeds have on capacities of the various links? What would be the impact on the demand for the link? What effect would the changed expressway speed standards have on the demand for mass transit?

Surveys of Community Characteristics. Intelligent reaction to a technically competent proposal also requires the capacity to judge the soundness of the proposal with respect to the values and expectations of affected parties. The capacity must exist to measure the impact in terms of the various definitions of community and to assess the preference orderings for the several alternatives by these communities. One important task that a CTS unit could perform would be to help narrow down value generalities to sets of criteria, objectives, and programs that are essential in any evaluation of projects or programs. Translation and specification of values does not take place automatically or without expenditure of effort. One significant role of the planner is to be a value technician for his clients (Reiner, 1967). This involves, first, help to the community or to its client in articulating its ends and delineating alternate sets of ends that the community might wish to consider—a job of value design. The value technician must also assist the community in remolding these values and goals into operational and programmatic form.

Community Characteristics Clarified. A closely related task is the discovery of the distribution of values and goals within the affected community. If there is general harmony, doubts such as arose in the Crosstown Expressway case of who spoke for whom will not arise. We have, of course, no illusions that every community has a well-developed and internally consistent set of values, goals, and criteria. We see the CTS unit as having precisely the function of helping the community as a client to clarify and articulate such a value system.

Education and Training. The very operation of a CTS would have long-range benefits. In addition to adding to the feeling of effective participation, it could be set up as an educational center for the community. It could serve as a means for vocational and professional upgrading in a field where there is a recognized personnel shortage, particularly of people from poverty and minority backgrounds. A well-functioning system of CTS's can also serve as a training ground for public-agency technical personnel and for those in policy-making positions, bringing them closer to the grass roots and to the affected clients.

What might such a CTS have offered in a case such as the Crosstown Expressway problem? First, because of the frankly critical position of the affected community, certain elements of the proposal that became controversial and that contributed to delays in making decisions would have been brought to the surface earlier. Second, the rather indefinite and at times tentatively offered alternatives could have been developed earlier and more specifically. Third, with regard to the objectives and values of the residents of the community, more detailed knowledge of housing preferences and of the potential use made of the neighborhood, its facilities, and transportation systems would have helped prepare a parallel community-development plan. Fourth, the existence of a CTS unit, at several critical junctures, would have helped resolve the problem of the information base on which the various proposals were built and the constraints that were said to limit the project. There were repeated conflicts concerning the number of dwelling units actually occupied, the number of families living in the area as renters and as owners, and the number of businesses and their intention to move or stay in the vicinity.

Administrative and Budget Constraints for a CTS

We envisage the CTS functioning on a relatively modest scale, but having the capacity to handle a variety of planning and development problems. As an example, we have developed a tentative budget: Table 1 gives a breakdown of expenses for a CTS with a budget of approximately $250,000 a year. Except for income from contract work, roughly balanced by increased expenses, we should expect state, federal, and local government agencies to fund the CTS unit.

A rough order of estimate for a client group might be one such unit per 50,000 people, creating an expenditure level of perhaps five dollars per person per year. Another reasonable estimate might be to follow the precedent of the Community Legal Services, which provides one office (in the case of Philadelphia) for about 50,000 population in the target area.

Opportunities for technical training should be budgeted from central planning commission budgets or funded by the Department of Streets, or such semipublic bodies as the Redevelopment Authority. These training opportunities, as we have suggested should also be open to residents. One form that these opportunities might take is to require 2 or 3 years of service with a CTS unit in exchange for a college or graduate-school education in a professional field. This approach is used in medical fields in a number of developing nations.

If a CTS unit is to function as a community organization for the whole range of reasons given above, two other aspects must be considered. The first is that the income of

TABLE 1 A Tentative Proposal for a Community Technical Services (CTS) Unit Budget Framework

Staff	Expenditures (dollars)
Technical	
senior planner	12,000
engineer	12,000
economist	12,000
sociologist	12,000
community worker	12,000
architect	12,000
additional salary for technical staff member who serves as director	3,000
benefits	25,000
subtotal	100,000
Administrative	
receptionist	7,000
secretary-typist (2)	14,000
bookkeeper	7,000
statistical clerk	7,000
draftsman	7,000
benefits	8,000
subtotal	50,000
Field staff (3)	21,000
benefits	4,000
subtotal	25,000
Consultants	
specialists in such subjects as pollution management, mortgage financing	30,000
Rental	5,000
Supplies, telephone, printing	5,000
Miscellaneous and contingency, at 15 percent	35,000
TOTAL (per year)	250,000

CTS employers, possible rental payments, and other expenditures have a small but measurable impact on the community economy. The second consideration is control. It is, of course, entirely within the spirit of the proposal that the management of a CTS be community-based. Thus, we could envisage day-to-day control as well as policy making a matter of concern of a local board. Such a board, administering the CTS and its budget, would set criteria for hiring personnel, designate research and survey operations, and approve the results of such work.

COMMUNITY ALERTING SERVICE

The Community Alerting Service is in use in Philadelphia. It covers information from the City Council, City Planning Commission, Redevelopment Authority, Zoning Board of Adjustment, State Liquor Control Board, Board of Education, and the Delaware Valley Regional Planning Commission.

Information available concerns all operations of these agencies, regular meeting dates, public hearings, location of meetings and hearings, and it identifies persons at the agencies to be contacted for information.

The Philadelphia Council for Community Advancement underwrites most of the cost of this service, and community groups pay minimal fees. Individuals and businesses, however, pay the actual cost of the service.

The city is divided into 11 districts, and the weekly listing provides information for all districts, by district. It also includes matters of citywide concern. A great effort is made to provide this information in enough time for communities to be able to use it. This means relying on the newspaper to find out the date of some hearings, because city hall is generally slower in announcing the date. Because most entries are listed by calendar number or bill number, it is easy to check on the future disposition of most actions. Thus, the service listed an application for certification of an extension of a school for the blind in zone 1 that was submitted in March 1971; a public hearing on the application was held on March 18 (listed in the March 12 report of the service). The April 30 report of the service listed this certification as granted. Unfortunately, this lag in reporting the results is not uniform, and one must search through several listings before finding out the disposition of a particular bill, variance, and so forth.

The Community Alerting Service is therefore a strictly informational service provided to communities who are then left to decide what to do. Such a service could, however, play a broader role. It could make a more active attempt to involve communities by providing (or listing) advocates for them. It could list not only what was happening, but who in each district, or in the city, might be able to help a community wishing to oppose an action. Further, the service could encourage more direct community participation in the listing service by training community people to perform the service for themselves. The process of communities dealing directly with city agencies in this manner might mean less lag in information diffusion and more direct concern by both community and city in such affairs. Finally, the service could follow up more energetically on the events occurring in the communities. For instance, it could report the progress and result of certain community fights with the actions listed, thus providing other communities with possible allies or simply experiential advice.

Thus, although the Community Alerting Service, as it exists, is just a service, with a little effort it could become an agency for advocacy.

REMAPPING

Remapping is an updating of formal zoning regulations for an area within the city. The remapping procedure in Philadelphia is based, as one of its directors noted, on compromise. If that compromise works well enough to result in successful remapping, it is because the Planning Commission is strong enough to control it. For instance, the Commission has the power at any point to abandon the remapping procedure in a particular community if there is not agreement. Further, they reserve the right of final review and generally act as liaison with the other important city agencies (City Council, Redevelopment Authority, and so forth) involved in the process. Nonetheless, the procedure allows for a good deal of community discretion, if not over major changes, at least over minor ones. The process can be described as consisting of the following 14 steps:

1. A community comes to the City Planning Commission and asks for remapping to be done in its area. (The Commission does not initiate remapping, both because of the formal structure of the procedure and because it is believed to be considerably easier to deal with communities that request remapping.) The communities generally learn of the possibilities for remapping through the Planning Commission area planners, or by seeing the process at work in neighboring communities.

2. A meeting with the community is held by the Planning Commission. A 10-man (this number is flexible) committee is chosen by the community to represent itself.

3. Zoning is explained verbally to the committee, because experience has shown that *ad lib* talks have more impact than written statements.

4. The committee begins a publicity program in the community through local newspapers, word of mouth, and so forth.

5. The Planning Commission works, block by block, with people for the first week only. After that, the people do all the leg work of finding out exactly what is in the community.

6. The Planning Commission begins to make contacts with the local Councilman, the Redevelopment Authority, and others interested in the community.

7. After the community submits the list of suggestions, the Commission goes over the list with staff planners.

8. The list of suggestions, with the planners' changes, is taken back to the community and discussed until a final list is prepared.

9. The committee calls a general community meeting to discuss this final list.

10. The list, as approved by the community, goes back to the Planning Commission for final approval.

11. After approval by the Planning Commissioners, an ordinance is prepared for presentation to the City Council.

12. The ordinance is presented by the district Councilman. There is usually no conflict here; Councilmen are willing to do this.

13. A public hearing is held by the Rules Committee.

The community is expected to support the ordinance and to handle possible dissident elements.

14. The City Council passes the ordinance, and the Mayor signs it.

The whole process takes about one year. Once remapping begins, most community committees stay in existence in a watchdog capacity.

Table 2 gives the zoning districts of Philadelphia's Zoning Code. Two conclusions can be drawn from the specific example of the remapping of the Haddington section of Philadelphia.

1. There is slight reduction of density for the area, mostly the result of converting much of R-9 and R-10 usage (row single-family, or two families, or apartments) to R-9A and R-10A usage (row single-family). In one section, on the other hand, an area shopping center was moved and reduced to a neighborhood shopping center, leaving a full block for new single-family housing.

2. The general mix of land uses in the area has been left the same. There was some effort to consolidate all industrial uses in one place, although general commercial uses remained generally in the same places. Again, there was an attempt to concentrate recreational areas; of the six parks, ranging from one block to several square blocks, that were there originally, only two remained in the remapping. The others were removed for housing.

It is evident that the remapping effort was more of a "tightening-up" of the neighborhood than an attempt to change its character in any way. Without knowing the history of the changes, it is impossible to know whether this was a result of citizen action, planner action, or mutual consent. It seems clear, however, that major changes in a neighborhood will come only through means other than remapping, such as urban renewal and forceful citizen action.

GUIDELINES FOR COMMUNITY-ORGANIZED OPPOSITION TO THE INTRODUCTION OF UNDESIRED FACILITIES

A public or private agency that is interested in expanding or relocating should look closely at a community where numerous emotional crises arise, at the capability of local community groups to communicate these crises, and at the local community response to these community-group messages (Malko, 1970). Is the message short, to the point, simple in language, and emotional? If so, community response is likely. To successfully mobilize against an intruding agency, it matters not what the crisis is; it matters whether or not the community-at-large responds to the

TABLE 2 Zoning Districts, Philadelphia Zoning Code

Type	Classification
Residential	
Single home, one family	R-1, R-2
Twin home, one family	R-3, R-4, R-5
Twin home, two families	R-5A
Row single-family or two families	R-7, R-8
Row single family	R-9A, R-10A
Row single-family or two families or apartments	R-9, R-10
Garden apartments (Districts vary in density.)	R-11, R-11A, R-12, R-13
Commercial	
Corner stores and small groups of 3 or 4 stores. No parking required.	C-1
Retail commercial. Large row of stores (strip commercial). No parking required.	C-2
Wholesale and retail commercial motels, offices. Parking required only for motels.	C-3
Similar to C-2, but does not permit same variety of users. Parking required.	C-7
Small group of stores with common parking area.	NSC (neighborhood shopping center)
Larger stores such as supermarkets and department stores; smaller stores are permitted. Parking required.	ASC (area shopping center)
Industrial	
Light industry; all uses inside building	L-1, L-2, L-3, L-4
General heavy industry; uses inside building.	G-1
General heavy industry; uses inside and outside building	G-2
Very heavy industry to include oil refineries, incinerators, steel works, rendering plants.	LR (least restricted)
Special	
Use only on existing playgrounds and parks	Recreational

Source: Philadelphia City Planning Commission.

community group, either by letter or at town meetings. Should a community group succeed in generating many well-attended town meetings with local politicians and agency people present, and should the meetings be orderly with a great deal of after-meeting follow-through, then the community group is likely to be an effective community-mobilizing force and thus present potential opposition to the expanding or relocating agency.

Before a community group can call for town meetings, it must be well known in the community. High "visibility" points, such as current and proposed programs, can draw attention to a community group, but a community group must guard against antagonizing other community groups in their area when aligning with these programs. Although audacity often works well when seeking funds and services from city agencies, it can fail when used against other community groups. From the point of view of an expanding or relocating agency, areas with many community-improvement programs can increase the recognition possibilities of a community group but can also limit the number of programs an expanding agency can bring as tradeoffs.

A new community group is limited to acquiring power by mobilizing large numbers of people, but this technique is awkward and certainly difficult to achieve. Most outside agencies won't hesitate to move into a community when only this mode of community-group power exists. Once a group is established and recognized in the community, it may seek power by cultivating friendships with the existing city power elite and also by assuming power with the image-building techniques of graphic and verbal publicity. A test of a community group's relative position of power in the community is whether agencies will seriously discuss community problems with them. Because successful community encounters with agencies depend, in part, on the community group's ability to portray a sense of orderliness and coordination, an expanding or relocating agency would do well to research a community group's past history in dealing successfully with other agencies and to take careful note of how the community group runs its meetings.

The success of a community group depends largely on the boundaries it claims as its own. Boundaries should be drawn to assist in expanding the community group's membership, to draw attention to the community group, to rationalize the boundaries for future planning, and to include certain individuals, businesses, and institutions that could assist the community group in programs and planning. Once a boundary is fixed, maps should be published and distributed to all major city agencies. A community group with no established boundary lacks a defined sphere of community influence and thus definable constituency. In general, an expanding or relocating agency should avoid community groups that equivocate when discussing area-wide community problems. Should a number of only marginally strong but vocal community groups exist, then the community group should consider developing a coalition. In general, an agency will and should avoid discussions with community groups having no established boundaries.

For whatever the reasons, community groups and agencies alike accept the working arrangement of community task forces. When each task force works with solutions in sight, establishes clear-cut objectives, and has all its work lead to some conclusions and direct actions, then task forces can be effective organizational tools in the hands of the community group. If this is not possible, then an agency with an eye for expansion will, and should, question the validity of the source, relevance, and priority of issues arising out of the community group. If a community group does not have the resources to sustain its efforts over many years, it will falter and eventually disappear. To an expanding or relocating agency this can mean the eventual removal of community opposition or the loss of a valuable ally.

Leadership is of paramount importance to a community group; if it does not have to answer to its community, if it fails to generate new leadership, if it fails to make relevant assignments for its staff and task force, and if it shirks its own responsibilities for community-improvement projects, then the community group will probably be ineffective. A good community leadership or lack of it will set the scene for community–agency discussions. When poor community leadership exists, an agency will determine its own destiny in that community.

An enterprising community group will list all potential resource people within and without the community. A community workshop, or something similar, under the direction of an exacting taskmaster should be formed to provide entry points for these people.

Local institutions with a taste for community acceptance could provide the community group with a structure of administrative procedures along with professional office staff, supplies, office space, and community/agency liaison workers. Program and proposal writers are always needed by community groups. To compensate for a lack of community administrative talent the community groups should seek programs that have outsiders doing the administrative work, with the community group determining program content and policy. Most community-generated and run programs can be administered in the beginning by outsiders, but the outsider should not have administrative roles in the community-group structure itself.

A community group with the organizational skill to recruit outside help and place it in the community, in addition to demonstrating an ability to replace this help with community people, will remain in the area for a long time. In general, a measure of a community group's ability to oppose an expanding or relocating agency is its ability to mobilize, organize, and administer both community people and outsiders.

Community groups should be cautious about receiving renewable funds from an agency, agency liaison people seeking social and political information about the community, agencies that are internally well organized, and agencies that appear magnanimously to bestow the community group with the responsibility of informing the community-at-large of the agency's plans.

Community groups should continually enlarge their list of allies, including influential politicians, city commissioners, and agencies and their staff. They should know these people and agencies well enough to be able to support the agency's pet projects, know the friendship pattern between them as well as their enemies, and know their funding sources along with the regulatory agencies that control them. They should be familiar with the formal and informal procedures of entering into the federal, state, city, and private dollar "pipelines." The community group should seek community representatives on all local agency boards, committees, and task forces.

If a community group is well entrenched in the establishment, it can demand and get packages of city services and expert advice from agency resource people. When requesting services, a community group should send a summary of the demand to all related and supportive agencies, addressed to a sympathetic individual in that agency. Hell-raising should be used only to set the scene for future demands, to assist in mobilizing the community around an issue, and for publicity.

Community-group meetings with agency representatives should be thoroughly researched and discussed before each meeting with an appropriate strategy and corresponding agenda resulting. If the community group is to sweep the agency's arguments under the table in the early minutes of subsequent meetings, a review of the community group should follow the meeting and decisions about the next step should be made. The community group should use as many as possible of the available clergy for daytime meetings and interested working people in the evening. General evening information "town meetings" should not be mixed with community-group business meetings. In general, no agency representative must be let "off the hook" during a meeting.

Before any formal discussions or negotiations with an agency begin, the community group should feel reasonably confident that sufficient pressure can be brought to bear on the agency to force it to adhere to any future agreements.

A community group can and should take the lead in negotiations by stating a list of demands, but it must insist that the agency refer to these demands as requests. An excellent place for a community group to begin reviewing an agency's position is in consultant work done for that agency. Once this basic research is done, a community group should publicly and explicitly state to the local community their relation with the agency, and as this relation develops, it should be put into contract form.

A community group should be suspicious of any negotiations that enter into a forum of simultaneous debates, that reject slow but effective bargaining techniques, or that lack an implementation commitment from the agency participants. Some set of bargaining rules and agenda should be followed with a careful selection of discussion points agreeable to both participants. Finally, a community group must never close off negotiations or dialogue with an agency once they have begun. This shuts the door to future agency commitments.

This report has attempted to answer the question: How can one, in advance, identify community or neighborhood groups that for one reason or another come to effectively oppose civic-improvement projects? With many or all of the above-mentioned characteristics, the chances of a community group's successful opposition is likely.

An expanding agency or institution must evaluate the neighborhood crisis potential of their proposed new site, the mobilizing and organizing abilities of local community groups, the number of active community-improvement projects in the area, the power-acquisition techniques available to local groups, the success of community groups in dealing with other agencies, whether a community group has carefully drawn physical boundaries, the characteristics and number of neighborhood leaders, the number of outside agencies aligned with the community group, and the internal capability of the agency to deal with community groups. How informed is the community group of the agency? How much money does a community group have at its disposal? How well known is a specific community group, and finally, how acceptable to the community is the agency's available package of tradeoffs?

FUTURE SCENARIOS

This second group of scenarios presents some possible outcomes if changes, both good and bad, are made in the distribution of discretionary powers.

SCENARIO 4

One prediction for 1980, for example, conjures up an image of incensed separate communities within metropolitan areas manning roadblocks to halt metropolitan projects. Abandoned roadbeds stop at the boundaries of communities, and citizen groups defy pleas, court orders, and police actions. Communities are pockmarked with partly demolished sites and cleared land waiting to be developed for hospitals, low-income housing, and local power plants. Attempts to develop mechanisms for producing equity between communities break down because of the controversies over definitions, weighting, and priorities. Central government authorities have declared a halt to all future public projects that benefit some communities more than others.

SCENARIO 5

Another 1980 fantasy is quite different. Policy makers and planners have highly developed skills of threat, intimidation, and least-cost selection. They are adept at withholding information until it is too late for community groups to act effectively. With a shifting power base, they carry out their expert plans for making the city into an admirable model of efficiency, cleanliness, and aesthetic beauty.

SCENARIO 6

Another 1980 alternative reflects the prominent participation of national action groups in community problems. Groups such as the Sierra Club, the Urban League, Kiwanis, and the American Legion lend their assistance to the solution of community–environment problems. The legal arms of these national groups and their own priorities for solutions to community problems have a very effective voice in shaping outcomes. Many small communities are the scene of contests between those mammoth citizen groups attempting to implement their own solutions. Local community interests do not get aired, nor can they be given much consideration by public officials who must placate the large and powerful groups and their local spokesmen.

SCENARIO 7

A final scenario is of organized community-planning groups set up for most neighborhoods of a metropolitan area. Centralized planning for cities, or for metropolitan areas as a whole, has largely ceased in favor of a semijudicial body that balances the expressed needs of the small communities. Community planning boards, originating in the middle sixties, are the focus for many other activities in addition to their original purpose, which was indigenous planning. Health, education, welfare, social activities, and other functions are managed through the community organizations. Based on local resources and population skills, the community planning functions are carried out in a way consistent with community needs and local politics. Community organizers help to present the issues and alternatives to the local population. Community planning receives its support from the capital program for the city but is permitted wide discretion in employing experts to assist in the technical aspects and to train neighborhood people in the process. The structure works well in employing local knowledge and expertise supplemented by technical help to yield feasible and politically acceptable solutions for neighborhood problems.

CONCLUSIONS AND RECOMMENDATIONS

For low-income communities to exercise a greater degree of discretion over the neighborhood environment implies greater control over four major functions: maintenance of existing properties, elimination of undesired land-use activities, prevention of noxious facilities from entering, and inducement of desired services and other land use. The strategies that have been described, including remapping, Community Technical Services, Community Alerting Service, and community organizing principles, all deal with some aspects of these community functions. (For another example of alternative strategy see Twentieth Century Fund Task Force on Community Development Corporations, 1971.) These strategies do not ensure greater community discretion or neighborhood satisfaction, either alone or in combination. In practice, as has been demonstrated, the strategies do not always mesh with the political system as it exists and operates.

To make metropolitan policy making more responsive to the needs of communities requiring the most attention, the demands of such communities must be felt. Community mobilization in low-income neighborhoods must first overcome the self-fulfilling defeatism and self-perceived marginalism that breed defeat. The community that does not mobilize is subject to severe costs because of the wedge left open for outsider opportunism and the city's expediency. Sometimes a community must run just to stay in place.

There is another relatively minor danger. Imitating suburban strategies can also lead to dysfunctional aspects. Just as many suburban areas are locked into the bind of having produced a sterile form of homogeneity (compatibility) at a severe cost to the overall metropolitan area, low-income neighborhoods might find as well that too much success can yield dissatisfaction. This is not a danger as yet, but mindless admiration for the middle-class mode may lead to ever-increasing metropolitan sterility.

ACKNOWLEDGMENTS

We are grateful to the many people who have helped to develop the ideas for this paper. In particular, we wish to thank Thomas Reiner of the Regional Science Department, University of Pennsylvania; David Cohen, formerly of the Philadelphia City Council; Ralph Hirsch and Barry Malko of the Philadelphia City Planning Commission; Barbara Teaford of the Delaware Valley Housing Association; and Yale Rabin of the NAACP Legal Defense Fund. We gratefully acknowledge partial support by the National Science Foundation (Project GS-2758).

REFERENCES

Altschuler, Alan A., 1970. Community Control: The Black Demand for Participation in Large American Cities. New York: Western Publishing Company.

Babcock, Richard, 1966. The Zoning Game. Madison: University of Wisconsin Press.

Boyce, David, Chris McDonald, and André Farhi, 1971. An interim report on procedures for continuing metropolitan planning. Philadelphia: Regional Science Research Institute.

Fagin, Henry, 1955. Regulating the timing of urban development. Law and Contemporary Problems, 20 (1955).

Malko, Barry, 1970. Notes on the development of a community opposition group. Research on conflict in locational decisions. University of Pennsylvania Regional Science Department Discussion Paper No. VI.

Michael, Donald, 1968. On coping with complexity: Planning and politics. Daedalus, 97 (4), 1179–1193.

Muglia, Allen, 1961. An inquiry into the philosophy and practice of zoning. M.A. thesis, University of Pennsylvania.

Natoli, Salvatore, 1971. Zoning and the development of urban land-use patterns. Economic Geography, 47 (1971).

Reiner, Thomas, 1967. The planner as value technician: Two classes of utopian constructs and their impacts on planning. *In* H. Wentworth Eldredge, *Ed.*, Taming Megalopolis, Vol. I, p. 232–247. Garden City, N.Y.: Doubleday (Anchor Books).

Reiner, Thomas, John Seley, and Robert Sugarman, 1971. The Crosstown controversy: A case study. Research on conflict in locational decisions. University of Pennsylvania Regional Science Department Discussion Paper XII.

Sager, Lawrence Gene, 1969. Tight little islands: Exclusionary zoning, equal protection, and the indigent. Stanford Law Review (April).

Trubeck, David, 1970. Exclusionary zoning: Cases, statutes, materials. New Haven, Connecticut: Yale Law School.

Twentieth Century Fund Task Force on Community Development Corporations, 1971. CDCs: New Hope for the Inner City. New York: Twentieth Century Fund.

U.S. Commission on Civil Rights, 1970. Land use control in relation to racial and economic integration. Washington, D.C.: U.S. Commission on Civil Rights. Staff Report.

U.S. National Commission on Urban Problems (Douglas Commission), 1968. Building the American city. 91st Congress, 1st Session. House Document No. 91-34.

Weiner, Peter, 1971. Report: Fifth Conference on Exclusionary Land Use Problems. Report prepared for the National Urban Coalition.

Williams, Norman, and Thomas Norman, undated (c. 1970). Exclusionary land-use controls. The case of north-eastern New Jersey. (Mimeo)

The Physical Environment and Urban Planning

M. GORDON WOLMAN
The Johns Hopkins University

For simplicity, almost all theoretical formulations of spatial phenomena assume the existence of a featureless plain on which to develop constructs of spatial relations. This justifiable assumption has led to a flowering of perceptive analyses. It flies in the face, however, of an old tenet that emphasizes the importance of the unique qualities of hills and valleys to planning and design of the urban scene. Whitehill (1968, p. viii) for example, quotes "Non potest civitas abscondi supra montem posita. . ." (One cannot hide a city located on a mountain), recognizing the significance of a hill to a town. The recent revival of interest in the environment and in landscape reemphasizes the importance that people have always attached to site, scene, and variety of the landscape. Theoretical literature accumulated over the past decades casts only a pale light on the questions to which planners seek answers in struggling to create a rational design of the urban scene.

Yet the goals are not necessarily antithetical. Ideally, planners might enjoy having theoretical frameworks supported by empirical observations that could be used to evaluate the effect of alternative uses of the natural environment. Such formulations might indicate the consequences of alternative actions or plans, including evaluation of economic and other values gained and lost by particular land-use or planning choices.

The present state of the art does not permit us to move with confidence from a knowledge of landscape processes and form to predictions of the results of future planning actions. Nevertheless, some examples are available that have predictive value, and a good deal of empirical evidence about the physical geography of existing or potential urban areas could be made available if those who could use it knew what it looked like. This paper attempts to set forth a few such examples that may be of some use to urban planners.

Of equal importance to the availability of information about the physical environment is the significance of the information to human settlement and culture. Here the history of geographic thought can be of some intellectual, if not practical, help to the urban planner.

During a moment of its history, geography provided what appeared to be a universal principle of the relation of man to the environment. Environmental determinism, as it came to be called, provided a simple framework with which to analyze the development and behavior of society. People believed that with a proper understanding of such things as landscape and climate, they could discern the underlying causes of successful political developments, dissolution of empires, siting of cities, and forms of agriculture. Subsequent study has demonstrated that simple determinism will not do. Neither the history nor the social structure of a people can be discerned without regard to the total assemblage of historical, cultural, and geographical elements. Man has proved capable of erecting cities and societies in a wide variety of terrains seemingly inhospitable from the standpoint of the natural or physical environment.

Along with the realization that the physical environment was one of many contributors to the cultural scene, it has also become evident that the same environment is perceived differently by different users and observers. Objective measures of environmental parameters do not in themselves assure a common reception and response to the environment by different groups or individuals (Kates, 1962).

The resurgence of concern for environmental deterioration, for rational approaches to planning for new towns, and for rapidly urbanizing areas has stimulated a comparable resurgence of interest in the environment as a guide to settlement, sometimes with a wistful hope that the balance of nature or that ecological imperatives would automatically unlock the proper mode of human settlement. A review of geographic thought suggests that more modest views of the explanatory magic of the geographic environment will prove more durable in the current effort to provide aesthetic and socially acceptable guidelines to development of urban areas. Environmental facts may provide a useful starting point for analysis, even an important element in evaluating alternatives; they will not, in themselves, provide self-evident guidelines to matters of value.

TWO MODES OF INFORMATION

Much information about the natural world is relevant to the design of cities. Although the physical geographer probably views the wares he has to offer with somewhat more enthusiasm than does the urban planner, probably a good deal more usable material is known than is at present used. A closer association of physical geographer and planner might facilitate this use and provide insight into relevant problems. Such an association might also give the planner a better conception of the physical geographer's possible contributions. To suggest the kinds of information that are available and a direction that additional effort might take, examples are given here to illustrate two distinctive approaches both to the kind of information available and to the mode of presentation. One approach deals with the dynamics of process and the other with attributes of the landscape and environment and their portrayal. The difference between the two is artificial: Whereas landscape refers essentially to a static condition, the significance of landscape to planning or to human activity often lies in the processes that take place on these landscapes, and not simply on the form of the land. In addition, with respect to both water and air, the important attributes are those directly related to process. Thus, the distinctions drawn here are principally justified by the degree of understanding of some of the relations involved and their value as illustrative examples.

WATER AND LAND

Over a period of years, for a given climate and a given condition of the land surface, the hydrologic cycle involving the movement of water, sediment, and dissolved substances from the land and through the channel system represents a kind of equilibrium. A change in any of the facets of the system leads to an alteration of the behavior of the cycle itself; thus, the hydrologic system involving both water and land is markedly altered by the construction of a city or town. Runoff to streams is a function of rainfall, evaporation, and transpiration of plants on the drainage basin. Covering the watershed in whole or in part with impermeable materials alters both low flows and peak flows. An increase in the amount of impermeable surface, coupled with an increase in the percentage of the area sewered alters the shape of the flood peak. Because seepage or infiltration is small, and gutters and storm drains transmit flow rapidly, the flood hydrograph is sharper and more peaked on urban lands than on rural lands (Figure 1). The time of runoff is shortened and the volume of direct runoff from a storm is increased. On a drainage basin under natural cover, a flood with a recurrence interval of 50 years has 4.4 times the discharge of the mean annual flood; whereas on a completely (100 percent) impervious basin, the same recurrence interval requires only twice the magnitude of the average flood (Figure 2). On basins that are both impervious and completely sewered with storm drains, the peak discharge from a given rainstorm may be as much as 4 to 8 times greater than on the natural basin. In contrast, small rains, which under natural cover might provide infiltration to the

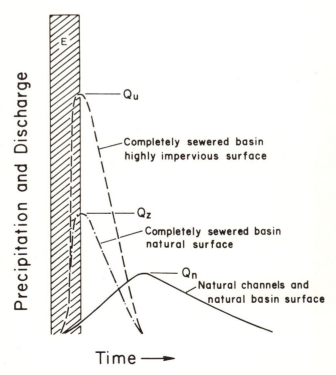

FIGURE 1 Differences in flood hydrographs associated with different land covers and sewerage. (From Anderson, 1970.)

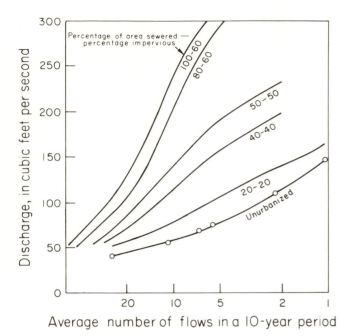

FIGURE 2 Effect of imperviousness on the magnitude of flood discharges and different recurrence intervals. (From Leopold, 1968).

groundwater table, no longer do so. As a consequence, during dry periods the base or low flow of small headwater tributaries declines as the impermeable urban cover expands.

Along with changes in runoff, the clearance of the watershed during construction exposes the land to rapid erosion. The yield of sediment increases as much as 5 to 50 times over that of rural areas during periods of construction (Table 1). Each person newly housed in suburbia contributes about 30 times his weight in sediment. After construction, the urban watershed provides little or no sediment, and the runoff from storm-water systems drains directly and rapidly to unprotected stream channels. In the eastern United States, changes in sediment yield have altered markedly with changes in land use. The process of urbanization leads to marked and rapid fluctuations in yield as land cover moves from pasture to construction to asphalt (Figure 3).

The consequences of rapid and direct flood runoff are increased erosion of the stream banks. Hammer (1970) has shown, for example, that in the Philadelphia area considerable channel enlargement has accompanied urbanization (Figure 4). For a drainage area that is 30 percent impervious, the channel area is roughly 200 percent above values found in surrounding rural areas of comparable size. Such erosion of stream channels may have significant consequences for the maintenance of many urban stream-valley parks. The assumption is often made that a natural stream can be protected and will remain both attractive and self-sustaining simply by maintaining a strip of greenery through a concrete landscape. Aside from the problems of trash, it is clear that the hydrologic changes accompanying urbanization will require that protective vegetation and revetments be installed to prevent removal of adjacent parklands by erosion.

To compensate for the increase in runoff resulting from the change in cover, reservoirs could be constructed well upstream on the watershed. Such reservoirs could be above or below ground and could, in some instances, be no more than expansions in the storm-drainage lines to provide limited storage. Elsewhere, rooftops and parking lots may provide temporary detention storage. Where surface reser-

TABLE 1 Sediment Yield from Drainage Basin under Diverse Conditions

River and Location	Drainage Area (Square Miles)	Sediment Yield (Tons/Square Mile/Year)	Land Use
Broad Ford Run, Md.	7.4	11	Forested
Helton Branch, Ky.	0.85	15	Forested
Fishing Creek, Md.	7.3	5	Forested
Gunpowder Falls, Md.	303	808	Rural-agricultural, farmland in county (1914–1943) 325,000 to 240,000 acres
Gunpower Falls, Md.	303	233	Rural-agricultural, farmland in county (1943–1961) 240,000 to 150,000 acres
Seneca Creek, Md.	101	320	Same
Building site, Baltimore, Md.	0.0025	140,000	Construction, entire area exposed
Little Falls Branch, Md.	4.1	2,320	Construction, small part of area exposed
Stony Run, Md.	2.47	54	Urban

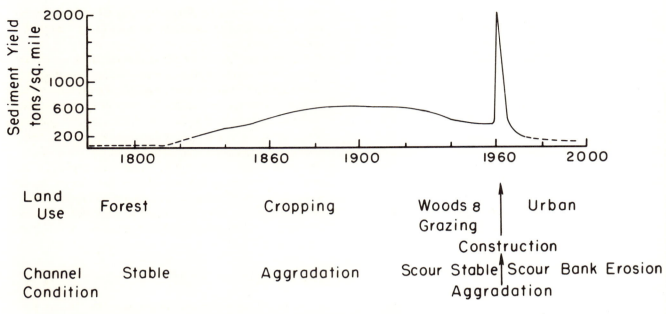

FIGURE 3   Schematic sequence: land use, sediment yield and channel response from a fixed area. (From Wolman, 1967.)

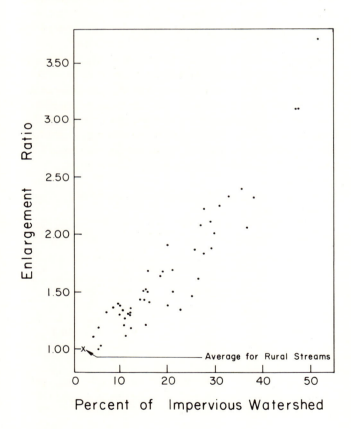

FIGURE 4   Enlargement of channels in urbanized areas compared to comparable channels in rural areas. (From Hammer, 1970.)

voirs are planned, it is important to recognize that reservoirs of limited size may fill with sediment even while construction is under way on the watershed. The quantities of sediment are so large that a pond or reservoir with a capacity of several acre feet may be filled by sediment produced by erosion during one or two summer thunderstorms. Timing of reservoir construction, measures for erosion and sediment control, and legal doctrine protecting downstream residents from later development upstream on the watershed are all required if the planning of urban development is to take adequate cognizance of the realities of land and water processes.

In addition to changes in the quantity of water and in the sediment content, urbanization also induces changes in the quality of streamflow, including the dissolved load, the organic constituents, and the temperature of the water. Studies of Long Island streams, for example, have shown that water in streams in urban areas may be 6–11 °F warmer during the summer than in the winter months, and they are subject to wide fluctuations in contrast to the stable temperature regimes of forested streams (Pluhowski, 1970). Similarly, studies of streams in areas that have been logged show increases in temperature of 15 °F when trees and brush are removed from the edges of the rivers (Brown and Krygier, 1970). Shallow ponds in urban areas, heated streets, a high proportion of direct runoff in contrast to groundwater flow, and removal of stream-bank vegetation are all facets of urbanization, and all contribute to increasing the temperature of the water.

Because streamflow from streets is plentiful, some people have hoped that urban rivers might be improved in water quality by the added inflow. Unfortunately, accumulating data suggest that the runoff from urban areas is of very poor quality. The data in Table 2, from a study in Chicago (American Public Works Association, 1969) indicate that the quality of street litter is comparable to treated sanitary sewage with respect to biochemical oxygen demand (BOD), but contains considerably less phosphorus and nitrogen. However, carbonaceous organic matter, total coliforms, and estimated fecal coliform organisms seem to be nearly as high or higher in the street litter as in sanitary sewage subjected to customary secondary treatment.

Although it is possible to ascribe some costs to the consequences or impact of these environmental changes associated with alteration of the land and water system during the process of urbanization, no generalizations can be made. For example, while an initial benefit is derived from leaving small channels in their natural state, and thus eliminating the cost of additional storm drainage, these benefits may be offset in part or in whole by maintenance costs required to preserve the channels later. In addition, for very small channels the absence of adequate low flows may create ponding, mosquito breeding grounds, and other nuisances. If these consequences are not foreseen, a later decision to place the stream in a storm drain may prove even more costly than additional initial expenditure might have been. This trade off involves three separate accounts, one from capital funds (related to the initial development), another from municipal capital funds for replacement, and a third from operations or taxes.

Because storm drainage is initially enormously expensive, people may think that maintenance or channel improvement could not conceivably match such costs. They should bear in mind, however, that lining a channel with concrete for a city block or two may cost a quarter of a million dollars, and labor costs for alternative vegetative measures, including maintenance, can easily amount to thousands of dollars a year.

This too-brief review of the alterations of the cycle of water runoff and land erosion simply suggests that information is available with which to evaluate the probable effects of urban developments on the behavior of the land surface and river system, both at the site of development and far downstream. To make such evaluations requires a knowledge of soils and climate of a region and their hydrologic interrelationships. Although by no means complete, in fact often fragmentary, such knowledge as there is must be presented in a way that is relevant to the planning process. Only recently has the effort begun to bring such information to bear in the planning and development of urban areas.

THE CLIMATE OF CITIES

For over a century we have known that cities change the local climate (Chandler, 1970). The well-documented variation in temperature has been given the name "urban heat island." Empirical studies have shown that the temperature in cities may be several degrees higher than that in the surrounding countryside, a relation shown for a 24-hour period for the city of Frankfurt in Figure 5. The minimum temperature at midnight is shown to be 2 °C warmer in the city center than on the outskirts. Elsewhere, differences of as much as 5 °C have been measured. Locally, the differential effect of different covers in the city itself can be seen by the contrast in temperature of a concrete and a grass surface when cooling in the late afternoon and evening (Figure 6). Both air and surface temperature of the grass are from 1 ° to 5 ° or 10 °C cooler than a courtyard or parking-lot pavement.

A simplified model, developed by Myrup (1969), illus-

TABLE 2 Comparison of Sanitary Sewage and Street-Litter Pollution Components

	Strength of Sanitary Sewage		Street[a] Litter per Gram	Pounds of Pollutants/Mile[b]			
				Sanitary Sewage		Street Litter	
Item	Raw	Treated		Raw	Treated	1 day	14 days
Biochemical oxygen demand (ppm)	85	11	5,000	85	11	0.8	11.2
Chemical oxygen demand (ppm)	238	34.7	40,000	238	34.7	6.4	89.2
Phosphorus PO$_4$ (ppm)		13.5	50	–	13.5	0.008	.112
Total Nitrogen as N (ppm)	16.8	11.0	500[c]	16.8	11	0.08	1.12
Total coliform/100 ml	[d]	28×10^4	13×16^6	–	25×10^8	47×10^{10}	66×10^{11}
Fecal coliform/100 ml	[d]	16,000	540[c]	–	14×10^7	39×10^5	55×10^6

[a] Assumed weighted average.
[b] Assumed value of 1.5 lb/day/100 ft of curb.
[c] From dust and dirt fraction.
[d] Not determined.
Source: American Public Works Association, 1969, p. 61.

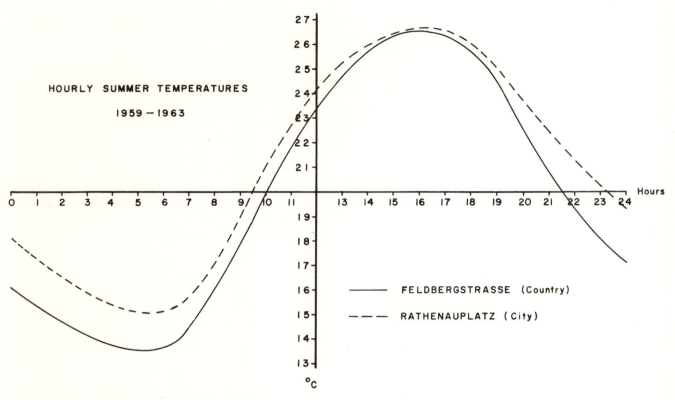

FIGURE 5 Average diurnal trend of temperature in the city and at the border of the city of Frankfurt. (From Georgii, 1970.)

trates some of the mechanisms controlling the development and magnitude of the heat islands and their possible relation to planning and design. Myrup's model is based on a simple energy balance in which the net supply of radiation from the sun is equated to the sum of the radiation lost by evaporation, by the movement of sensible heat to the air, and by the movement of heat into the soil. By evaluating these four parameters, Myrup was able to construct a model of the temperature of cities that compares well with some of the empirical information. Although the model predicts summer temperatures at the surface 6 °C higher during the day and about 4 °C at night, differences comparable to those actually experienced, the maximum differences between city and country occur during the day rather than at night, as shown in the temperatures for Frankfurt (Figure 5).

The model indicates that the absence of evaporative surfaces in the city is of prime importance in creating the heat island. This importance is suggested by a comparison between a city park and the surrounding city center (Figure 7). The maximum difference in temperature is on the order of 12 °C, a figure closely approximated by values obtained in a field study. The critical importance of evaporation is amplified by sensitivity analyses that indicate that a change from about 10 to 20 percent in the area of park-

land in a city decreases daytime temperatures about 1.5 °C. The overall decrease in daytime temperatures when 20 percent of the city is evaporating surface or parkland is about 3.5 °C.

The presence of the heat island is attributed to a variety of factors in addition to the reduction in evaporative areas. These include the reduction in wind speed associated with buildings, man-made production of heat, the change in surface materials, and the presence of pollutants. "Rough" irregular buildings may contribute to the dissipation of heat near the city center, a tendency counter to the "smooth" surface of grassland in parks; however, through evaporation the park compensates for the decreased roughness. The larger the city, the higher the critical wind speed needed to eliminate the heat-island effect (Figure 8).

Detailed studies of the concentration and dispersion of pollutants of city air have also demonstrated spatial and temporal patterns of distribution associated with traffic patterns and with characteristics of climate. Although these distributions are by now familiar (Figure 9), giving an oblique view of the sulphur-dioxide distribution in St. Louis at 4 a.m. and 6 a.m., is included primarily because of the computer mapping technique that it illustrates. The oblique projection provides a striking illustration of the magnitude

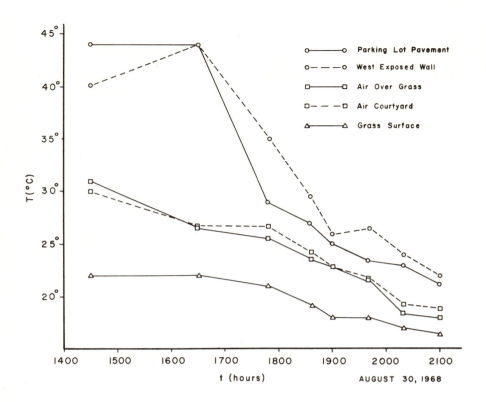

FIGURE 6 Cooling of different surfaces and the air above them in an urban region on a clear night in a continental polar air mass. (From Landsberg, 1970.)

of the concentration of sulfur dioxide and its variation in time and space.

At a very different scale, detailed studies of the micrometeorology of the air spaces and circulation between buildings indicate that not only are gross changes in wind structure and pollution associated with cities, but important variations occur in temperature, in wind speed, and hence in pollutant distribution even on different sides of the street and with different street widths and building heights. For example, Georgii (1970) observed that at low wind speeds (velocity less than 2 m/sec), concentration of carbon monoxide was nearly horizontally stratified across a street, with highest concentration at street level and very little circulation. In contrast, at higher velocities (about 2 m/sec) circulation extends to street level and lines of equal concentration are diagonal, with highest concentra-

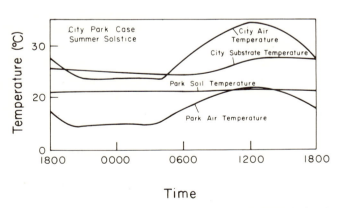

FIGURE 7 Air and soil temperature for a city park area calculated for the summer solstice. Temperatures calculated for the city center are also shown for comparison. (From Myrup, 1969.)

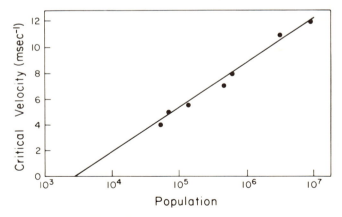

FIGURE 8 Relation between city size (P) and the critical wind speed for elimination of the urban heat-island effect. (From Oke and Hannell, 1970.)

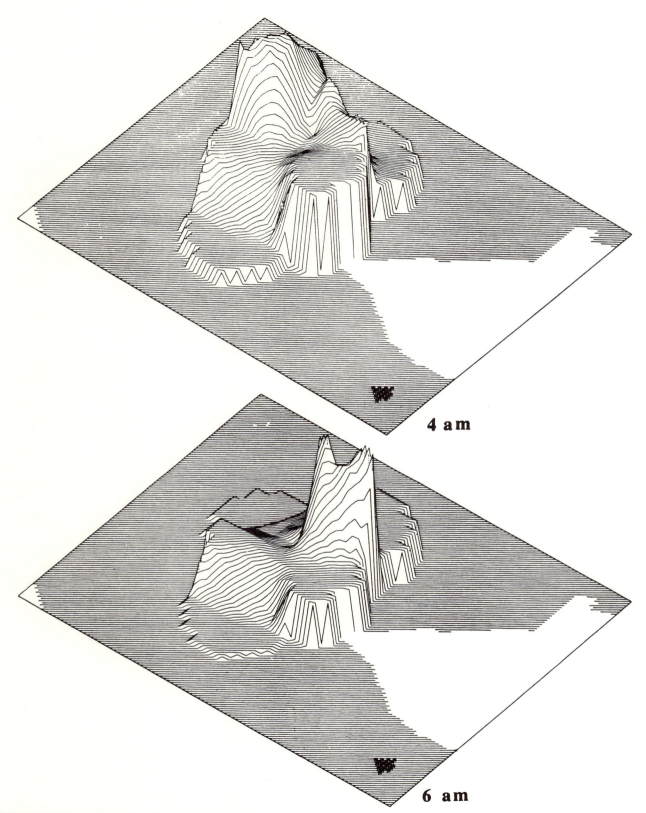

FIGURE 9 Computer mapping of the sulfur dioxide (SO_2) surface in oblique view for St. Louis, Missouri, December 20, 1964, at 4 and 6 a.m. (From Warntz, 1971.)

tions on the leeward side (Figure 10). The relation between the dynamics of the circulation and the geometry of streets and buildings is illustrated in Figure 11. The model study of the effect of a tall slab building downwind from a smaller building (an increasingly common relation with the increase in tall slab buildings in cities) indicates that wind speeds 3 m above the ground may be increased more than twofold, depending on the spacing between the buildings and their relative heights.

In some ways all these observations may seem to be esoteric and of limited practical value. It is evident, however, that the dynamics of the behavior of the air over cities, on both a micro and macro scale, may be greatly influenced by features of urban layout and design. Thus the illustrative data suggest that design and planning alternatives can be utilized to mitigate the effects of the materials and activi-

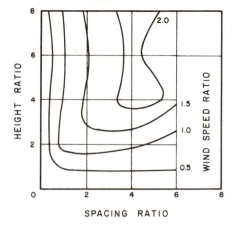

HEIGHT RATIO = $\dfrac{\text{HEIGHT OF LOW BUILDING}}{\text{HEIGHT OF SLAB BUILDING DOWNWIND}}$

SPACING RATIO = $\dfrac{\text{SPACING BETWEEN BUILDINGS}}{\text{LOW BUILDING HEIGHT}}$

WIND SPEED RATIO = $\dfrac{\text{ACTUAL WIND SPEED}}{\text{WIND SPEED WITHOUT BUILDING}}$

FIGURE 11 Variation in wind speeds between a small building and a large slab building. (From Sexton, 1970.)

ties of the urban scene on the climate to which citizens are exposed. Myrup (1969) suggests for example that evaporative surfaces such as parks might be installed on existing rooftops. Similarly, appropriately spaced parkland of climatologically significant dimensions might well be a part of a conscious design of new or renewed urban areas. Parenthetically, it is interesting to note the obvious fact that temperature differences of a few degrees may represent significant subjective differences in comfort levels. A study by Johnson and others (1969) suggests that when city temperatures are about 80–85 °F, reduction of temperatures by a few degrees might result in significant reduction of power costs in the New York region owing to the reduced demand for air conditioning. To the extent that the profile of a city street, including the width of the street itself and the height and roughness of the surrounding buildings, can be designed, such design might well provide more satisfactory conditions for the dissipation of accumulated pollutants as well as heat in the urban scene.

ATTRIBUTES OF THE LANDSCAPE

Mapping is so much a part of the planner's art that to speak of the use of maps may be carrying coals to Newcastle. The

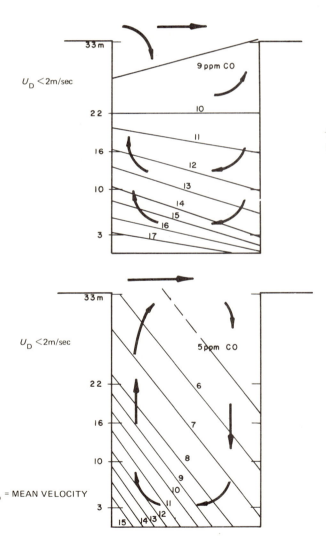

FIGURE 10 Effect of wind speed on circulation between buildings and distribution of carbon monoxide at successive levels above the street. (After Georgii, 1970.)

use of maps, however, not only to portray information graphically but to suggest the interrelations among diverse spatially distributed attributes, warrants continuing emphasis.

Both the development of sophisticated technology, including computers and remote sensing devices, and renewed emphasis on the significance of the natural environment have stimulated a desire to create new kinds of maps portraying relevant information. Much of this effort, however, either assumes the existence of a topographic map or fails to realize that such a map provides perhaps the greatest possible concentration of stored information. Under some circumstances the topography alone, on Knob Hill in San Francisco, for example, may provide a reasonable approximation of the much-beloved rent surface of the economic geographer. Many developing areas have inadequate topographic maps, and many might even use 5-ft contour maps to great advantage if they were available.

Recently the concept of landscape mapping, however, has been extended to include a variety of parameters that represent interrelations of physical and biological facts with meaningful values of interest to society, or attempts to develop methods of portraying what appear to be intrinsic values of landforms. These efforts, involving physical and biological features, range from computer maps of specific attributes of the landscape to more pictorial portrayals of specific features believed to be important starting points for allocating different land uses.

Computer mapping of land-use opportunities, for example, has been utilized in studies of resource management and in evaluating alternatives for urban river valleys. In such studies the computer offers a technique for data storage and portrayal on a grid system. Scales can be developed for categorizing such diverse parameters as human-population density, service-utilization patterns and accessibility, soil type, animal populations, drainage, relief, vegetation, and road access. Where theoretical or empirical relations can be derived to provide relative ranking or value among such parameters, the computer can be programmed to map areas of successive values or, for example, to designate the interaction or overlap of conflicting values. Figure 12 presents such a value map for a portion of Maine with a potential for recreational development. Although it is a rather simple case, the map focuses on areas of potential conflict or accord among competing users.

Mapping techniques developed by McHarg (Wallace and McHarg, 1966) provide a more graphic illustrative technique for demonstrating distinctive features of the landscape (U.S. Geological Survey, 1970). Because the method is familiar to planners, we focus our attention here on the environmental attributes mapped and on the sources of information on on which they depend (Table 3). The location of water courses, gradients of hill slopes, areas of standing water, land subject to flooding, permeability of soils, and areas of recharge to groundwater are customarily shown. Each item often requires a wealth of background information, often of a complex kind. For such mapping efforts to be meaningful, the information must be relevant and the process of mapping expeditious. Under this spur, natural scientists have begun to seek ways to meet the demand. For example, expeditious mapping of areas subject to flooding requires the translation of complex hydraulic and hydrologic relations into simple mapping techniques. Some investigations have indeed shown that a variety of techniques, including topographic features, soils, and vegetation may be used to extend mapping of areas subject to flood at relatively low cost (Table 4). Such techniques are based on prior geographic analyses that have successfully related the geometry of channels and floodplain heights to hydrologic characteristics related to the frequency of flooding.

Growing interest in the environment has provided the impetus for more elaborate or comprehensive mapping of all aspects of the environment for possible use in urban planning. Thus geologic hazards, thickness of the surficial mantle of soil, location of sand and gravel, depth of groundwater, mechanical properties and permeability of soils, degree of fracturing of rocks, landslide susceptibility, location of potential landfill sites, and bedrock geology are all currently the subject of detailed study and mapping by public and private agencies (U.S. Geological Survey, 1970; McComas and others, 1969). Among the most encyclopedic attempts of this kind is the recently published *Physical Environment of Saskatoon, Canada* (Christiansen, 1970).

Although perhaps the lion's share of attention has been given to depicting land and water as they affect urban planning, significant use is now being made of meteorologic and climatic information in urban layout and design. The list of potentially important parameters (Table 5) is striking in itself. Urban climatologists have pointed out that the scale of the relevant information varies, depending on the problems to be solved. The prevailing wind, for example, a macro-scale feature, may be important in aligning streets to take advantage of wind direction for ventilation or to protect against chilling blasts in winter on the plains. Meso-scale phenomena, however, such as down-valley breezes in mountainous terrain or onshore winds from lakes and bays may dominate in other landscapes. Each of these factors has, in fact, been used in planning new cities (Landsberg, 1970).

At the same time, familiar generalizations must give way to more thorough analyses of complex phenomena. We cannot assume, for example, that the prevailing wind direction, based on time alone, is sufficient to assure that homes upwind from commercial centers, in turn upwind from industrial plants, will provide the most satisfying design. It may well be that only those winds within a range of velocities and associated with specific conditions of atmospheric

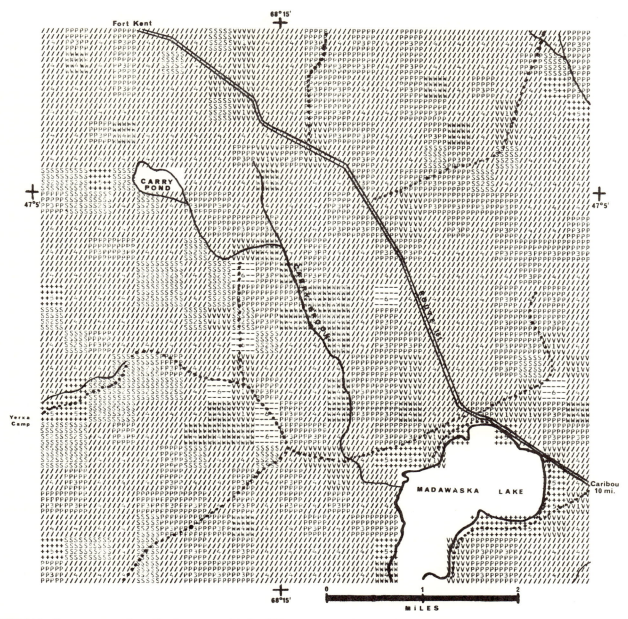

FIGURE 12 Computer mapping of land-use potentials for different purposes in a wooded area in Maine. Allocation of forest between four uses—vacation homes, ski development, pulpwood, and wilderness—1968 (long-run), Township 16, Range 4, Aroostook County, Maine. (From Beardsley, 1970).

This area is mapped to show where one use has a higher potential on a particular site than any of the other uses. It also shows where no one site has an advantage. The following symbols are used:

- v = vacation-home sites
- s = ski-development sites
- p = pulpwood sites (long-run)
- w = wilderness sites
- + = high-value land—no one use dominates
- / = medium-value land—no one use dominates
- _ = low-value land—all uses have poor potential.

Wilderness is determined by the inverse of proximity to roads. Each use is given equal importance. Pulpwood potential is measured by soil quality.

TABLE 3 Parameters Used in Land-Use Mapping

Plan for the Valleys	Plan for the Potomac
Valley floors	Surface water
Unforested valley walls	Floodplain
Forested valley walls	Steep slopes (over 12 percent)
Forested plateau	Piedmont—crystalline rocks
Unforested plateau	Piedmont—sedimentary rocks favorable for groundwater development
Lakes	Coastal plain—unconsolidated sediments
Promontory sites	Coastal plain—favorable for groundwater development
Open plateau	

Sources: Wallace and McHarg, 1966; Potomac Planning Task Force, 1967.

stability will cast a pall over living areas, and such winds may not in fact be the prevailing winds in point of time.

At the micrometeorological scale, as mentioned earlier, design of street and building spaces may have a vital effect on the atmosphere experienced by city dwellers. As Table 5 shows, there are myriad factors at this scale, including exposure to solar radiation and orientation with respect to wind-driven rains, that affect not only comfort but urban services such as snow removal and storm drainage.

At this time of American consciousness a discussion of the relation between physical geography and urban planning would be deficient if it failed to mention the burgeoning effort to cope with the concept of environmental impact. All the examples cited thus far are but small pieces of the complex phenomena currently characterized as environmental impacts. The necessity, however, for all agencies at the federal level and many other institutions, both public and private, to prepare environmental-impact statements demanded by the Environmental Policy Act has expanded the interest and the range of citizen and professional perception. To meet this formal demand, some studies have begun to develop checklists or inventories to formalize the impact of such activities as transportation, industrial activity, or construction of public works. Although most of these deal with the kind of phenomena discussed above, a number of new parameters, including aesthetics of the landscape and the quality of views and vistas have made their appearance (Leopold and others, 1971).

It is possible, of course, to expand *ad infinitum* the list of needs and demands for data to meet them. Unfortunately, important lacunae lie between the obvious importance of some information and the precise values of having it. For the most part, the state of the art permits us to suggest a set of potential effects, in fewer instances it permits us to measure accurately the impact or magnitude of effects, and still less often it enables us to place a positive or negative value on the impact. I have tried in this paper to illustrate a few situations where this is nearly possible. The relation of value to the spatial distribution of attributes of the natural scene merits some closing words of caution as well as speculation.

Mapping of diverse features of the landscape does not in itself provide value judgments as to the appropriate use of specific parts of the landscape. Although rational suggestions can be made that lands subject to flood should be reserved for open spaces, competing interests in scarce flatland may make the appropriate decision doubtful. Similarly, it can be shown that the cost of construction on hill slopes, including provision of drainage and control of erosion and sedimentation, may add materially to the cost of dwellings. This expense does not lessen the desirability of homesites on hills, however, and a map of slopes provides only the background for evaluating alternatives.

Data from the well-known percolation test, used to measure permeability and to evaluate the suitability of soils and subsurface rocks for septic tanks, provide an interesting example of the dilemma of judgment. From Figure 13 it can be seen that the area required for seepage on the Howard soil is less than that on the Valois soil, which, in turn, is less than the amount required on the Alden soil as a result of the successively slower infiltration rate on each of these. For the same reasons, one might expect the results depicted on Figure 13, where it is evident that the survival rate in terms of years of service is greatest for the Howard soil and least for the Alden soil. The scale of years and the survival curve in Figure 13, however, suggest a different problem. After 12 years, only 50 percent of the septic-tank seepage fields have survived on the soil best adapted to septic tanks. Thus the fundamental problem is not soil receptivity, but whether septic tanks are an appropriate waste-disposal mechanism. The appropriateness of the system depends not only on the receptivity of the soil but on the expected long-term performance of the septic tanks, the distance of the development from sewage-treatment plants, the distance to other population centers, and the probability that poor performance will result in contamination of surface streams, lakes, and groundwater supplies.

Attempts to directly relate the spatial distribution of attributes of the physical environment in the cities to economic or aesthetic considerations are by no means new or entirely fruitless. The success of builders in selling lakefront

TABLE 4 Techniques of Mapping Areas Subject to Flood

Method	Principles	Principal Methodological Drawbacks	Approximate Cost[a]
Physiographic	Topographic features: correlation flood levels, the floodplain—return period, 1–2 years Terraces: stepped topography	Inadequate correlation Topographic form and flooding Omission of backwater effect	$1–$4/mi of channel (estimated)
Pedologic	Soil development Stratification Drainage	Distinguishing colluvial and alluvial soils Terrace soil similarities Indistinct association soil and flooding	$1–$4/mi (estimated)
Vegetation	Distinctive vegetation assemblages Vegetation form related to high water Microvegetation related to high water	Inadequate correlation Assemblages or species with flooding Soil moisture and flood effects undifferentiated Plant deformation not correlated with specific flood height	Unknown
Occasional flood Highest of record Major Recent, major	Aerial photos, remote sensing of floods Historic records, recorded flood profiles Regional stage frequency relations Topography from stereoscopic air photos	Records unavailable Errors in spatial transposition Subtle topographic variation	$200/quadrangle ($4/mi converted)
Regional flood of selected frequency	Regional stage frequency relations Regional physiographic relations and generalized hydraulic computations	Errors in spatial transposition Variability of hydraulic conditions Omission of backwater effect	$4/mi (estimated); $1.50–$4/mi
Flood profile and backwater curve	Definition of flood profile from high-water marks or detailed hydraulic computations	Detailed topographic information required	$400–$1,000/mi (includes topographic mapping)

[a]Does not include preparing map.
Source: Wolman, 1971.

TABLE 5 Meteorological Factors of Interest in Urban Planning and Design[a]

Problem	Meteorological Parameters
Air pollution	
General planning	Synoptic aspects
Chimney design	Inversion of temperature, temperature profile below inversion
Drift of noxious fumes and so forth	Local wind movement, especially under inversion
Building design	
Strength of structures	Extreme wind gusts
Orientation, eave design	Sunshine, radiation; wind direction and velocity
Heat load	Solar radiation; nocturnal cooling
Weathering	Extreme air and sun temperatures, rainfall
Waterproofing, drainage	Heavy rainfall
Labor scheduling	Periods of wet weather, extreme temperatures
Air-conditioning	Dry- and wet-bulb temperatures, wind speed, solar radiation
Power and communication	
Wind generators	Wind speed
Spacing of aerial conductors	Wind gusts
Anomalous propagation	Temperature and humidity inversions, especially below 500 ft
Power supply	Hot and cold spells, thunderstorms
Transport	
Road construction and maintenance	Extremes of temperature, heavy rainfall
Rail construction	Extremes of radiation temperature
Road accidents	Rainfall, snow, frost, fog
Aviation runways	Wind, visibility, temperature and wind profiles

Source: C. E. Hounam, 1970.

the 70-year period continued to attract nearly half the total development.

With the improvement in understanding of physical and biological phenomena and their relation to urban systems, coupled with the expanding development of analytic tools, we can expect increasingly perceptive and fundamental evaluations of the relation between man and environment. The use of systems analysis as a technique for evaluating alternatives with the help of high-speed computers makes possible the investigation of more complex phenomena, even if only by simulation of the potential effects of particular phenomena. A combination of the dynamics of natural processes and their relation to spatial distribution of both human activities and natural features is suggested by analyses of the relation between

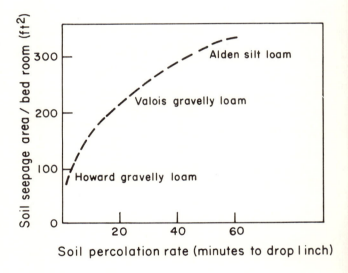

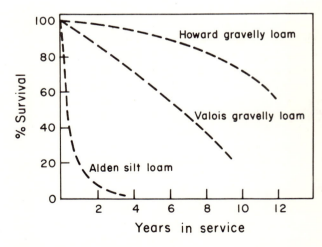

FIGURE 13 Effect of percolation rate on area required for septic-tank seepage and on survival of seepage fields. (From Olson, 1964.)

property on artificial lakes in suburbia attests to a knowledge of consumer wants or needs. Scholars have also shown that less spectacular features of the land have markedly influenced patterns of urban growth.

In a study of the growth of Minneapolis and Saint Paul, Borchert (1961) showed that the type of land was directly related to the density of urban development. In addition, the expansion of the Twin Cities took place with relatively little change in the percentage distribution of the urban densities on the different types of land (Figure 14). Thus while the metropolitan area expanded, the relative percentages of development in the four categories of land changed very little, and flat, well-drained land throughout

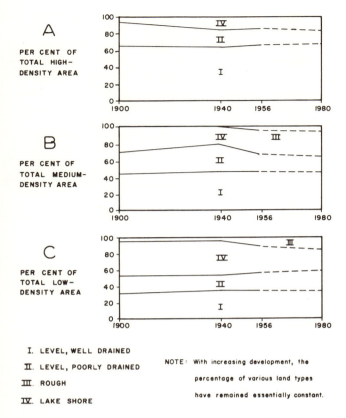

FIGURE 14 The relation of (A) high-density, (B) medium-density, and (C) low-density settlement to physical classes of land. (From Borchert, 1961.)

the size and characteristics of a river-drainage net and the disposal of treated-sewage effluent.

As the area of a metropolitan region expands and the distance to the urban center increases, the distance that wastes must be transported to existing sewage-treatment plants also increases. When additions to an existing plant are required, economies of scale associated with such large treatment plants may be offset by the long distances of transport. Because treatment rarely removes all wastes, the residual from a large treatment plant may also exceed the capacity of the available watercourses on which the treatment plant was originally constructed. At some point, the incremental costs of successive enlargement of the major plant exceed the costs of a number of small treatment plants, dispersed along smaller stream channels within the drainage network, each requiring shorter transport of wastes. Economy of scale in treatment is not necessarily the best solution (Broaddus, 1970). The optimum location and design will vary from place to place; it is becoming evident that, in some instances, dispersal may be preferable. This is particularly true in areas that are short of water, where the reuse of treated waste water may be economical, provided that wastes are not transported large distances, and can no longer be economically returned for reuse.

CONCLUSIONS

Three conclusions can be made on the relation between the physical environment and urban planning and development.

First, the separation between man and nature or between the physical environment and man-made phenomena is both artificial and misleading. Wolpert's essay, "Community Discretion over Neighborhood Change," pp. 41–54, demonstrates that the spatial distribution of facilities has a differential impact on different parts of the community, as do the magnitude and spatial distribution of natural processes. The absolute height of a flood, for example, is only one part of the needed information. The impact of a flood of that height will be assessed differently depending on where one lives, one's opportunities to move, and a host of other social conditions. It is the integration of these relations rather than the separation that constitutes the planning contribution.

A second conclusion was mentioned at the outset as a cautionary note. Geographic knowledge and the history of geographic thought have demonstrated that simple environmental determinism does not provide an adequate guide to human settlement. Information about the environment is essential to thoughtful planning because it helps to provide an evaluation of the consequences of alternative courses of action. The mere choice of information to be evaluated constitutes a decision about values, yet the values associated with alternative actions do not lie in inches of runoff or in acres of grassland. Such values must be determined by society.

Last, a great deal more is known about the environment than is currently used in planning and developing urban areas. At a minimum, sufficient knowledge of many processes exists to predict that the modifications of the environment inherent in the development of cities will lead to a sequence of changes at a given location and often at distances far removed from the site of the disturbance. We should not be surprised at the chain of so-called inadvertent modifications of the landscape that follow development. Acceptance of this simple truth might in itself lead to more comprehensive, as well as more thoughtful, approaches to the use of the landscape.

We hope that some of the illustrations here will not only be new but will strike a responsive chord among those who are faced with the problems of deciding where and how cities should grow. The evidence suggests that such decisions will remain matters of judgment reflecting the diverse values of human interests. The history of geographic thought exposes the fallacy that human affairs are wholly determined by the environment in which they occur. At the same time, this history shows that man's capacity to adjust to and manage the environment has played an important, if not a controlling, part in human affairs throughout history.

REFERENCES

American Public Works Association, 1969. Water pollution aspects of urban runoff. Washington, D.C.: U.S. Department of the Interior, Federal Water Pollution Control Administration, WP-20-15. 272 pp.

Anderson, D. C., 1970. Effects of urban development on floods in Northern Virginia. U.S. Geological Survey, Water Supply Paper 2001. Washington, D.C.: U.S. Government Printing Office, 22 pp.

Beardsley, W. A., 1970. A research procedure for conflicts and complementarity in the allocation of forest lands. Ph.D. dissertation, Johns Hopkins University. 167 pp.

Borchert, J. R., 1961. The Twin Cities urbanization area: Past, present and future. Geographical Review, 51 (1961), 47–70.

Broaddus, John J., 1970. Scale economies of waste treatment regionalization. A case study of York County, Pennsylvania. M.A. thesis. Catholic University of America. 19 pp.

Brown, C. W., and C. A. Krygier, 1970. Effects of clear cutting on stream temperature. Water Resources Research, 6 (1971), 1133–1139.

Chandler, T. J., 1970. Urban climatology–Inventory and prospect. *In* Urban Climates, WMO Technical Note 108, WMO 254, T.P. 141, pp. 1–14.

Christiansen, E. A., *Ed.,* 1970. Physical environment of Saskatoon, Canada. Ottawa: National Research Council of Canada.

Georgii, H. W., 1970. The effects of air pollution on urban climates. *In* Urban Climates WMO Technical Note 108, WMO 254, T.P. 141, pp. 214–237.

Hammer, T. R., 1970. Criteria for measurement of stream channels as an indicator of peak-flow history. University of Pennsylvania, Regional Science Research Institute Discussion Paper 36. 56 pp.

Hounam, C. E., 1970. The meteorological factor in design. *In* Building Climatology, WMO Technical Note 109, WMO 255, T.P. 141, pp. 218–219.

Johnson, S. R., J. D. McQuigg, and T. P. Rothrock, 1969. Temperature modification and costs of electric power generation. Journal of Applied Meteorology, 8 (1969), 919–926.

Kates, R. W., 1962. Hazard and choice perception in flood-plain management. University of Chicago, Department of Geography Research Paper 78. 197 pp.

Landsberg, H. E. 1970. Micrometeorological temperature differentiation through urbanization. *In* Urban Climates, WMO Technical Note 108, WMO 254, T.P. 141, pp. 129–136.

Leopold, L. B., 1968. Hydrology for urban land planning–A guidebook on the hydrologic effects of urban land use. U.S. Geological Survey Circular 554, p. 9.

Leopold, L. B., F. E. Clarke, B. B. Hanshaw, and J. R. Balsley, 1971. Procedure for evaluating environmental impact. U.S. Geological Survey Circular 645. 13 pp.

McComas, M. R., K. C. Hinkley, and J. P. Kempton, 1969. Coordinated mapping of geology and soils for land-use planning. Illinois State Geological Survey, Environmental Geology Notes, No. 29, p. 11.

Myrup, L. D., 1969. A numerical model of the urban heat island. Journal of Applied Meteorology, 7 (1969), 908–918.

Oke, T. R., and F. G. Hannell, 1970. The form of the urban heat island in Hamilton, Canada. *In* Urban Climates, WMO Technical Note 108, WMO 254, T.P. 141, pp. 113–127.

Olson, G. W., 1964. Using soil surveys for problems of the expanding population in New York State. Ithaca: New York State College of Agriculture, Cornell Extension Bulletin 1123, p. 31.

Pluhowski, E. J., 1970. Urbanization and its effect on the temperature of the streams on Long Island, New York. U.S. Geological Survey Professional Paper 627-D. pp. D1–D109.

Potomac Planning Task Force, 1967. Report of the American Institute of Architects. Washington, D.C.: U.S. Government Printing Office.

Sexton, D., 1970. Building climatology. Wind deflection by buildings. *In* Urban Climates, WMO Technical Note 109, WMO 255, T.P. 142, p. 59.

U.S. Geological Survey, 1970. San Francisco Bay region environment and resources planning study. USGS Open File Reports, Basic Data Contributions, Technical Reports and Interpretative Reports.

Wallace, D. A., and I. I. McHarg, 1966. Plan for the valleys. Washington, D.C.: U.S. Government Printing Office. 40 pp.

Warntz, William, 1971. Computer graphics and theoretical geography. U.S. Army Topographic Laboratories, Special Report, ETL-ST-71-1, pp. 79–112.

Whitehill, W. M., 1968. A topographical history of Boston. (Second edition). Cambridge, Mass.: Harvard University Press. 299 pp.

Wolman, M. G., 1967. A cycle of sedimentation and erosion in urban river channels. Geografiska Annaler, 49 (1967), 385–395.

Wolman, M. G., 1971. Evaluating alternative techniques of floodplain mapping. Water Resources Research, 7 (1971), 1383–1392.

Spatial Perspectives on Economic Change among American Cities

LESLIE J. KING
McMaster University

INTRODUCTION

The United States is today inhabited by a highly urbanized society (Hoyt, 1962; Berry, 1970). It is a nation of cities, and the mechanisms, forms, and prospects associated with this urbanization strongly influence and shape most facets of its contemporary life.

As concomitants of this high level of urbanization, many complex patterns of interaction and interdependence bind the different cities together. These patterns find expression, for example, in the technically sophisticated networks of communications, in the often overcrowded corridors along which people, goods, and services move, and in the myriad contact fields whereby ideas, innovations, and information are spread from one urban center to another. With this intricate web of cities and connecting links, it is not surprising that problems in one or two centers are often quickly multiplied and accentuated and require corrective actions and controls that are increasingly more difficult and expensive to mount. Past epidemics, economic setbacks, power blackouts, or even the interruption of airline services at a single major airport have borne witness to these difficulties.

An increasing number of official reports are therefore acknowledging the existence and importance of these patterns of intercity interaction and interdependence. For example, a National Academy of Sciences report on urban research (Committee on Social and Behavioral Urban Research, 1969), stressed the following point with respect to public services at the local level: "It must be recognized clearly that ours is a very mobile society, and that the failure of public services in one community may lead to difficulties in another that may be far removed geographically."

A recently published report on urban policy in Canada (Lithwick, 1970) emphasizes the same point in even stronger terms, no less appropriate for the United States scene than for that of Canada:

The introduction of space, joined with the central role of economic development, leads us to take a systemic view of the urbanization process. Space leads to a dispersal of urban activities, but the economy ties those activities together into an overall, highly connected, and hierarchically patterned system. Urbanization therefore determines not only the growth of individual urban units, but the evolution of the whole urban system. This evolution is what urbanization is all about. It conditions the efficiency and productivity of the economy and hence its further development. An approach that fails to appreciate the totality of this urban network—that fails to see the impact of city A on city B, and through it the feedback into the whole urbanization-development process—ultimately will be unable to cope meaningfully with urban reality.

Such acknowledgments imply a need for integrated regional planning—a need for planning policies that take into account the various interdependencies and links between regions and cities that are capable of attaining such desired objectives as economic equalization and steady and balanced economic growth. Hirsch (1966) has suggested that these particular objectives are in fact the powerful forces behind the current push toward regional planning (also National Goals Research Staff, 1970; and *Growth and Change*, 1971). We should like to be able to achieve a level of expertise in planning intercity and interregional relations comparable to that of national economic planning. Some of the tools that might prove useful in this task have already been crudely fashioned, such as the different techniques, including interregional input–output models, that have been developed by regional scientists and others (Isard, 1960). National economic planning only became a reality, however, after the development of a system of national-income accounts and the structuring of a theory of income determination that took into consideration both monetary and fiscal variables (National Science Board, 1969). The state of the art in regional analysis is certainly nowhere near this advanced level. Considerable progress is being made toward the development of a system of regional accounting, but much of the work is still only in the conceptual stage (Hirsch, 1964; 1966). On the theoretical side there exists a patchwork of different formulations stemming from the work of geographers, planners, regional scientists, and economists (Von Böventer, 1964). But the lack of any all-embracing synthesis lends weight to Friedmann's (1964) contention that, "At the national level there is at present no systematic comprehensive examination of the spatial dimension of economic growth."

So far, geographers have not contributed a great deal of information that might be useful in overcoming the different conceptual difficulties and technical problems now hindering the development of effective regional planning policies. For the most part, geographic research has focused on static situations and on narrow definitions of urban and regional economies. By contrast, the formulation of effective planning policy, whether at regional or national levels, demands a sound appreciation of the dynamics of the systems being planned and the ability to identify critical control variables. Geography's record in this arena is, nevertheless, probably as good as that of any other discipline, including economics, which was until recently a most reluctant participant in research and discussion related to urban and regional analysis.

A fairly extensive geographic literature dealing with the static structure of urban economic systems does exist, and notwithstanding the foregoing criticisms, the perspectives and emphases illustrated in this literature may prove valuable in designing future research efforts and in establishing related priorities. The brief and selective review of this work that follows, concentrates on three topics: the work on central-place systems, the analyses of intercity transportation-flow patterns, and the economic-base studies. These are not the only significant contributions made by geographers toward examining national and regional systems of cities, but much has been written on these topics that affords adequate illustration of some of the geographer's perspectives. Admittedly, they do not very explicitly illustrate those topics relating to the mathematical and statistical analysis of spatial series, thought by some geographers to be among their more useful contributions to social-science research (Taaffe, 1970).

THE STATIC STRUCTURE OF URBAN SYSTEMS

The first contribution to be noted in this context is that of the so-called central-place studies. These studies for the most most part have dominated urban-geography research over the past decade or so, and some of the associated methodological developments, particularly the interest in theoretical formulations and related mathematical and statistical analyses, have had an even broader impact on geography as a social science.

Drawing much of their inspiration from seminal works by the German scholars Christaller and Losch (Christaller, 1933), research workers have examined in detail the structure of trading relations between urban communities as service centers and the dispersed rural farm population who are the consumers. The findings have focused principally on the existence of hierarchies in both the number of different population-sized centers and their associated trade areas; on the relation between the size of a city, the complexity of service functions that it offers, and the size of the area that it serves; on the relation between the distance lengths of shopping trips and the type of goods and service demanded; and on certain algebraic and geometrical formulations of the number, size, and locational arrangement of cities in any particular region (Berry, 1967). More recently, there has also been a growing interest in more formal mathematical models of central-place systems (Dacey, 1966; Curry, 1967; Papageorgiou, 1971), and in a reexamination of many of the existing findings in the light of a new emphasis on the psychosociological aspects of consumer shopping behavior (Golledge, 1967).

These central-place studies have been made not only of many different urban–rural settings, both in this country and abroad, but also of intraurban commercial structure and shopping behavior. Many of the descriptive generalizations apply equally well in both settings.

As a framework for the detailed analysis of intercity relations and of the roles of cities in the national and regional economies, central-place theory is obviously inadequate. It is primarily a static formulation, although various cross-sectional analyses have stemmed from it. But a truly dynamic theory of central-place systems has yet to be written. Central-place analysis is also very much a partial analysis. It ignores all economic sectors that cannot properly be regarded as service activities geared to the market of the surrounding tributary area, and it emphasizes the demand side of the market system, almost ignoring supply considerations. The central-place model has also proved inadequate as a model of market areas within metropolitan areas (Berry, 1971). On the positive side, central-place theory has provided useful constructs in analyses of spatial diffusion (Hudson, 1969).

Closely related at times to the central-place studies have been the geographic analyses of intercity and interregional transportation networks and flow patterns. These studies fall into two broad categories. Numerous detailed statistical analyses have been made of observed flow patterns, exemplified by Taaffe's studies of airline-passenger movements (Taaffe, 1962). These studies have yielded a number of inductive generalizations. Examples of these generalizations include Taaffe's statements about the hierarchical organization of the zones of traffic dominance assoicated with different-sized cities, the increasing dominance in the traffic flows of a few large centers shown in cross-sectional analyses, and the existence of traffic shadow zones around many of these major urban centers. These studies have provided additional support for many of the central-place findings, particularly on the hierarchical structure of the urban system. In contrast to the central-place formulations, which as logical-deductive ones did proceed from certain basic, albeit rather weak, assumptions about consumer and entrepreneurial behavior, these transportation analyses appear even more footloose in underlying theory. In this first category, we might also include a smaller subset of analyses that have focused on the geometrical properties of transportation networks and have sought to generalize about the relative locations of nodes (cities) in these networks in terms of their relative accessibility and their membership in particular decompositions of the networks (Haggett and Chorley, 1969). Again, the thrust has been primarily descriptive.

A second broad category of transportation studies includes those that have been prescriptive rather than descriptive in their findings. For example, Werner (1968) has outlined a method whereby he identifies the transportation route "that minimizes total cost when the region containing the two terminal points is partitioned into any number of polygonal subregions that are homogeneous in those factors that determine cost." Other geographic studies in the same spirit can be cited (MacKinnon and Hodgson, 1970; Sen, 1971; Werner, 1969). By their very nature these studies emphasize analytic solutions, iterative procedures, or simulation techniques, and so far they have usually referred, with one or two exceptions, to hypothetical rather than real-world situations.

In summary, the work of transportation geographers has thrown some additional light on the hierarchical patterning of intercity flows and transactions, and it has yielded solutions to some technical problems in network analysis that may well prove useful in designing future systems.

The third and final review topic is that of economic-base studies in urban geography. Geographer J. Alexander (1954) was one of the early contributors to the now voluminous literature on the significance of the distinction between basic or export activities and nonbasic or local activities in the urban economy. The subsequent development of this concept and its application and evaluation in problems of forecasting urban development has fallen, however, more to economists and planners. The work of geographers on the minimum-requirements approach in the estimation of the export-local components deserves mention as an exception to this statement (Ullman and others, 1969). Most geographers have preferred to concentrate on taxonomic schemes that would allow for the classification of cities by the mix of economic activities they support. The achievements along these lines have been impressive (Berry and Horton, 1970), at least in refining classificatory procedures, but unfortunately the classifications seem to have added little information on the functioning of the urban economic systems.

The brief foregoing review of some of the work now in progress in urban geography reveals a major research challenge facing urban geographers: to develop and test models of the intercity relations and interdependencies that deal not only with variations over space but also over time. Until this difficult task is accomplished, it is doubtful whether a sound base can ever be built for regional and other forms of spatial planning.

PROBLEMS OF SPATIAL FORECASTING

In the literature of econometrics, numerous techniques are suggested that are adaptable to problems of spatial forecasting. With Casetti and Jeffrey (Jeffrey and others, 1969; King and others, 1969; Casetti and others, 1971; King and others, 1971), I have been involved in research on some aspects of economic changes among the cities of the United States, using conventional single-equation models and least-squares estimation procedures. The data are published statistics on employment and unemployment levels. The sets of findings reported here are not all closely related, but they have as a common theme the analysis of temporal change in city economic series, with particular emphasis on the decomposition of the different urban time series into additive components. These components are related to certain distinctions made first between national, regional, and local generating mechanisms and, second, in unemployment patterns between short-term fluctuations, structural change, and overall growth.

TRENDS IN URBAN EMPLOYMENT GROWTH

In one study, an attempt was made to differentiate between cities in the nation with reference to the form of their employment growth paths over the decade from 1957 to 1969

(King and others, 1972). The data used were the bimonthly levels of total employment in major labor-market areas, and these were available as continuous series for some 128 areas.

A particular form of factor analysis (Sheth, 1969), hitherto unused, as far as we know, in regional analysis, was employed on two sets of the standardized data. The first set had the effect of city size removed, but retained the effect of differences in the rate of growth between cities. The second set was standardized to remove both the effects of size and rate while retaining the differences in the timing of growth between the cities.

Analysis of the first data set yielded a single reference curve, which alone accounted for 92 percent of the variance of the standardized city curves around the mean standardized curve. The city scores on this reference curve ranged from 5.8 for San Jose, California (positive scores were indicative of faster-than-average growth), to −1.4 for Fall River, Massachusetts (indicative of slower-than-average growth). High positive scores predominated generally in the West and Southwest, although Spokane, San Francisco, Fort Worth, and Corpus Christi provided notable exceptions, and large negative values characterized many cities in the east and eastern north–central states.

The analysis of the second data set yielded three reference curves that together accounted for 92 percent of the variability in the timing of growth around the mean curve for this data set. The first of these curves was identified with variance in the general timing of growth over the period, cities with positive parameters on the curve being most heavily affected by the 1958 recession and showing most of their employment growth in the post-1964 period; cities with negative parameters showed growth evenly distributed throughout the period. Large positive values were typical of the heavy manufacturing cities in eastern Michigan, Indiana, Ohio, and western Pennsylvania, whereas negative parameters characterized cities in the eastern areas of the manufacturing belt, in the South, Southwest, and on the West Coast. The second curve identified the differential impact of short-term cyclical fluctuations on local employment growth. Cities that are cyclically unstable had large positive parameters (for example, Erie, Flint, Kenosha, and Muskegon), whereas more stable economies had very small values (for example, Fresno, Los Angeles, San Bernardino, and San Diego). The third reference curve provided a measure of the importance of seasonal factors in producing short-term fluctuations in local labor markets, and generally this effect was more pronounced in cities west of the Mississippi than in those to the east.

A significant result of the two preceding analyses was that an eightfold classification of the cities was possible (with the seasonal reference curve omitted), which threw some light on the relation between the rate of economic growth and the susceptibility to cyclical fluctuations (Table 1). As many as 48 of the fast-growing cities were also cyclically stable, which is at least consistent with the thesis propounded by Borts (1960) that fast-growing cities containing progressive firms are better able to withstand cyclical fluctuations in employment. The relation is, of course, much more complex than this, and these results only show the need for further research.

TRANSMISSION OF ECONOMIC FLUCTUATIONS AMONG CITIES

The problem here is to determine how economic fluctuations are transmitted through a set of urban economies and how the impacts on the different cities vary, both in their intensity and in their timing. The question of determining the intensity of impact has to do with the relative cyclical stability of different city economies. The question of the timing is now of prime concern.

Bassett and Haggett (1971), who have paralleled our efforts with their research on towns in southwestern England, have posed the particular problem well. Noting the work of the National Bureau of Economic Research in this country

TABLE 1 Classification of Cities

Group	Sign of Parameter			Growth Characteristics		Cities in Group
	RF1	RF'1	RF'2			
1	+	−	−	Fast/Early/Cycle	Stable	48
2	+	−	+	Fast/Early/Cycle	Unstable	6
3	+	+	−	Fast/Late/Cycle	Stable	0
4	+	+	+	Fast/Late/Cycle	Unstable	1
5	−	−	−	Slow/Early/Cycle	Stable	21
6	−	−	+	Slow/Early/Cycle	Unstable	9
7	−	+	−	Slow/Late/Cycle	Stable	11
8	−	+	+	Slow/Late/Cycle	Unstable	32

Source: King and others, 1972.

on the analysis of economic time series and its findings on business cycles, and on "the establishment of reference months for phases in the cycle and the identification of leading indicators," they suggest the following:

The concept of leading indicators may be extended in the spatial domain to that of leading areas, i.e., within a national or regional economy, which regularly display their peaks and troughs some months ahead of other areas and thus provide early indicators of turning points in local business cycles (Bassett and Haggett, 1971, p. 390).

In an initial investigation of this problem, using bimonthly unemployment data for some 33 metropolitan centers in the Midwest, we found that "there were strong and simultaneous effects among cities focused on Pittsburgh, Youngstown, Indianapolis, and Detroit," and that both the Indianapolis and Detroit clusters lagged about 3 to 5 months behind the Pittsburgh–Youngstown cluster (King and others, 1969). The analysis involved a regression of each city series on the national series, with seasonal effects also considered, and then the intercorrelation of the city residual series. These correlations were run with different lags and the lag associated with the highest correlation for each city pair was identified. Among the cities in each group there were high intercorrelations and simultaneous interaction (zero lags). Unfortunately, the data used were for the period May 1960–September 1964, which embraced the 1961 recession and subsequent recovery; this must be taken into consideration when these findings are being analyzed. The influence of national developments over the period was strong (Table 2) and, as a result, many important regional effects may have been hidden.

This line of analysis was subsequently extended to embrace the 140 major labor-market areas using data for May 1960–July 1965. A model was constructed that related local city unemployment to a structural component and to a weighted national unemployment index (King and others, 1971). The model was of the following form:

$$U_{jt} = c_j + b_j t + d_j t + a_j W_{j, t + n_j} + e$$

where U_{jt} is the level of unemployment in city j at time t; c_j, b_j, and d_j are the parameters for a quadratic time trend in structural unemployment; a_j is a parameter measuring the cyclical stability of city j in response to national factors; and $W_{j, t + n_j}$ is the national unemployment series weighted by the city's industry mix and lagged by n_j. The nature of the time lags is of interest here. (The n_j values are in Appendix A.) The results show that the midwestern cities consistently lead the nation by at least 2 months (one time interval) and in the case of Pittsburgh, Youngstown, Steubenville, Wheeling, Gary, and Muskegon the lead is 4 months. By contrast, the megalopolis and New England cities mirror the national trend, while most of the other cities, especially those in the West, follow by 2–4 months.

Again, we do not place too great a significance on these particular results, but consider them sufficiently provocative to warrant closer examination. The use of more extended data series and some disaggregation by type of industry might prove fruitful; a different approach, disaggregated by industry type, was tried by C. E. Trott (1969). He considered three export industries in Lima, Ohio, and analyzed the cross-spectral relations between these and their counterparts in seven other Ohio cities. The phase angles divided by the frequencies gave him estimates of the time lag.

DECOMPOSITION OF SPATIAL ECONOMIC SERIES

In an earlier paper stemming from our research, we made the following remarks (Jeffrey and others, 1969):

The extension of the investigation of economic time series to a multiregional system requires consideration of sets of time series. For each region or city within the system there are either one or several time series that may reflect causative factors associated not only with trends and oscillations, but also spatial factors that may affect the whole system, or segments of it.

In accordance with this suggestion, we have pursued certain lines of investigation in which the city economic series are decomposed into a national component, a regional component, and a local or unique component. In the paper previously mentioned, the national component

TABLE 2 Correlation between National Series and the City's Unemployment Series, 1960–1964

Akron	0.91	Grand Rapids	0.88
Canton	0.89	Kalamazoo	0.88
Cincinnati	0.89	Lansing	0.87
Cleveland	0.88	Muskegon	0.71
Columbus	0.87	Saginaw	0.87
Dayton	0.87	Evansville	0.78
Hamilton	0.83	Fort Wayne	0.78
Lorain	0.77	Gary	0.72
Steubenville	0.72	Indianapolis	0.85
Toledo	0.80	Terre Haute	0.84
Youngstown	0.63	Louisville	0.77
Wheeling	0.81	Chicago	0.93
Erie	0.87	Davenport	0.70
Pittsburgh	0.77	Peoria	0.87
Detroit	0.84	Rockford	0.87
Flint	0.78	Milwaukee	0.86
		Racine	0.82

was first removed by regressing the city series on the national series. A bifactor analysis was then employed to test the hypothesis that certain regional components could be identified in the residential series. The existence of five such groupings among the midwestern metropolitan areas, centered on Chicago, Detroit, Indianapolis, Cleveland, and Pittsburgh, was confirmed by the analysis. In developing the rationale for this type of hypothesis one can draw on the information about hierarchical structures in the urban system that is to be found in the geographic literature reviewed earlier. The use of the bifactor model in testing such hypotheses is limited, however, by the fact that some form of an *a priori* grouping of the cities (the variables) is demanded.

Jeffrey (1970) has pursued the question of identifying regional components using the Sheth factor analysis model to which we referred earlier. His results confirm the existence of strong spatial-contiguity effects in the responses of cities to subnational cyclical impulses.

In the multiple-regression model previously mentioned, the parameter a_j is a measure of the cyclical stability of city economies in response to national fluctuations. (See values in Appendix A.) If the parameter is unity, the city's fluctuations match those of the nation; if it is greater or less than unity, then the city experiences more or less severe fluctuations, respectively. The values given in Appendix A have a mean of .98 and a range from 1.8 for Wheeling, West Virginia, to .4 for Denver, Colorado. In general, the cities of the Atlantic Seaboard, the Deep South, the Great Plains, and the Mountain States are cyclically stable, whereas the most cyclically unstable ones are concentrated in a belt running from Saginaw, Michigan, to Altoona, Pennsylvania; in the Tennessee Valley; and in the Pacific Northwest. High a_j values are also characteristic of Minneapolis–St. Paul, Terre Haute, Fort Wayne, and Worcester.

An explanation for the variability in these a_j values has been sought in terms of export-base theory (the demand elasticity of export industries appears relevant), city size, industrial diversification, and overall growth performance (Jeffrey, 1970; Rodgers, 1957). Jeffrey found that for the 140 urban areas, cyclical instability was positively related to specialization in durable-goods manufacturing and inversely related to industrial diversification and total and competitive employment growth. Some of these relationships were originally considered in Rodgers (1957).

TESTING FOR SPATIAL-TEMPORAL TRENDS AT REGIONAL LEVELS

The possible existence of regional components in urban economic time series suggests testing for the existence of growth poles. A rapidly expanding literature is available on the topic of growth poles and their role in economic development. Originally conceived for particular economic sectors, the concept has been developed more recently in a spatial sense, referring to regions or locations that might exert a propulsive effect on economic growth in the surrounding region (Lasuén, 1971).

Geographers have developed procedures to handle two problems in the empirical analysis of such polarization effects. They have devised a method for identifying the locations of growth poles using cross-sectional temporal data for a set of cities (Casetti and Semple, 1968), and have established a procedure for testing hypotheses that polarized growth did occur with respect to particular city growth poles (Casetti, King, and Odland, 1971). Although both these procedures are empirical, they make possible precise examinations of certain questions of spatial structure that are consistent with the economic-process theory relating to growth poles.

STRUCTURAL IMBALANCE IN THE URBAN EMPLOYMENT PATTERNS

The question of the importance of so-called structural unemployment in the overall employment situation of the nation is still a subject of debate among economists. Structural employment is that form of unemployment that results in the long run from changing technology, different consumer preferences, shifts in the location of industry and population, and the inability or failure of the labor market to adjust to these situations.

In one study, intercity variations in the level of structural unemployment were interpreted as reflecting a state of disequilibrium in the national urban system, and the hypothesis that the variability of these levels should decrease over time was tested (Casetti, King, and Jeffrey, 1971). The analysis focused on the values for c_j in the regression model mentioned earlier and also examined the mean and variance terms for the structural component among the cities in 1960 and 1965. This convergence hypothesis seemed appropriate in view of the government's attempts to improve the employment situation in certain redevelopment areas. However, the data for the 140 major labor-market areas did not support the hypothesis. The reduction in structural unemployment, which was marked among the depressed cities of West Virginia and Pennsylvania, was matched by major increases in all West Coast cities and by some increases in New England communities. The implications of this observation in the analysis of the relation between employment opportunities and migration patterns are currently under investigation.

CONCLUSION

We have attempted to illustrate how the analysis of urban economic time-series data can be structured to yield insights into the spatial organization of the national urban system. Much of this work has been concerned with parameter estimation and with the discussion of the variability in the different parameter values among the cities. We are confident that the effort has been justified, although the limitations of the available data have cast doubt on the validity of some of the numerical values that we have obtained. Our work has further emphasized the recognized need for more powerful tools with which to estimate the parameters of spatial-temporal series (Chisholm and others, 1971), and so improve the prospects for effective regional planning.

A review of the work so far indicates one extension that might move us somewhat closer to our stated goal. This would involve systems of equations approaches in which the effects of interaction among cities would be handled explicitly by variables on the right-hand side of each city equation that relate to other cities in the system. Work is proceeding along these lines.

APPENDIX A The Regression Equations

City	c_j	b_j	d_j	a_j	n_j	R^2	d
Albany, N.Y.	−1.91[a]	−.0416	.0010	.63[a]	1	.41	.72[a]
Albuquerque, N.M.	−1.07[a]	−.0700	.0012	1.03	−1	.53	.87[a]
Allentown, Pa.	0.24	.1040	−.0015	.82[a]	0	.83	.64[a]
Altoona, Pa.	4.67[a]	.0139	−.0010	1.11	1	.65	.34[a]
Asheville, N.C.	−3.18[a]	−.0664	.0008	1.25[a]	0	.68	.73[a]
Atlanta, Ga.	−0.78	−.0676	.0008	.95	1	.85	.95[a]
Augusta, Ga.	0.12	−.0328	.0006	.80[a]	−1	.74	.85[a]
Austin, Tex.	0.42	−.0474	.0006	.69[a]	1	.62	.97[a]
Baltimore, Md.	2.26[a]	−.0255	−.0001	.65[a]	1	.68	.72[a]
Baton Rouge, La.	0.84	−.1364	.0017	1.11	1	.86	.56[a]
Beaumont, Tex.	−0.18	−.0254	.0002	1.33[a]	1	.73	.61[a]
Binghamton, N.Y.	2.51[a]	.0239	−.0004	.63[a]	−1	.41	.72[a]
Birmingham, Ala.	3.24[a]	−.0276	−.0001	.83[a]	1	.90	.76[a]
Boston, Mass.	1.23	.0353	−.0004	.49	−1	.46	.87[a]
Bridgeport, Conn.	0.40	−.0832	.0011	1.21	0	.79	.71[a]
Brockton, Mass.	3.80[a]	.1234	−.0026	.72	0	.31	.88[a]
Buffalo, N.Y.	0.04	.0857	−.0013	1.06	0	.80	.78[a]
Canton, Ohio	−1.24[a]	.0307	−.0005	1.40[a]	1	.95	1.40[a]
Cedar Rapids, Iowa	−2.32[a]	−.0107	.0003	.89	0	.67	.77[a]
Charleston, S.C.	0.45	−.0460	.0007	.73[a]	−2	.50	.39[a]
Charleston, W.Va.	1.50[a]	−.0269	.0003	1.06	0	.44	.50[a]
Charlotte, N.C.	1.41[a]	−.0231	.0004	.58[a]	0	.43	.80[a]
Chattanooga, Tenn.	−2.57[a]	.1582	−.0031	1.50[a]	−2	.85	.51[a]
Chicago, Ill.	−2.13[a]	.0038	−.0001	1.14	0	.68	.92[a]
Cincinnati, Ohio	−.33	.0211	−.0002	.82[a]	0	.89	1.64[a]
Cleveland, Ohio	−1.77[a]	.0134	−.0002	1.21[a]	1	.94	1.12[a]
Columbus, Ga.	3.40[a]	−.0612	.0006	.68	1	.66	.45[a]
Columbus, Ohio	.38	−.0321	.0005	.62[a]	1	.88	1.09[a]
C. Christi, Tex.	−0.80	−.1240	.0017	1.11	1	.71	.36[a]
Dallas, Tex.	−0.43	−.0460	.0007	.88	1	.77	.77[a]
Davenport-Rock Island-Moline, Iowa	−2.61[a]	−.0533	.0004	.72[a]	1	.67	.59[a]
Dayton, Ohio	−1.28[a]	−.0053	.0001	.91	0	.84	.95[a]
Denver, Colo.	2.49[a]	.0165	−.0002	.42[a]	−1	.34	.50[a]
Des Moines, Iowa	−1.02	−.0033	−.0006	.69[a]	0	.46	.54[a]
Detroit, Mich.	1.73[a]	.0284	−.0006	1.56[a]	1	.92	.61[a]
Duluth-Superior, Minn.-Wis.	2.29[a]	.1578	−.0025	.99	−2	.39	.41[a]
Durham, N.C.	0.48	.0133	.0002	.68[a]	−2	.30	.69[a]
El Paso, Tex.	1.68	.0000	.0003	.71	−1	.32	.47[a]
Erie, Pa.	−0.30	−.0421	.0005	1.56[a]	1	.83	.70[a]
Evansville, Ind.	−0.98[a]	−.0516	.0006	1.25[a]	1	.85	.55[a]
Fall River, Mass.	1.49[a]	.0673	−.0005	1.10	0	.48	1.21[a]
Fresno, Calif.	−2.21	.0130	.0002	1.28	−1	.36	.47[a]
Flint, Mich.	−2.93[a]	.0550	−.0006	1.35[a]	1	.80	.86[a]
Ft. Wayne, Ind.	−3.63[a]	−.0062	.0000	1.56[a]	1	.82	.48[a]
Ft. Worth, Tex.	−.40	.0139	−.0004	.88	0	.72	1.00[a]

APPENDIX A Continued

City	c_j	b_j	d_j	a_j	n_j	R^2	d
Gary, Ind.	−1.02[a]	.0580	−.0009	1.01	2	.76	.56[a]
Grand Rapids, Mich.	−1.77[a]	−.0212	.0003	1.17[a]	1	.84	.88[a]
Greensboro-High Pt., N.C.	−2.25[a]	−.0884	.0013	1.12	0	.76	.86[a]
Greenville, S.C.	−1.64[a]	−.0064	−.0005	1.09	−2	.60	.94[a]
Hamilton, Ohio	1.54[a]	.0063	−.0009	.97	0	.80	.71[a]
Harrisburg, Pa.	−1.77[a]	.0163	−.0006	1.24[a]	1	.70	.50[a]
Hartford, Conn.	0.66	−.0372	.0005	.66[a]	0	.74	.77[a]
Houston, Tex.	1.11[a]	−.0025	−.0001	.59[a]	1	.68	.96[a]
Huntington, W. Va.	4.42[a]	−.0802	.0001	1.33[a]	1	.68	.61[a]
Indianapolis, Ind.	−0.38	−.0516	.0004	1.16	1	.79	.57[a]
Jackson, Miss.	0.34	−.0037	.0001	.57[a]	0	.36	.64[a]
Jacksonville, Fla.	−1.69[a]	−.0097	.0001	.94	0	.75	.96[a]
Jersey City, N.J.	1.50	.0014	.0000	.94	0	.41	.77[a]
Johnston, Pa.	1.34[a]	.1654	−.0038	1.65[a]	1	.88	.40[a]
Kalamazoo, Mich.	−2.02[a]	−.0346	.0004	1.20[a]	1	.86	.85[a]
Kansas City, Mo.-Kan.	−0.73	−.0670	.0008	1.14	−1	.63	.42[a]
Knoxville, Tenn.	−3.44[a]	−.0581	.0005	1.51[a]	−1	.82	.57[a]
Lancaster, Pa.	−2.34[a]	−.0493	.0007	1.04	1	.71	.76[a]
Lansing, Mich.	−2.91[a]	.0441	−.0005	1.27[a]	1	.85	.88[a]
Lawrence-Haverhill, Mass.	1.13	−.0232	.0007	.89	0	.48	1.53[a]
Little Rock, Ark.	−1.58	−.0406	.0006	.96	1	.48	.74[a]
Lorain, Ohio	−0.38	−.1213	.0017	1.43[a]	1	.91	1.17[a]
Los Angeles, Calif.	−0.52	−.0378	.0009	1.11	−1	.58	1.06[a]
Louisville, Ky.	−0.13	−.0838	.0008	1.19	1	.80	.74[a]
Lowell, Mass.	0.96	−.0575	.0008	.77	0	.37	.79[a]
Macon, Ga.	0.74	−.0136	.0003	.75[a]	−1	.44	.62[a]
Madison, Wis.	−0.07	.0115	.0000	.45[a]	−1	.46	.48[a]
Manchester, N.H.	−0.03	−.0094	.0000	.87	0	.61	.72[a]
Mempnis, Tenn.	2.66[a]	−.0298	−.0002	.72[a]	1	.44	.79[a]
Miami, Fla.	0.55	.2610	−.0041	1.07	0	.65	.15[a]
Milwaukee, Wis.	−1.42[a]	.0316	−.0004	.78[a]	0	.70	1.00[a]
Minneapolis-St. Paul, Minn.	−2.43[a]	−.0402	.0008	1.10	−1	.55	.72[a]
Mobile, Ala.	−1.21[a]	−.0471	.0005	1.07	−1	.68	.49[a]
Muskegon, Mich.	2.30[a]	−.1586	.0021	1.20[a]	2	.73	1.07[a]
Nashville, Tenn.	−0.01	.0000	−.0001	.68[a]	−1	.46	.72[a]
New Bedford, Mass.	2.05[a]	−.0838	.0012	1.24[a]	0	.58	1.08[a]
New Britain, Conn.	−2.58[a]	−.0652	.0014	1.37[a]	0	.71	.84[a]
New Brunswick, N.J.	1.18	.0312	−.0004	.76	0	.40	.74[a]
New Haven, Conn.	0.09	.0000	−.0001	.83	0	.61	.99[a]
New Orleans, La.	3.41[a]	.0240	−.0009	.48[a]	2	.82	.61[a]
New York, N.Y.	1.83	.0119	−.00013	.61[a]	0	.54	1.00[a]
Newark, N.J.	1.68	.0198	−.0004	.73	0	.37	.71[a]
Newport-News, Va.	1.35[a]	−.0869	.0011	.54[a]	1	.77	.57[a]
Norfolk, Va.	1.29	−.0669	.0010	.58[a]	1	.70	.92[a]
Oklahoma City, Okla.	0.30	−.0019	.0002	.60[a]	−1	.62	.96[a]
Omaha, Neb.	0.69	.0247	−.0003	.43[a]	−2	.38	.57[a]
Paterson-Clifton-Passaic, N.J.	2.43[a]	−.0364	.0005	.74	−1	.48	.78[a]
Peoria, Ill.	−0.07	.0000	−.0002	.97	1	.69	.62[a]
Philadelphia, Pa.-N.J.	1.02	.0610	−.0010	.90	0	.56	.77[a]
Phoenix, Ariz.	0.49	−.0070	.0003	.77	−1	.34	.75[a]
Pittsburgh, Pa.	3.63[a]	.1038	−.0026	1.52[a]	2	.89	.62[a]
Portland, Me.	2.48	−0.402	.0005	.60[a]	0	.31	.44[a]
Providence-Pawtucket-Warwick, R.I.	1.03	−.0010	.0000	.94	0	.46	.87[a]
Racine, Wis.	0.66	−.0337	.0005	.99	0	.57	.73[a]
Reading, Pa.	−2.19[a]	−.0149	.0001	1.18	0	.80	1.19[a]
Richmond, Va.	−0.23	−.0436	.0006	.60[a]	1	.69	.70[a]
Roanoke, Va.	−0.31	−.1945	.0022	1.26[a]	2	.89	.54[a]
Rochester, N.Y.	0.29	−.0003	.0000	.76	1	.38	.59[a]
Rockford, Ill.	−0.96	−.0243	.0002	1.07	1	.81	.60[a]
Sacramento, Calif.	0.54	−.0052	.0006	.82	−1	.45	.54[a]

APPENDIX A Continued

City	c_j	b_j	d_j	a_j	n_j	R^2	d
Saginaw, Mich.	−4.06[a]	.0455	−.0007	1.45[a]	1	.88	.73[a]
St. Louis, Mo.	−1.11	−.0100	.0000	1.11	0	.62	.64[a]
Salt Lake City, Utah	−2.85[a]	.0208	.0011	1.03	−2	.47	.76[a]
San Antonio, Tex.	1.30	.0182	−.0002	.45[a]	0	.26	.68[a]
San Bernardino-Riverside-Ontario, Calif.	−0.30	−.0802	.0016	1.06	−1	.69	.75[a]
San Diego, Calif.	4.89[a]	.0593	−.0006	.49[a]	−1	.34	.44[a]
San Francisco, Calif.	0.27	−.0034	.0003	.82	−1	.42	.69[a]
San Jose, Calif.	1.48	−.0447	.0012	.78	−1	.40	.41[a]
Savannah, Ga.	−1.24	−.0447	.0008	1.11	0	.77	.84[a]
Scranton, Pa.	4.98[a]	.1108	−.0025	1.09	1	.73	.83[a]
Seattle, Wash.	−2.75	−.0046	.0006	1.21	0	.43	.42[a]
Shreveport, La.	0.03	.0000	−.0001	.97	−1	.43	.71[a]
Spokane, Wash.	0.16	.0437	−.0009	1.09	0	.33	.41[a]
Springfield, Mass.	2.06[a]	.0264	−.0004	.70	1	.52	.79[a]
Stamford, Conn.	0.60	.0436	−.0004	.54[a]	0	.38	.71[a]
Steubenville, W. Va.	1.20[a]	.0667	−.0010	1.38[a]	2	.68	.42[a]
Stockton, Calif.	0.95	.0463	−.0003	1.10	−2	.34	.51[a]
Syracuse, N.Y.	0.27	−.0384	.0003	.97	1	.60	.66[a]
Tacoma, Wash.	−3.07	−.0189	.0006	1.59[a]	0	.37	.46[a]
Tampa-St. Petersburg, Fla.	0.74	−.0299	−.0001	.92	0	.91	.88[a]
Terre Haute, Ind.	−2.37	−.0546	.0004	1.29[a]	1	.46	.55[a]
Toledo, Ohio	−3.35[a]	.0785	−.0012	1.56[a]	1	.84	.42[a]
Trenton, N.J.	0.08	−.0229	.0000	1.05	0	.65	.74[a]
Tulsa, Okla.	−1.26	.0031	−.0001	1.05	0	.76	.85[a]
Utica-Rome, N.Y.	3.63[a]	−.0066	.0002	.77	1	.39	.58[a]
Washington, Md.-Va.	0.47	.0000	.0005	.43[a]	−1	.37	.92[a]
Waterbury, Conn.	3.79[a]	−.0371	.0004	.77	0	.58	.97[a]
Wheeling, W.Va.	0.05	.0000	−.0002	1.82[a]	2	.73	.56[a]
Wichita, Kan.	−0.48	−.0499	.0008	.93	0	.52	.87[a]
Wilkes-Barre, Pa.	4.76[a]	.0000	−.0009	.99	1	.78	1.03[a]
Wilmington, Del.-N.J.-Md.	−0.13	.0033	−.0002	.97	1	.46	.54[a]
Winston-Salem, N.C.	1.02	.0205	−.0003	.74	−2	.38	.64[a]
Worcester, Mass.	−1.40	.0427	−.0004	1.28[a]	1	.57	.75[a]
York, Pa.	−.85	.0711	−.0012	.99	1	.79	.42[a]
Youngstown, Ohio	−.97	.0203	−.0004	1.43[a]	2	.73	.31[a]

[a] Significant at the 95 percent level. (Note that with respect to a_j, the null hypothesis in the t test is $a_j = 1$.) The d values in the right-hand column are the Durbin–Watson statistics for autocorrelation in the residual series of each city; the 95 percent confidence level is used.

Source: Jeffrey, 1970.

REFERENCES

Alexander, J. W., 1954. The basic–nonbasic concept of urban economic functions. Economic Geography, 30 (1954), 246–261.

Bassett, K., and P. Haggett, 1971. Towards short-term forecasting for cyclic behaviour in a regional system of cities. In Regional Forecasting, M. Chisholm, A. E. Frey, and P. Haggett, Eds., pp. 389–413. London: Butterworth and Co.

Berry, Brian J. L., 1967. Geography of market centers and retail distribution. Englewood Cliffs, N.J.: Prentice-Hall.

Berry, Brian J. L., 1970. The geography of the United States in the year 2000. Transactions of the Institute of British Geographers, 51 (1970), 21–53.

Berry, Brian J. L., 1971. The passing of central-place theory, Research Institute Lectures on Geography, Special Report ETL-SR-71-1, U.S. Army Topographic Labs., Ft. Belvoir, pp. 113–118.

Berry, Brian J. L., and Frank E. Horton, 1970. Geographic perspectives on urban systems with integrated readings. Englewood Cliffs, N.J.: Prentice-Hall.

Borts, G. H., 1960. Regional cycles in manufacturing employment in the United States, 1914–1953. New York: National Bureau of Economic Research.

Casetti, E., and R. K. Semple, 1968. A method for the stepwise separation of spatial trends. University of Michigan, Department of Geography. MICMAG Discussion Paper No. 11.

Casetti, E., L. J. King, and D. Jeffrey, 1971. Structural imbalance in the U.S. urban-economic system, 1960–1965. Geographical Analysis 3 (1971), 239–255.

Casetti, E., L. J. King, and J. Odland, 1971. The formalization and testing on concepts of growth poles in a spatial context. Environment and Planning.

Chisholm, M., A. E. Frey, and P. Haggett, 1971. Regional Forecasting. Proceedings of the Twenty-Second Symposium of the Colston Research Society. London: Butterworth and Co. 470 pp.

Christaller, W., 1933. Die zentralen Orte in Süddeutschland. Jena: Fischer. Translated by C. W. Baskin, The Central Places of Southern Germany. Englewood Cliffs, N.J.: Prentice-Hall.

Committee on Social and Behavioral Urban Research, 1969. A strategic approach to urban research and development. Social and behavioral science considerations. Washington, D.C.: National Academy of Sciences. 45 pp.

Curry, Leslie, 1967. Central places in the random spatial economy. Journal of Regional Science, 7 (1967), 217–238.

Dacey, M. F., 1966. A probability model for central place locations. Annals, Association of American Geographers, 56 (1966), 550–568.

Friedmann, J., 1964. Regional development in post-industrial Society. Journal of American Institute of Planners, 30 (1964), 87.

Golledge, R. G., 1967. Conceptualizing the market decision process. Journal of Regional Science, 7 (1967), 239–257.

Growth and Change, 1971. A Journal of Regional Development, 2 (1971).

Haggett, P., and R. J. Chorley, 1969. Network analyses in geography. London: E. Arnold. 348 pp.

Hirsch, W. Z., Ed., 1964. Elements of regional accounts. Baltimore: The Johns Hopkins Press.

Hirsch, W. Z., Ed., 1966. Regional accounts for policy decisions. Baltimore: The Johns Hopkins Press.

Hoyt, H., 1962. World urbanization. Expanding population in a shrinking world. Urban Land Institute Technical Bulletin, 43 (1962). 50 pp.

Hudson, J. C., 1969. Diffusion in a central place system. Geographical Analysis, 1 (1969), 45–58.

Isard, W., 1960. Methods of regional analysis. Cambridge, Mass.: The M.I.T. Press.

Jeffrey, D., 1970. Economic impulses in an urban system. Ph.D. dissertation, Ohio State University.

Jeffrey, D., E. Casetti, and L. King, 1969. Economic fluctuations in a multiregional setting: A bi-factor analytic approach. Journal of Regional Science, 9 (1969), 397–404.

King, L. J., E. Casetti, and D. Jeffrey, 1971. Cyclical fluctuations in urban unemployment levels in U.S. metropolitan areas. Tijdschrift voor Economische en Sociale Geografie.

King, L. J., E. Casetti, D. Jeffrey, and J. Odland, 1972. The analysis of spatial-temporal patterns in United States metropolitan employment growth, 1957–1969. Growth and Change, 3 (1972).

Lasuén, J. R., 1971. A generalization of the growth pole notion. Paper given at Colloquium on Regional Inequalities of Development, I.G.U. Commission on Regional Aspects of Economic Development, Vitoria, Brazil.

Leven, C. L., Ed., 1970. An analytical framework for regional development policy. Cambridge, Mass.: The M.I.T. Press.

Lithwick, N. H., 1970. Urban Canada problems and prospects. Ottawa: Central Mortgage and Housing Corporation. 50 pp.

MacKinnon, R. D., and M. J. Hodgson, 1970. Optimal transportation networks. A case study of highway systems. Environment and Planning, 2 (1970), 267–284.

National Goals Research Staff. 1970. Toward balanced growth: Quantity with quality. Washington, D.C.: U.S. Government Printing Office.

National Science Board, 1969. Report on the Special Commission on the Social Sciences of the National Science Board, Knowledge into action. Improving the nation's use of the social sciences. Washington, D.C.: National Science Foundation.

Papageorgiou, G., 1971. A generalization of the population density gradient concept. Geographical Analysis, 3 (1971), 121–127.

Rodgers, A., 1957. Some aspects of industrial diversification in the United States. Economic Geography, 33 (1957), 16–31.

Scott, A., 1965. Policy for declining regions: A theoretical approach. In Areas of Economic Stress in Canada, W. D. Wood and R. S. Thomas, Eds., pp. 73–93. Kingston: Queen's University Press.

Sen, L., 1971. The geometric structure of an optimal transport network in a limited city-hinterland case. Geographical Analysis, 3 (1971), 1–14.

Sheth, J. N., 1969. Using factor analysis to estimate parameters. Journal of American Statistical Association, 64 (1969), 808–823.

Taaffe, E. J., 1962. The urban hierarchy; an air-passenger definition. Economic Geography, 38 (1962), 1–14.

Taaffe, E. J., Ed., 1970. Geography. Englewood Cliffs, N.J.: Prentice-Hall.

Trott, C. E., 1969. A cross-spectral model of an urban system. Ph.D. dissertation, Ohio State University.

Ullman, E. L., M. F., Dacey, H. Brodsky, 1969. The economic base of American cities. Seattle: The University of Washington Press.

Von Böventer, E., 1964. Spatial organization theory as a basis for regional planning. Journal of the American Institute of Planners, 30 (1964), 30–100.

Werner, C., 1968. The law of refraction in transportation geography: Its multivariate extension. The Canadian Geographer, 12 (1968), 28–40.

Werner, C., 1969. Networks of minimal length. The Canadian Geographer, 13 (1969), 47–69.

Wood, W. D., and R. S. Thoman, Eds., 1965. Areas of Economic Stress in Canada, Kingston: Queen's University Press.

Fundamental Issues Concerning Future Settlement in America

RICHARD L. MORRILL
University of Washington

The American landscape, the result of the imprint of man on the natural environment, is beautiful and ugly, empty and crowded, prosperous and depressed. In recent years many authors have speculated on the forms that the American landscape may take in a postindustrial age (Berry, 1970a; Ewald, 1968). Others are more concerned with the obvious ugliness, abuse, and poverty of much of the landscape, from a national to a local scale. The many strategies that have been suggested to ameliorate these problems have been, in turn, attacked as uneconomic, unconstitutional, or unrealistic.

I have tried here to evaluate possible alternative future landscapes from a broad geographic, social, and economic perspective, with as little prior bias toward particular outcomes as possible, but with a personal emphasis on national goals of equity over, if necessary, goals of efficiency.

THE FREEDOM OF THE FUTURE IS LIMITED BY THE DECISIONS OF THE PAST

Our ability to determine what the landscape of the future will be like is greatly restricted because most of tomorrow's landscape will be inherited virtually unchanged from yesterday. People and their activities are located in particular places; the material investment in improvements and modifications to the land is stupendous, at least $3 trillion. The human nonmaterial investment in current place-oriented behavior is just as overwhelming. The investment of a few years can have only a marginal effect in altering the human or natural features of the landscape or modes of behavior, especially if we realize that most material and nonmaterial investment and effort is applied to the enhancement or conservation of existing investments and patterns of behavior. Over time, the landscape does change significantly, nevertheless, and we must appreciate both the probable impacts of present decision making on the landscape and the kind and magnitude of investments that would be required to effect any desired improvements or changes.

GOALS FOR THE FUTURE AMERICAN LANDSCAPE

Goals for American society are usually expressed in a vague rhetoric of widely accepted concepts of growth, prosperity, quality of life and of the environment, equality, and freedom (Commission on National Goals, 1960; National Goals Research Staff, 1970; Eberhard, 1971; Hauser, 1971; Friedmann, 1971; Hansen, 1971). History has shown that these goals are not all easily achieved nor are they even very compatible. In practice, the overriding goals have been economic growth, a high *per capita* product, and the preservation of national independence and economic freedom. More recently, this pattern has been modified by concern for some aspects of equality and for conservation of the quality of the environment. Many recent critics would substitute a goal of environmental quality for economic growth. Some, including myself, would make social and economic equality and justice the primary goal (Harvey, 1970). We must be realistic and realize that we probably cannot achieve all these goals equally or simultaneously. We have not even been able to maintain the legislatively ordained stable growth and full employment, let alone conserve the environment or achieve social and economic justice (U.S. Congress, 1946). What, then, are the implications of emphasizing the various goals: growth, environmental quality, and social and economic equality.

The goal of economic growth, measured by increasing annual total and *per capita* gross national product, is generally accepted by most of the effective economic and political decision makers of our society (National Goals Research Staff, 1970, p. 24; Moroney, 1970; Morrill and Wohlenberg, 1971). Pursuit of this goal has created the most affluent society in world history, at least in *per capita* terms. One serious problem of this approach is that the efficient expansion of a private economy requires concentration of power, and therefore tends to result in severe social and economic inequality, making it partly incompatible with a goal of social justice. Poverty and social injustice are not really paradoxes in our society, although they are often claimed to be: They are expected consequences of differential control over economic resources in a competitive order. As a result, achievement of minimal standards of social and economic welfare at the bottom depends on a prodigious total national product, but even so, it instills in the less successful a feeling of severe relative deprivation (Miller, 1971). This problem obtains not only within a population in a given place or region, but between different regions. Differential control and access to economic resources and markets results in severe regional social and economic inequality. The efficient expansion of the private economy has required spatial as well as distributional concentration of economic growth and prosperity. Again, marginal regions are better off in times of general rapid growth, but suffer especially in periods of stagnation (Hansen, 1970; Morrill and Wohlenberg, 1971).

The second serious problem, to be felt even more in the future, is that the projected increase in gross national product is so enormous that many, especially those with ecological training, fear devastating and perhaps irreversible damage to the natural environment. Projected demand for fuels, water, and land resources are so great that such growth may be possible only at the expense of future generations, at the expense of less-developed countries and peoples, and at the risk of severe ecological imbalance. The severity of these risks is objectively still unknown, although it is obvious that pressure on resources will be very great. As long as the private economy does not bear the long-term social and economic costs of resource depletion, air and water pollution, congestion and overcrowding, the risk of the overuse and damage of resources is great (Jarrett, 1966). Some of these costs are being charged to the private producer, although much is being borne by the public sector. Thus, for example, petroleum consumption, automobile use, and steel consumption are overencouraged to the extent that the current price of gasoline does not reflect the real costs of air pollution, health impairment, traffic congestion, lost time, and land withdrawn from higher-valued uses (National Goals Research Staff, 1970, p. 72). Owing to the great metropolitan and regional concentration of economic activity, environmental damage is territorially limited geographically, and for that reason, it is more severe and occurs sooner in time (e.g., New York and Los Angeles air pollution, Lake Erie water pollution).

A goal of ecological balance urged by many environmental critics of society, implies an arresting of further damage to the environment, a restoration of many damaged environments, and a shift from an emphasis on annual gross national product (growth) or "throughput" to achieving a high wealth or standard of living biomass (Jarrett, 1966). An emphasis on recycling of resources, and even more, on maximizing the time horizon of a given product or resource use or investment is basically incompatible with the traditional operation of a free market economy, which requires maximizing "throughput" (annual revenues) as the main incentive for investment. However, an ecological-balance goal is no more compatible with an aim of social and economic equality because of the competitive nature of the economy. With a normal 5 percent unemployment, greater underemployment, and a chronic labor surplus as the most important causes of poverty, and even perhaps of racial discrimination, any decrease in growth or gross national product and attendant decrease in employment will only aggravate inequality and poverty (National Goals Research Staff, 1970, p. 73). As desirable as the goal is, therefore, and despite eloquent support from intellectuals (including geographers), it is not likely to gain the support of either the rich, whose power depends on growth, or the poor, whose hope also depends on growth.

A goal of social and economic equality could be partly achieved if growth were so great that full employment resulted. The ecological effects of such extreme growth, however, could be severe. The inescapable conclusion is that greater equality, without excessive growth and with a concern for ecological balance, can be achieved only by some basic shifts in social and economic values and structures. A higher degree of public interference in the economy is inevitable, but probably not as revolutionary as some hope and others fear. The wealth (and annual product) of the United States is already sufficient to afford the elimination of poverty, slums, poor health, and many other manifestations of inequality (Morrill and Wohlenberg, 1971). A simple but radical redistribution of income toward greater income equality is required; this is most easily achieved through a far more generous guaranteed-income plan, but preferably through basic reform of the processes that determine prices, employment, wages, and salaries. With respect to regional inequality on local and national scales, a solution is again not possible without greater public involvement, especially in the decisions of where to make the investment in new opportunities. A shift in values from economic efficiency toward social equity is apparent in both income redistribution and public interference in the location of economic activities, but probably both greater class and regional equality are possible with very little effect on economic efficiency or corporate profitability. It is still difficult to believe we are ready to pay such a price (Hauser, 1971, p. 17).

DETERMINANTS OF THE LANDSCAPE

In a nation so characterized by individualism and the rhetoric of freedom, it must surely be true that the composite landscape is the result of countless decisions of individual citizens and that where and how the citizen lives is his choice. At a microgeographic level the landscape does bear the imprint of the traditional freedom of at least the middle- and upper-class individuals to do just as they want with their property. At the more basic level of the setting—rural, urban, or metropolitan—and the region, however, the choice of the individual becomes circumscribed. The truth is that the significant decisions on the location of economic opportunities, and therefore on where people will live, are made in the private-business sector (Perloff, 1960). In a competitive society, the rational firm or investor will expand or locate new facilities, creating new opportunities, in those locations that seem to offer secure and sizable profitability. Businesses seem to believe in and follow demographic projections of metropolitanization, thus creating, by their investment, a self-fulfilling prophecy. Over recent decades a higher and higher proportion of these new opportunities have been located within larger and larger metropolitan areas and in particularly favored regions. In general, the views and preferences of government, prospective or actual employees, and even most stockholders are irrelevant. The majority of the American population say they would prefer not to live in a metropolis (New York Times, 1969; Hansen, 1970, p. 246); various levels of government express concern for depressed regions, parts of cities, and nonmetropolitan America generally (President's National Advisory Committee on Rural Poverty, 1968; Glazer, 1970; National Goals Research Staff, 1970); but the business world makes the real decisions.

The freedom of the individual is reduced to taking it or leaving it. The displaced worker in a declining area can choose to remain there in underemployed poverty, or he can move to the metropolis; this situation contrasts with Friedmann's strange logic that since people went to the metropolis, they must love it (Friedmann, 1971, p. 19). The propriety of the fact that the important decisions are made by capital and that people (labor) are conceived as a factor of production to shift according to the needs of businesses is, in general, unquestioned. I stress the point, since it is essential to realize that the present landscape is mainly a product of private, especially larger-scale business decisions, as the future landscape will be, unless society chooses to modify the process of decision making.

The general public as individuals and as government has affected the macrogeographic landscape to some extent. Mainly through the allocation of defense expenditures and military installations, as well as highway, agricultural, and other funds, the government has been able, since 1940, to decentralize economic growth to parts of the South and West (National Goals Research Staff, 1970, p. 47–48). The Tennessee Valley Authority represented an even more direct intervention in investment decisions. Earlier government investments in economic opportunities included various irrigation and reclamation schemes, and more indirectly, the railroad land grants and the highly permissive attitude toward resource exploitation.

The determination of many people to move to California, and later to Florida and Arizona, whether or not job opportunities existed, probably did increase economic growth over what it otherwise would have been. Having moved, the people represented both a potential labor force and market to which investors responded. This shift of population was aided by the somewhat greater freedom of part of the retired population to choose their region and place of residence (Ullman, 1954).

Within the metropolis the middle and upper classes are afforded considerable choice in residential and job location, but the poor have very restricted choice in both. Increasing separation of work and job, again a result of private-business decisions, works an increasing hardship on the poor, just as more higher-paying jobs are moving to the suburbs (Advisory Commission on Intergovernmental Relations, 1968).

PROBLEMS AND TRENDS OF THE AMERICAN LANDSCAPE

Although much of the American landscape—scenic, rural, even urban—is beautiful and represents a mutually beneficial relation of man and environment, there is also much evidence of environmental abuse and neglect, misallocation of resources, unrealized potential, and human poverty. At the macro or regional scale, the fundamental issues are the problems of metropolitan and regional concentration of activities and people and their pollution as well as the concomitant rural and regional stagnation and decline. At the local level, some major issues are the frequent ugliness of the microhuman landscape, in turn a function of poverty, freedom of property, and poor taste; the relative location of jobs, residences, businesses, and social and economic groups; and the kind of transportation systems to serve them. I concentrate here on the regional problem.

METROPOLITAN CONCENTRATION: SETTLEMENT POLARIZATION

For at least 100 years the process of urbanization has transferred millions from rural areas and smaller settlements to towns, cities, and metropolises. The primary basis for rapid urbanization was the efficiency of manufacturing that set off a spiral of increasing demand and productivity and encouraged the commercialization and mechanization of agriculture. Commercial and service activities located together in urban settlements, for reasons of agglomeration economies; industrial activities located together for reasons of both agglomeration and scale economies. Service centers, a hierarchy of central places from countless hamlets to New York City, spread across the landscape to serve the dispersed American population. Industry located both in the better located service centers, especially ports and transport junctions, and in clusters of settlements close to water power and coalfields (Berry and Horton, 1970, pp. 21–36).

The railroads bringing cheap long-distance overland transportation, extended settlement across the country and remain a necessary condition for concentration in larger urban centers, both within the northeastern core of the nation and within regions. The accessibility of resources and markets varied greatly from place to place. The sufficient condition for concentration has been the realization of greater and and greater scale economies (permitted by the cheapness of rail transport). Thus metropolitanization, the concentration of most net economic and population growth in the highest level of the urban systems, was already well under way by 1900 and was made possible by the railroad (and industry-scale economies), not by the automobiles. The car, in fact, was expected to result in decentralization, but the forces of concentration have been stronger. The car has led to the decline, relocation, or even the disappearance of countless hamlets and villages as rural residents shift their focus to larger towns; and, of course, it has led to decentralization of residences and jobs within the metropolis (Berry and Horton, 1970, pp. 207–227, 440–482).

The nature of railroad diffusion, the discriminatory pattern of rail rates; the antebellum differentiation between North and South in labor, land, immigration, and other policies, as well as in slavery; postbellum discrimination against the South; and especially the industrial head-start and concentration of capital, talent, education, and technology were among the reasons for the overwhelming dominance of the northeastern core (Anderson, 1968). Even in 1970, after at least three decades of some regional decentralization, a core region of only 15 percent of the area of the conterminous United States still has 45 percent of the population, 55 percent of the income, 65 percent of the manufacturing, and a far higher proportion of the higher levels of economic decision making (Ullman, 1958).

This historic concentration of wealth was economically rational and efficient for investors from the dominant region, but did establish the pattern of dependence of the rest of the country on resource exploitation in agriculture, mining, and forestry. Despite economic discrimination the Far West enjoyed fair incomes because a few people shared rich resources, but the absolute level of development was below potential (Perloff, 1960). In the South the excess population, racial conflict, and dependence on agriculture resulted in endemic underemployment and poverty and underutilization of human and natural resources. This long-term exploitation of the South from outside as well as by a small aristocracy inside is taking a long time to overcome (Nichols, 1969).

Since the 1940's the West and South have experienced fairly rapid development. The spectacular growth of California resulted from massive military and defense investments and the migration of millions in search of amenities, whether or not jobs were available, which in turn encouraged branches of northeastern industries (National Goals Research Staff, 1970, p. 51; Berry and Horton, 1970, p. 35). To some extent the process is occurring in Florida. In Texas, moderate growth of population and industry was based more on indigenous resources, mainly petroleum, and to a considerable degree on local determination. In the Piedmont, especially, and in much of the small-town South, industries were attracted that chose not to adapt to higher-cost labor in the Northeast (Maddox and others, 1967).

REGIONAL INEQUALITY

Gross regional disparities are less than they were in the 1920's, but they remain great. Figure 1 shows those areas of the country with a net poverty gap in 1960; that is, areas in which the money necessary to bring all families just up to the nonpoverty threshold could not be raised by transfer from the more wealthy in those areas (Morrill and Wohlenberg, 1971, Chap. 6). This severe condition, reflecting lack of job opportunities, unfavorable industrial and occupational structures, and labor surplus, is characteristic of most of the South, much of the Plains, and even peripheral parts of the Northeast and West. This condition occurs in two thirds of the area of the country with two fifths of the people. Despite development, income levels in the South remain far below those in the Northeast. What improvement the periphery has experienced appears to be somewhat contrary to the natural course of private economic events and to be a result of government intervention, regional determination (Texas), and irrational patterns

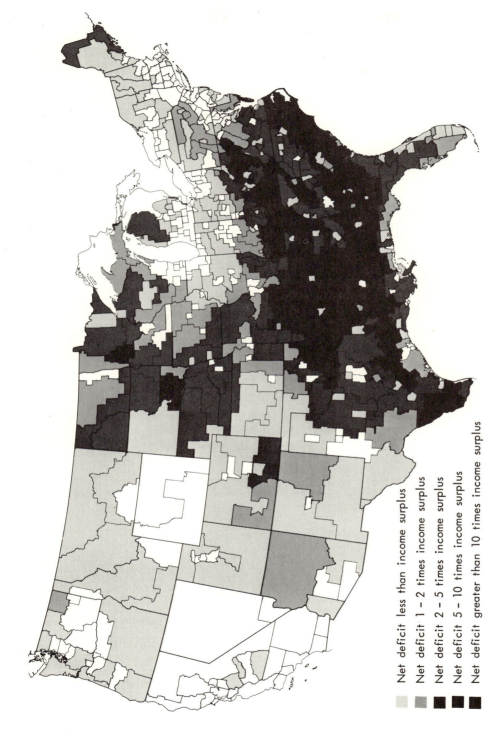

FIGURE 1 Economic areas with poverty gaps greater than income surplus in 1960. There are 338 areas.

of migration (California, Florida). The persistence of so much regional poverty over so much territory is a consequence of the imagined unprofitability of increasing the variety and quality of economic opportunities in nonmetropolitan portions of the country. It is a national problem in that millions are condemned to poverty because of their location preferences, so many human resources are underutilized, and there is no simple or automatic solution.

RURAL-URBAN MIGRATION

If economic opportunities are most efficiently located in the Northeast and in other metropolitan regions, then the economically rational solution is for the surplus population to move there from the periphery. Millions have done so, especially from the South, Appalachia, and the Great Plains, but more millions have refused to move, because they prefer their home areas and because they realize that prosperity is by no means assured, even if they move to the richest northeastern metropolises, which contain absolutely large numbers of poor people themselves (Morrill and Wohlenberg, 1971).

Within regions, the upward shift of people and activities from rural and small-town areas to the metropolis has been an economically rational response to the increasing mechanization and productivity of agriculture, forestry, and mining that has released millions from these activities. It has also been a response to the preference and seemingly optimal location of the growing sectors of the industrial and service economy for the larger agglomerations. On balance, the process of urbanization has brought tremendous benefits (Friedmann, 1971, p. 19; Ewald, 1968, pp. 138-157). Perhaps the greatest benefit has been the creation of a giant rich and productive national economy and the world's highest living standard. Concurrently it has made possible far wider access to better education and cultural opportunities and has helped to lead to liberalization of social attitudes; many costs of the imperfect process may be seen on the landscape, however.

Tens of millions have migrated from rural areas, because few alternatives appeared to replace opportunities lost in the ever more efficient primary sectors. Many become satisfied, but available data on preferences clearly reveal that today, at least, the large majority of those not native to metropolitan areas claim that they wish to leave but have been forced into the metropolis for economic survival. Millions are unable to adapt or to find higher-paying jobs and represent only a shift from rural to urban poverty (Elgie, 1970, pp. 35-54; Hansen, 1970; President's National Advisory Committee on Rural Poverty, 1968).

The results of this out-migration on the rural, small-town areas are mixed. For some, exodus of the surplus population has been sufficient to enable most of those remaining to enjoy a decent living standard on large efficient holdings (Eberhard, 1971, p. 9). In such cases, however, the absolute level of service activities and the number of places falls. Probably in the majority of rural areas, the ideal has not occurred. Instead a stagnation or relative decline in *per capita* as well as in gross levels of income and services has taken place, because too many refuse to leave and because so often the marginal members stay. The most productive and educated migrate, leaving an unfavorable aged population with high underemployment and high dependency levels (Parr, 1966; Morrill and Wohlenberg, 1971, pp. 134-135). This condition has existed in many areas for far too long to be treated as a temporary adjustment to technological change. Partly because so many fear the metropolis and doubt their ability to compete, and because they have discovered that opportunities there are also restricted, they remain and add to the competitive weakness of labor in nonmetropolitan areas (Morrill and Wohlenberg, 1971, pp. 134-135).

In those parts of the Northeast, California, and Florida where the metropolitan areas are closely spaced (about 100 mi apart), the rural areas do not lag because people can remain in their home setting or shift to a rural setting and still commute easily to the metropolis, thus transferring income from the city. Also the farmers are conveniently situated with regard to local market and suppliers (Berry, 1970b). In much more of the country, the metropolitan areas are fewer and further apart, or lacking in opportunities themselves. About half the area and a quarter of the population are beyond commuting range to viable metropolises. This problem emphasizes the dilemma—the conflict between the desire and determination of so many people to remain in rural areas or home regions and the reality of metropolitan economic advantages. So many regions are relegated to primary activities only, and so many people are thereby denied normal participation in the nation's wealth. At present the economic consensus is that these people are irrational romantics, delaying the equilibrium process of regional income convergence.

CONDITIONS IN METROPOLITAN AMERICA

At least half the problem of metropolitan concentration is the cost to the cities, not to the country. First, there are the social and economic costs of the rural migrants themselves. These are poverty jobs, underemployment and unemployment, delinquency and broken homes, the high cost to the cities of dealing with rural migrants and their problems, and the depressing effect of excess rural migration on wage levels of the unskilled (Hansen, 1970, pp. 241-244; Glazer, 1970). Next are the increasingly severe costs of pollution, waste disposal, water supply, traffic congestion, and public security (because of crime and delinquency), for which the single most important variable may be the sheer population of the metropolis. The larger the city, the higher are rents and land values inflated, and the more difficult it is to ensure either the public or private space desired.

Although the largest cities are the greatest generators of wealth and culture, as well as the most profitable sites for most private economic activities, much of the great cost outlined above is not borne by the private sector, but by the public sector and by individuals (Hoover, 1968; Perloff and Wingo, 1968). The measurement of these costs is so difficult that we do not know whether metropolitan locations are actually optimum for most economic activities if all costs are considered. Sketchy evidence suggests that, on an average, unit economic costs for manufacturing, services, and transportation fall as metropolitan size increases to perhaps 1,000,000 population or more; whereas social costs of congestion, pollution, space provision, and crime begin to climb markedly after about 500,000. Although the nation would be much poorer and duller without our greatest metropolises, there is mounting reason to wish that they not become far larger yet, or that not too many more places join their ranks and assume their severe problems.

In summary, the polarization of settlement resulting in metropolitan concentration and rural stagnation is a severe problem, because of the mounting costs and disorders of the metropolis and the poverty and waste of resources of much of the countryside. Above all, in a democratic society, perhaps the wishes of many people not to live in the overcrowded giant metropolis should receive more attention.

PROSPECTS

Many scenarios for the American future have been suggested. Doxiadis and Gottman, extrapolating certain present trends to one extreme, project a supermetropolitan America, in which most of the population will reside in a few giant megalopolises of from 10 to 50 million people (Doxiadis, 1970). This outcome assumes a higher-than-probable total population growth, solutions to the horrendous social and transportation problems plaguing much smaller places today, the willingness or desire of the people to live in these world cities, and, I believe, a basic change in social behavior. There is no denying, however, that current trends point in this direction.

Berry, Friedmann, Meier, and Webber, extrapolating along the potential of communications and transportation innovation, project an opposite outcome; a large-scale return to country living (Friedmann, 1965). This is theoretically possible for the middle and upper classes, who will have short work weeks, who can accomplish their work by remote communication, and who will be able to commute by fast efficient means to even distant metropolises. A return to country living is also possible for the retired and for those poor who choose to live on a guaranteed income; the metropolis, then, can be abandoned to the working lower classes. This outcome rests on somewhat tenuous assumptions, especially with respect to transport technology and cost. It involves the risk of even greater social polarization.

Although it is impossible to forecast the future, the rational man has no choice but to try to anticipate it (National Goals Research Staff, 1970, pp. 23-24). Therefore, between these extremes, I shall describe the landscapes suggested by a cautious extension of trends: In the absence of radical public intervention, the future pattern of settlement may be remarkably unchanged from the present.

There are not strong reasons to expect investors to shift from the current profitable pattern: location in large metropolitan areas (over 250,000 or especially over 500,000 population), with a predominant and growing share in the fringes and a declining share in the city centers; location in towns and cities that are satellite (25-50 mi) to the largest metropolitan areas (over 2,000,000 population). These trends may produce undesirable outcomes, such as continuing job and population concentration and more rapid physical expansion of the largest metropolitan areas, leading to aggravation of the problems associated with greater size, especially waste disposal and traffic congestion. There may be extreme pressure on land and water resources in the coalescing major metroplitan areas in the Northeast, California, and Florida. There will probably be greater class and racial polarization, with almost all the richer people moving to suburb and exurb, abandoning the central city to the elderly, jobless, poor, and black, and risking increased social and political turmoil. Population stagnation would probably result, together with continuing relative economic decline of most rural and small-town areas. Population decline may be halted as more of the elderly choose rural areas in which to retire, and if a national guaranteed income is established that is sufficient to permit those who wish to remain in or shift to rural areas to subsist in genteel poverty and not to compete for scarce jobs. These possibilities, however, will do little for the nonmetropolitan economies. Friedmann argues that greater affluence, leisure, and mobility will extend metropolitan benefits much farther (100-200 mi) in the future. I doubt that this will occur before 1985—after these rural romantics are forced from their preferred areas (Friedmann, 1965).

This effect on the landscape would be unfortunate, because of the economic costs of extreme concentration—locally and regionally—on water supply, waste disposal, transport provision and traffic amelioration, pollution control, and provision of open space. Also involved would be the corollary economic costs of underutilization of land and natural and human resources in noncongested areas; the social costs of crowding, traffic congestion, crime, and racial tension in the metropolis; and of either forced migration or of a rural life restricted by poverty. Above all, the effect on the landscape would probably be contrary to the desires of a majority of people.

The prospects and recent experience are perhaps not as extreme as painted above. In fact, in most less-successful regions of the country there are at least a few moderately growing and fairly successful cities, not prosperous enough to meet regional needs, but indicating that prospects—and potentials if the rules of the game were to change—are not really hopeless.

ALTERNATIVE FUTURE SETTLEMENT PATTERNS

Because of the nature of the American economic system, the simplest alternative is to follow a policy of public noninterference, to accept the consequences of a market solution, and in the American tradition, to adjust to and overcome problems as they arise (Downs, 1970, pp. 3-12; Friedmann, 1971, p. 21).

An alternative advocated by a coalition of rural people and rural interests who would preserve their way of life and increase rural opportunities and of those who view the American metropolis as inherently unhealthy, is to undertake a program of rural industrialization—a dramatic reversal of all economic–geographic trends of the century (President's National Advisory Committee on Rural Poverty, 1968).

Another alternative, developed in Europe and enjoying wide verbal support in the United States today, is to pursue a policy of encouraging the growth of a set of smaller metropolises (or growth centers) in the regions that are at present less successful—a compromise plan of regional decentralization from the Northeast and California, but local concentration to viable centers (Darwent, 1969).

CONTINUATION OF CURRENT POLICIES AND PRACTICES

The regional and local concentration of people and activities resulting from extension of current trends, has been described. The costs of dealing with metropolitan problems will be great, and many people will be unhappy, both in the metropolises and in the areas left behind. I believe that making a megalopolitan world sufficiently livable would be extremely costly—financially and socially—and less desirable than other possibilities. Still the prospects are not really bad, and it would be foolish to underestimate the capacity of this society to evolve an acceptable future. Many people do prefer metropolitan living. Large metropolitan concentrations of people are not inherently un-

pleasant. London, Paris, and Moscow are aesthetically pleasant, culturally rich, and physically secure, and they have efficient transportation. Physiologically, people do not need a bucolic life. If pollution and waste-disposal problems can be solved—the solution is largely a matter of technology and money, which we have, if our propensity for violence and crime can be reduced—a far more difficult achievement, if full nonpoverty employment can be achieved—probably impossible without greater public intervention, and if racial discrimination and conflict can be eased—again unlikely without full employment and more direct public control of discrimination—then our giant cities could become satisfactory homes for most people. From an ecological viewpoint, too, the concentration of man's activities in smaller regions and metropolitan areas, if socially and technologically feasible, might be expected to exert less direct pressure on the natural ecology of the larger part of the country than would a more widespread development.

The private car is both a prodigious polluter and a prodigious space consumer. If the nation's population were to be even more concentrated in large metropolises and crowded regions, then it would probably be necessary to restrict greatly the private use of the car and to substitute public transit (Ewald, 1968, p. 146). This may be welcomed by some planners and intellectuals, but will undoubtedly be rejected by the vast majority of people and businesses. Generally, to make giant metropolises more livable would require the acceptance of greater restrictions on individual and business freedom, especially on the use of real property and cars, a very high price to pay in our society (Downs, 1970, p. 11).

RURAL ECONOMIC GROWTH

In the 1971 Congress, several Senators from the Agriculture Committee, supported by the Department of Agriculture and many farm and other organizations, introduced legislation to authorize federal expenditures of several billions of dollars to help establish industry in rural areas (defined as places away from metropolises and with under 35,000 inhabitants). Some metropolitan areas profess to want fewer rural migrants, lending wide support to and belief in the desirability of a rural economic resurgence, which would permit many more to live in settlements that they apparently prefer.

There are industries that can survive in rural areas and small towns that are efficient at smaller scales of output, and it may be reasonable to give them some incentive (President's National Advisory Committee on Rural Poverty, 1968). To advocate or anticipate any large-scale rural industrialization is, however, unrealistic and even unnecessary to the objective of aiding rural America (Hansen, 1970, Chap. 9). Most of the economic activities—goods and services—that are expected to expand or relocate in the foreseeable future require or prefer metropolitan settings for competitive reasons of size and quality of labor pool, availability of business and related services, access to suppliers and markets, willingness of capital to invest, and efficient scales of output.

A program of rural industrialization, concentrating aid in places with populations of under 25,000, is therefore an inefficient and probably hopeless endeavor tending to attract only marginal, short-lived, unstable, and low-paying activities. It is also unnecessary, because the problem is to enable people to live in rural areas, not necessarily to provide industrial work there. Ideally, the right growth-center strategy, to be discussed later, has the special virtue of allowing metropolitan investment opportunities while permitting rural residence.

It is indeed possible to foresee some degree of rural industrialization as a result of a policy of creating more metropolises. Already in Europe and the United States, both higher-paying manufacturing and service activities show some evidence of locating or relocating in urban locations, 25 to 50 mi or more outside the larger richer metropolises. For example, Manhattan is viewing the exurbanization of some corporate headquarters with considerable alarm. The difficulty is that this is occuring in only a few already prosperous regions. The sheer high productivity of American industry and agriculture, together with greater affluence and leisure, suggests as well a probable resurgence of handicraft industries in the United States, a process already begun in Scandinavia. Much of this industry would probably be located in rural or small-town areas, some of which might tend to be in fairly crowded, high-amenity areas such as California.

It is reasonable to support some programs for rural areas, including a decent guaranteed income, especially for the retired and for Indian reservations. These programs should include subsidies of acceptable levels of education, and to compensate for the expense of training those who must leave the area to find work; and loans and tax incentives for industries that have a reasonable chance of surviving when paying nonpoverty wages (Hansen, 1970, Chap. 9). It is not reasonable, however, to look to rural industrialization as the means of accommodating the population growth of the country, or to encourage or subsidize inefficient industries that cannot freely compete with those in metropolitan areas. I believe that an exception should be made for Indian reservations, that the government—if necessary—should subsidize good employment opportunities on reservations, to allow those who wish to remain in their communities. This would be extremely small compensation for the generations of exploitation and degradation.

GROWTH-CENTER ALTERNATIVE: THE DEVELOPMENT OF A CLOSER NETWORK OF SMALLER METROPOLISES

A growth-center policy can mean many things. To some it may mean accommodating the future growth of our larger metropolises by a set of new towns that are actually satellite cities (Alonso, 1970). Such a policy is designed to make the metropolitan region more livable and may help to alleviate uncontrolled suburban sprawl, but it is not any answer to the problem of regional metropolitan concentration and rural stagnation or, for that matter, of social division or poverty.

Following is a discussion of a growth-center policy that would develop several smaller metropolises in regions that are at present stagnant or less developed, so that virtually all the population would be within commuting distance of metropolitan work opportunities and quality services. The policy is designed to redistribute future growth and income among regions (Klaasen, 1970; Darwent, 1969), and its purpose is to achieve greater regional equity and balance. In itself, a growth-center policy does not affect the distribution of income among individuals, nor is it, as some proponents evidently believe, any fundamental solution to poverty, which is caused more by structure than by region (Morrill and Wohlenberg, 1971, Chap. 6).

ADVANTAGES AND PROBLEMS OF A GROWTH-CENTER STRATEGY

The advantages of a growth-center policy include allowing more people to reside in regions and settings of their choice, fuller utilization of human and natural resources of neglected areas, and removal of excess pressure from overcrowded larger metropolises. A further advantage would be the equalization of regional income and opportunity and experimentation with new forms of urban residential, business, and transport structures (Hansen, 1970, pp. 251–254). Problems (not necessarily disadvantages) that would arise in implementing a growth-center policy include higher levels of public intervention in the private economy, involving probably much tighter control of land in growth centers; interference with the normal flow of investment capital; and thus a perhaps unwise transfer of economic opportunities from areas better suited to them. High short-term costs of building and developing the growth centers, including opportunity costs of foregoing possibly more productive investments elsewhere, would be involved as well as possible high, long-term costs of subsidy of inefficient, nonviable growth centers. Metropolises might also have adverse ecological effects on present rural and small-town areas (Downs, 1970).

The principal and most popular advantage of growth

centers for a region is that although industrial jobs may be concentrated for efficient competition, people can live, if they wish, in rural or small-town settings, and, to a much greater degree than at present, in the region of their choice. Greater freedom is thus granted to the prospective employee, and consequently less is reserved for the investor. Encouraging a network of smaller metropolises in poorer regions will result in fuller utilization of local human and natural resources, but we cannot say categorically that the national aggregate utilization of human and natural resources will be any greater. Because so much labor is relatively immobile, and because of the normal costs of exploiting and transporting most raw materials, it is highly probable that a growth-center policy would result in fuller resource use—but even then such use will not necessarily be more or even as efficient or productive as a more highly concentrated settlement pattern. There may even be a sacrifice of some efficiency in favor of greater equity if a growth-center policy is pursued, but no conclusive evidence exists either way. Downs (1970, p. 7) argues that British experience illustrates the futility of growth centers, but Cameron (1970) shows that induced growth can be highly successful, given appropriate activities and linkages.

The creation of a variety of urban opportunities in growth centers leads to greater regional equity or income equalization. In general, economic history indicates that economic growth of poorer regions or countries does not damage richer regions, but rather increases the profitability of exchange.

Locally, growth centers can have favorable impacts on a relatively poor surrounding countryside. Commutation transfers enough income to the local communities to support better retail trade and services, especially schools and health facilities. Local farm income should improve, owing to the metropolitan market itself, more competition among suppliers, better transport, and work opportunities other than those on farms (also Berry, 1970).

The large metropolitan areas (over 250,000 population) added about 20 million people in the 1960's. Although declining birthrates should somewhat reduce this volume in the future, 60–70 million more people will still have to be accommodated between 1970 and 2000 (Downs, 1970, p. 4). An effective growth-center policy might be able to transfer a quarter to a half of this growth to the centers and their near hinterlands, so that existing large metropolitan areas would need to accommodate an increment of only about 5 percent or less per decade. The metropolitan areas would be able to devote more of their resources to improve the quality of life for their residents, instead of using them mainly to adjust to rapid growth.

Many innovative proposals have been made for possible desirable and efficient patterns of residences and businesses in cities and for transport systems to serve them. These proposals are most difficult to implement in existing large cities, but the addition of very large and integrated complements of housing, factories, and businesses to smaller cities would permit valuable experimentation (Ewald, 1968, pp. 149–152). The very process of designing and building a growth center could provide a constructive and helpful avenue for public and private cooperation as an alternative to declining military and defense activity (National Goals Research Staff, 1970).

An effective growth-center program would not be a simple matter of adopting some permissive legislation. The level of public financial involvement and design control would be unprecedented, and the very creation of viable growth centers cannot but constitute a new degree of public involvement in the private economy. Creation or vitalization of several new metropolises with 50,000–500,000 population from small cities with 10,000–200,000 population obviously depends on the shifting of hundreds of thousands of jobs that do not yet exist and deflecting billions in investments from the existing metropolises where they otherwise would have been placed (Downs, 1970; Eberhard, 1971; Hauser, 1971; Friedmann, 1971; Hansen, 1971). There would have to be a cross section of activities from the private sector. In all but the most favored locations, significant federal tax incentives, investment credits, and loan guarantees will be required. These might not be constitutional, but experience in Europe suggests that they would be necessary (Downs, 1970; Cameron, 1970).

Indeed achievement of sufficient representation of stable, high-skill, and high-wage activities might well require legislation restricting their location in already successful metropolitan areas without very strong justification. Creation of even 100 new metropolises, housing 20 million additional people, would require perhaps a quarter of all private and public capital investment available for new growth over the next three decades—a massive shift of opportunities that the present metropolises, themselves beset with poverty and unemployment, will hardly be happy to forego (Friedmann, 1971, p. 20). The large majority of new opportunites would not, however, be affected, and no places are called on to reduce absolutely their economic base.

I and many others believe that it would be socially and ecologically desirable if a few of the very largest places, New York, Los Angeles, Chicago, perhaps Philadelphia, Detroit, San Francisco, Boston, Washington, and Cleveland, were to be stabilized at their present size. It is, however, patently impossible to impose such restraints and maintain a free society, so such an objective is best forgotten (Downs, 1970, p. 7).

Experience in Europe also suggests that successful growth centers will require a high degree of public control over land use and land transactions other than ownership, to prevent speculation and chaotic development. Ironically, however, there is also the opposite risk that excessive planning design will result in too limited variety, too few businesses and services, and too formal a landscape (Ewald, 1968, pp. 147–149).

A second basic concern is whether the very high cost of growth centers constitutes as good an investment as the alternative of not as controlled an investment. Investment to accommodate the additional population and to improve living standards would be made anyway. Will that portion channeled to growth centers be as productive as it would otherwise have been? Relative productivitiy depends on two uncertainties. Will the high productivity of new plants compensate for the very high cost of the necessary new overhead capital? Will the location of many growth centers be so inherently poor that long-term subsidy or even failure may be expected? In addition, will the shift tend to make it more difficult for the larger and older metropolises to invest in needed replacement, modernization, beautification, and social amelioration?

Because the growth centers will have new industrial plants and the most modern and efficient social and economic infrastructure, they should be very effective and productive units; postwar reconstruction in Europe and Japan supports this assumption. Incremental growth in existing places should require far less capital, probably less than half, because of the existing infrastructure (Downs, 1970, pp. 7–8). Yet in the long run this growth will require costly rehabilitation, replacement, and extension. No definite conclusion can be reached on this problem, but over the long run, logic suggests that there will be no significant difference between the final total of private and public costs. The greater problem will surely be the risk of a shortage of needed capital replacement in older places, if the public shifts its support to the more exciting new places.

It may be suggested that if the less-successful regions and places had been well located and endowed, they would have become prosperous without artificial help, and that the free market demonstrates the nonviability of such areas (Friedmann, 1971, pp. 19–20). This is a fundamental criticism of the growth-center idea, based on economic-geographic concepts of comparative advantage. The idea that some areas and places are innately inferior or unusable is akin to the idea that poverty is caused by the innate inferiority of the poor. The reasoning is faulty, very partial, and unhistoric. American economic history is filled with examples of areas and places that were once poor and marginally successful but became large and prosperous because of change in technology, demand, and above all transportation. Indeed the railroad was a form of artificial help, and served to substantiate what was formerly potential. In recent decades we can point out the spectacular success of such places as Los Angeles, Phoenix, Salt Lake City, Oklahoma City, and Las Vegas, which at one time seemed hopeless. Less-developed regions or places seem, and usually are, inferior to more-developed areas and places until an investment is made.

The idea that some areas of the country are inherently inferior or unable to compete successfully rests on a now obsolete concept of comparative advantage and the controlling importance of either resources or transportation. The truth is that the less-successful regions are precisely those that depend most on resource exploitation and expensive transportation of resources (Morrill and Wohlenberg, 1971). For almost all expanding sectors of the economy, access to raw materials and proximity to very local markets and suppliers is of declining importance (Berry, 1970a, p. 345). Most areas of the United States, even those that are least successful at present, have adequate rail and highway connections.

The implication is clear: The probable success of a place almost anywhere depends much more on the inherent productivity of its constituent enterprises and labor, of its innovative ability, and of the quality of linkages to markets and suppliers than on the existing characteristics of the local area. The principal short-run problem would be the inadequate quality and quantity of labor in some regions (Hansen, 1970). Thus, although there are some patently absurd natural landscapes that are best suited for wilderness preservation, there are certainly many more acceptable locations for possible growth centers than will ever be needed, and there is no question of building totally new cities from a wilderness, but of the deliberate improvement of existing moderately successful places with adequate transport and some infrastructure.

In summary, as far as economic cost is concerned, a concentrated decentralization or growth-center strategy to accommodate part of the future growth will probably yield somewhat more and cost somewhat less than allowing present trends to continue. This is because many people who refuse to move to large existing metropolises will be able to enjoy the advantages that metropolises can bestow, and the very large metropolises will not need to devote such large resources to accommodate excess rural migration and too-rapid growth. On the social-political side, a growth-center policy responds to the recognized desires of many people to live in what are now less-successful regions and places, not because they were innately inferior, but because the private economy chose to invest elsewhere.

To realize the potential benefit of a growth-center strategy, the problem of the size and spacing of the centers must be confronted. It is widely recognized that metropolitan areas of over 250,000 population have certain scale advantages of local markets and labor supplies and in the provision of a variety of cultural, sports, and business services

(Hansen, 1970, pp. 249–251; Berry, 1970b). Much of the population does not demand such amenities, however, and there are many prosperous and attractive smaller cities with populations of from 25,000 to 250,000. Planning for a 250,000 minimum would be an unnecessary rigidity. A variety of sizes from 50,000 to 500,000 population would be more realistic, because of the great size of the country and the variations in population density. With a 250,000 population minimum, either a very large number of places at an impossibly great cost would be required, or a large proportion of less successful, nonmetropolitan America would not in fact be within reasonable commuting range. A minimum spacing between centers of 100 mi is necessary, except in areas of extremely low density (under two persons per mi^2) to ensure the necessary access to opportunities and transfer of benefits to the periphery.

CONCLUSION: TOWARD A FUTURE SETTLEMENT PATTERN

From this essay emerges an advocacy of establishing a set of growth centers in less-successful or less-urbanized regions to accommodate part of the future urban growth. This policy would permit more of the population to live in the regional setting of their choice, and indirectly, but much more efficiently, accomplish the aims of rural industrialization to revitalize nonmetropolitan America. At the same time, excessive pressure on the largest metropolises and metropolitan regions would be relieved, but these areas would continue to grow. If such a policy were adopted, however, we should realize that it would require greater public involvement, especially in land-use control and the location of future private investment, than has heretofore been accepted in our culture. This will also be true if we are serious about solving metropolitan problems (Hauser, 1971, pp. 14–17). I believe that the gain in freedom of choice for large numbers of people more than offsets the small loss in discretion for far fewer firms, and that the change in priority is justified on economic grounds of regional equity and political grounds of public demand.

REFERENCES

Advisory Commission on Intergovernmental Relations, 1968. Urban and rural America: Policies for future growth. Washington, D.C.: U.S. Government Printing Office. 186 pp.

Alonso, William, 1970. What are new towns for? Urban Studies, 7(1970), 37–56.

Anderson, Stanford, *Ed.*, 1968. Planning for diversity and choice: Possible futures and their relation to the man-controlled environment. Cambridge, Mass.: M.I.T. Press. 340 pp.

Berry, Brian, J. L., 1970a. Geography of the United States in the year 2000. Ekistics, 29 (1970), 339–351.

Berry, Brian, J. L., 1970b. Commuting patterns: Labor market participation and regional potential. Growth and Change, 1 (1970), 3–11.

Berry, Brian, J. L., and Frank E. Horton, 1970. Geographic perspectives on urban systems: With integrated readings. Englewood Cliffs, N.J.: Prentice-Hall. 564 pp.

Cameron, Gordon, 1970. Growth areas, growth centers, and regional conversion. *Scottish Journal of Political Economy,* 17 (1970), 19–38.

Commission on National Goals, 1960. Goals for Americans. Englewood Cliffs, N.J. Prentice-Hall. 372 pp.

Darwent, D. F., 1969. Growth poles and growth centers in regional planning: A review. Environment and Planning, 1 (1969), 5–32.

Downs, Anthony, 1970. Alternate forms of future urban growth in the United States. Journal of the American Institute of Planners, 36 (1970), 3–12.

Doxiadis, C. A., 1970. Man's movement and his settlements. Ekistics, 29 (1970), 296–321.

Eberhard, John P., 1971. The hidden agenda. Growth and Change, 2 (1971), 9–13.

Elgie, Robert, 1970. Rural inmigration, urban ghettoization, and their consequence. Antipode, 2 (1970), 35–54.

Ewald, William R., Jr., *Ed.,* 1968. Environment and policy. Bloomington: Indiana University Press. 459 pp.

Friedmann, John, 1965. The urban field. Journal of the American Institute of Planners, 31 (1965), 312–320.

Friedmann, John, 1971. The feasibility of a national settlement policy. Growth and Change, 2 (1971), 18–21.

Glazer, N., *Ed.,* 1970. Cities in trouble. Chicago: Quadrangle Books. 276 pp.

Hansen, Niles M., 1970. Rural poverty and the urban crisis. Bloomington: Indiana University Press. 352 pp.

Hansen, Niles M., 1971. The problem of spatial resource allocation. Growth and Change, 2 (1971), 22–24.

Harvey, David, 1970. Social process, spatial form, and the redistribution of income in an urban system. 22nd Colston Symposium. London: Butterworth and Co. 470 pp.

Hauser, Philip M., 1971. The population issues. Growth and Change, 2 (1971), 14–17.

Hoover, Edgar, 1968. The evolving form and organization of the metropolis. *In* Issues in Urban Economics, H. Perloff and L. Wingo, Jr., *Eds.,* pp. 237–289. Baltimore: Johns Hopkins Press.

Jarrett, Henry, *Ed.,* 1966. Environmental quality in a growing economy. Baltimore: Johns Hopkins Press, 173 pp.

Klaasen, L. H., 1970. Growth poles in economic theory and policy. *In* Review of Concepts and Theories of Growth Centers. Paris: United Nations (UNESCO).

Maddox, James G., E. E. Liebhafsky, V. W. Henderson, and H. M. Hamlin, 1967. The advancing south. New York: Twentieth Century Fund. 72 pp.

Miller, Herman P., 1971. Rich man, poor man. New York: Thomas Y. Crowell. 46 pp.

Moroney, J. R., 1970. Factor prices, factor proportions, and regional factor endowment. Journal of Political Economy, 78 (1970), 158–164.

Morrill, Richard L., and Ernest Wohlenberg, 1971. The geography of poverty. New York: McGraw-Hill. 148 pp.

National Goals Research Staff, 1970. Toward balanced growth:

Quantity with quality. Washington, D.C.: U.S. Government Printing Office. 226 pp.

New York Times, 1969. Rural poverty. Gallup Poll, May 5, p. 41.

Nichols, V., 1969. Growth poles: An evaluation of their propulsive effects. Environment and Planning, 1 (1969), 193-208.

Parr, John, 1966. Outmigration and the depressed area problem. Land Economics, 42 (1966), 149-159.

Perloff, Harvey, 1960. Regions, resources, and economic growth. Baltimore: Johns Hopkins Press for Resources for the Future. 716 pp.

Perloff, H., and L. Wingo, Jr., *Eds.,* 1968. Issues in urban economics. Baltimore: Johns Hopkins Press.

President's National Advisory Committee on Rural Poverty, 1968. Rural poverty in the United States. Washington, D.C.: U.S. Government Printing Office. 641 pp.

Ullman, Edward, 1954. Amenities as a factor in regional growth. Geographical Review, 44 (1954), 119-132.

Ullman, Edward, 1958. Regional development and the geography of concentration. Papers, Regional Science Association, 4 (1958), 179-206.

U.S. Congress, 1946. Employment Act, 79th Congress. Second Session. U.S. Code, Title 15, Chap. 21, Secs. 1021-1022.

Contemporary Urbanization Processes

BRIAN J. L. BERRY
University of Chicago

INTRODUCTION

The organizers of this symposium, with all due disciplinary bias, started with the premise that new and vital geographical perspectives now emerging are capable of improving our understanding of urban problems and of contributing to their solution. Can this in truth be said about contemporary urbanization processes? In dealing with urbanization processes, we are tempted to try to infer where these processes will lead in the next decades and to attempt to identify leverage points for the alteration of trends if we do not like what we foresee.

This procedure has its dangers, however. To illustrate, let us examine what happened to two demographic forecasts that were made of the populations of the city and metropolitan area of Chicago in the 1960's. These forecasts were made by the Population Research and Training Center of the University of Chicago and the Real Estate Research Corporation. Both were under private contract to the City of Chicago, and both used trends to 1960 as base (Table 1).

Both groups of forecasters erred in predicting the growth of the population of Chicago because they did not foresee the mounting racial tensions that led whites to leave the central city at twice the expected rate; and they overpredicted the population growth of the metropolitan area, because although the area grew at about the same rate as the nation, they did not foresee the recent startling announcement from Washington's Center for Metropolitan Studies that national birth rates plummeted in the last 8 years to simple replacement levels. The surprising shift in trend is the cause of the failure of all forecasts; behavioral changes run counter to historically derived expectations.

What other surprises can be extracted from the few 1970 Census results that are currently available? What do they imply for our knowledge of contemporary urbanization processes, and in turn for urban policy?

POLARIZATION AND THE EXPANSION AND INNER DIFFERENTIATION OF DAILY URBAN SYSTEMS

Let us return to the question of racial polarization. If on one axis of a graph we plot the rate of population change during the period 1960–1970 for each of the nation's central cities, and on the other axis we plot percentage points by which the black population increased during the same period, a clear inverse relation appears (Figure 1). The greater the increase in size and concentration of the ghetto, the more rapid the decrease of the central city's white population, a decrease that runs at about twice the rate of the black increase. Small wonder then that the largest net emigration losses in the decade were registered by the following counties and cities:

County or City	Emigration (in thousands)
Kings, N.Y. (Brooklyn)	280
Wayne, Mich.	276
New York, N.Y. (Manhattan)	219
Cook, Ill.	219
Philadelphia, Pa.	207
St. Louis City, Mo.	183
Allegheny, Pa.	130
Baltimore City, Md.	118
Suffolk, Mass.	110
Milwaukee, Wis.	105
Orleans Parish, La.	102

Source: Current Population Reports, 1971.

One result of these emigration losses is that when the spatial pattern of population growth for the decade is studied, as in Figure 2, the zones of greatest growth are not the counties with the greatest "degree of urban orientation," as defined traditionally by the U.S. Department of Agriculture, using criteria of population size and density (Figure 3) (U.S. Department of Agriculture, 1970). The high-growth zones are the outer reaches of the commuting fields surrounding the nation's central cities (Figure 4) (U.S. Bureau of the Census, 1969). To be sure, population decline was again spatially most extensive in those areas beyond daily commuting contact of economic centers of metropolitan status, as it had been in the decade 1950-1960 (Figures 5 and 6). During the 1960's, metropolitan counties (as defined by the Bureau of the Census) gained 5,307,000 people through net immigration, whereas non-metropolitan counties lost 2,294,000 through net emigration. In a comparison of population in the 1960-1970 with that in 1950-1960, 955 counties showed net migration gains, and 2,169 experienced net emigration in the past decade; in the preceding decade the corresponding numbers were 677 and 2,455. The difference is important, however, because it is caused in large measure by the extension of growth into outlying sections of the daily commuting regions. These regions extend far beyond the reaches of the conventional image of metropolitan areas created and publicized by the federal statistical establishment and consequently used in many federal definitions and programs.

The first characteristic of contemporary urbanization that should be emphasized thus is that the centralization of the population into metropolitan areas is being counterbalanced by a reverse thrust of decentralization. The situation is very different from that during the last years of the nineteenth century, from which we derive the concept of urbanization and its adjunct, the metropolitan area, now in vogue in the corridors of the Bureau of the Census. At that time, Adna Ferrin Weber (1967) observed that "the most remarkable social phenomenon of the present century is the concentration of population in cities," and he considered the tendency toward population concentration to be "all but universal in the western world" (Weber, 1967). Hope Tisdale (1941-1942) later called this tendency toward population concentration and the increase in the number and size of the points of concentration "the process of urbanization." She saw urbanization as "a process of becoming," which implied a movement "from a state of less concentration toward a state of more concentration" (Tisdale, 1941-1942). Weber, Tisdale, and a host of others were acknowledging that by 1900 the industrial city within the nation-state had arrived, physically concentrated, core-oriented, and carrying with it a distinctive way of life (Wirth, 1938). Urbanization could be conceived as a socio-economic process resulting in the creation and growth of points of population concentration. By simply drawing boundary lines around the concentrations, a relatively un-ambiguous series of observational units (cities) could be defined and studied.

If growth extended beyond the corporate limits of the city, all that was required was to bound the larger metropolis. Thus, in keeping with what was then an appropriate procedure, in 1910 the Bureau of the Census introduced the idea of metropolitan districts. The concept was stated most succinctly by the Bureau in 1932:

... the population of the corporate city frequently gives a very inadequate idea of the population massed in and around the city, constituting the greater city, ... and (the boundaries of) large cities in a few cases ... limit the urban population which that city represents or of which it is the center.... If we are to have a correct picture of the massing or concentration of population in extensive urban areas ... it is necessary to establish metropolitan districts which will show the magnitude of each of the principal population centers.

The metropolitan district of 1910 was defined for every city with over 200,000 inhabitants. Little altered, similar definitions were applied in 1920, 1930, and 1940, although by 1940 the size had been decreased to 50,000. In 1950 and 1960 the concept was little changed, although the criteria defining it had become more elephantine. Paraphrased, the criteria are as follows:

The general concept of a metropolitan area is of an integrated economic and social unit with a recognized large population nucleus ... each standard metropolitan statistical area must contain at least one city of at least 50,000 inhabitants (exceptions are permitted). The standard metropolitan statistical area will then include the county of such a central city, and adjacent counties that are found to be

TABLE 1 Forecasted and Actual Population of Chicago (in thousands)

	Actual Populations		Projections (Using 1960 Base)		
	1960	1970	1970[a]	1975[b]	1980[a]
City of Chicago					
White	2,713	2,207	2,427	2,257	2,234
Nonwhite	838	1,158	1,173	1,363	1,540
TOTAL	3,551	3,365	3,600	3,620	3,774
Balance of Metropolitan Area					
White	2,588	3,465	3,525	3,665	4,496
Nonwhite	82	147	175	91	347
TOTAL	2,670	3,612	3,700	3,756	4,843
Total Metropolitan Area					
White	5,301	5,672	5,953	5,922	6,733
Nonwhite	920	1,305	1,349	1,544	1,886
TOTAL	6,221	6,977	7,302	7,476	8,619

[a] Forecasts made for the City of Chicago by the Population Research and Training Center, University of Chicago.
[b] Forecasts made for the City of Chicago by Real Estate Research Corporation.

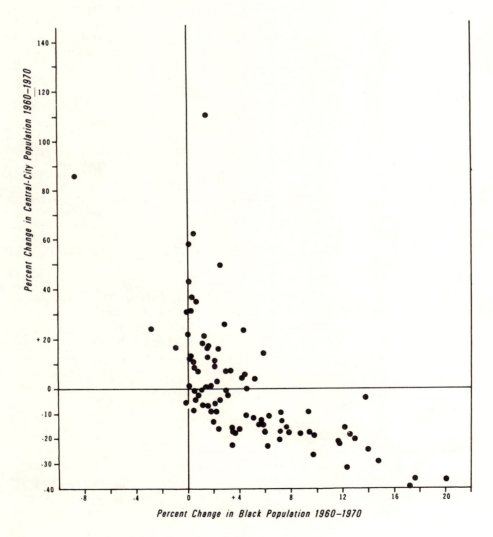

FIGURE 1 Changes in central-city populations related to increases in the percentage of black population, 1960–1970.

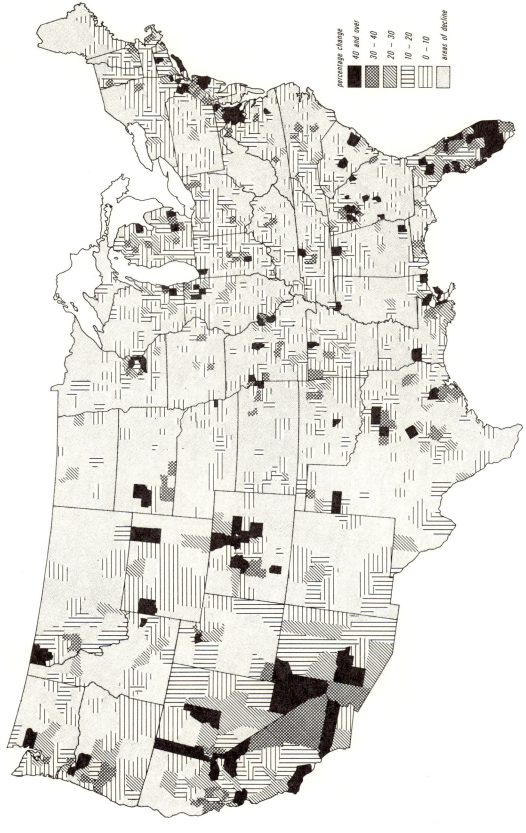

FIGURE 2 The spatial distribution of population growth, 1960-1970.

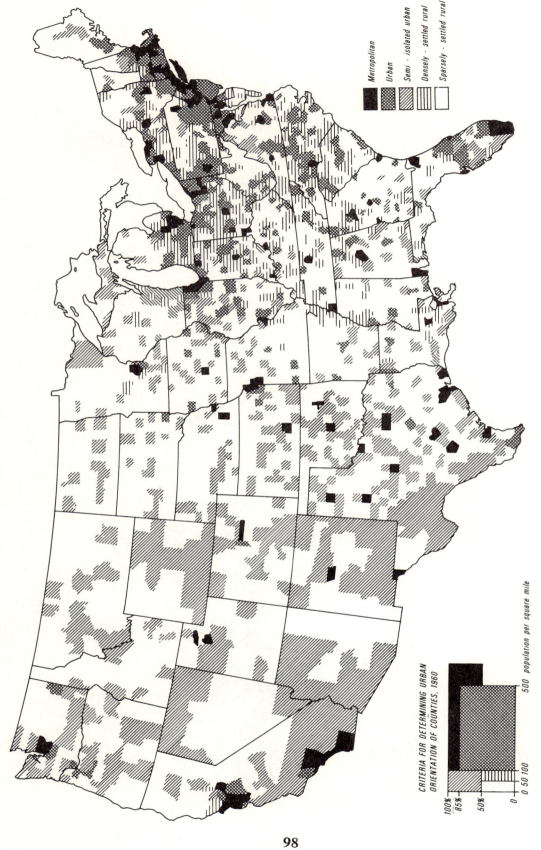

FIGURE 3 The U.S. Department of Agriculture map of urban orientation in 1960, based on population density of percentage of the population classified as "urban."

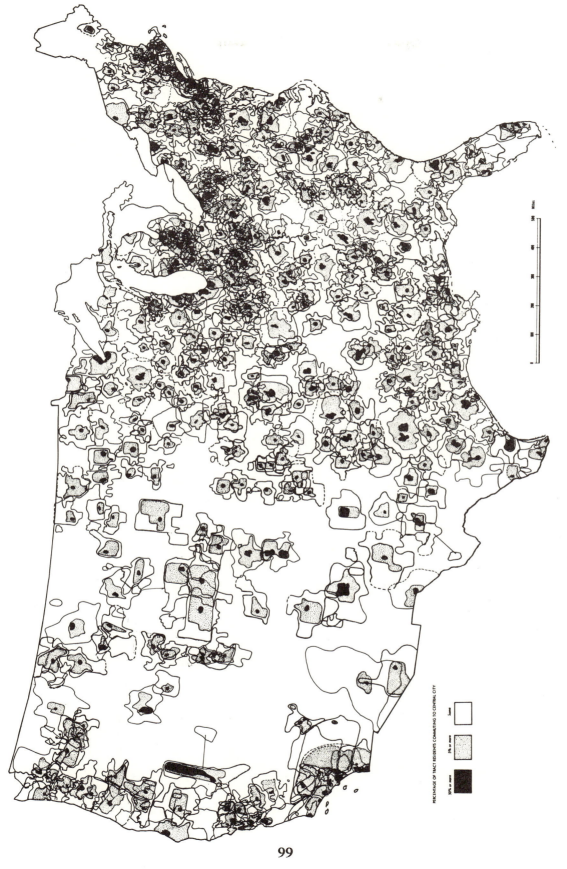

FIGURE 4 Commuting fields of the nation's major central cities in 1960.

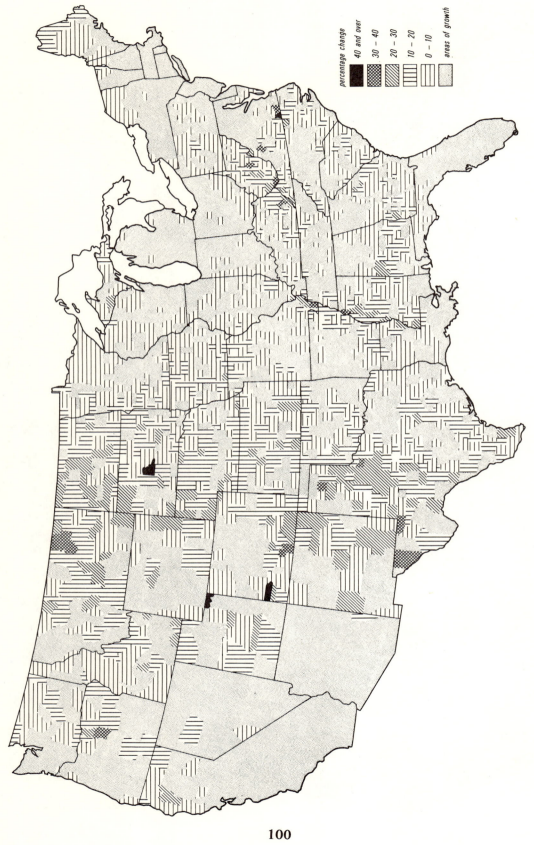

FIGURE 5 The spatial distribution of population decline, 1960–1970.

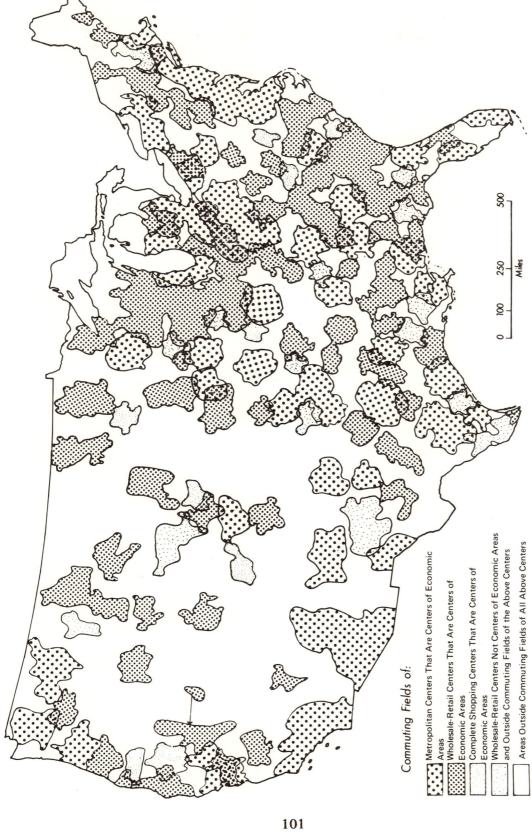

FIGURE 6 Commuting fields classified by hierarchical status of dominant central city.

metropolitan in character and economically and socially integrated with the county of the central city. In New England the requirement with regard to a central city as a nucleus still holds, but the units making up the area are the towns rather than counties. The county (or town in New England) is the basic statistical unit. A Standard Metropolitan Statistical Area (SMSA) may contain more than one city of 50,000 population. The largest city is considered the nucleus and usually gives the name to the area. The name may include other cities in the area. Standard metropolitan statistical areas may cross state lines. . . . One of the basic criteria for measuring economic integration to determine whether additional counties should be included in an area definition is the relation of place of residence to place of work, involving outlying counties and the county of the central city.

The 1970 census data are being published, using the same types of unit, with only minor changes of criteria to relieve the worst underbounding problems presented by the 1970 criteria in the face of new processes of urbanization.

As we saw in the maps of population change 1960–70, however, metropolises today have so burst their nineteenth-century boundaries that broad daily urban systems now transcend all the traditional definitions ("central cities," "urbanized areas," and even the "standard" limits of "metropolitan statistical areas"). They form a network now blanketing all except the most sparsely settled parts of the country, embracing the daily activities and travel of 90 percent of the nation's population.

As these systems developed, they imprinted regular patterns on the nation. Initially these patterns were core-oriented and conical in form. To quote a description of New York (Hoover and Vernon, 1959),

If we think of the region as a huge conical structure in which altitude represents the concentration of human activity, we find Newark, Jersey City, Paterson, Elizabeth, Yonkers, and Bridgeport—each with a population of over 100,000—protruding as lesser peaks from its sloping flanks. Yet by any measure one cares to devise, the apex of the whole structure is on the island of Manhattan.

The growth and spread of similar cones around each city brought to the nation orderly rhythms of opportunity and welfare; as altitude fell, so did population densities, income, and educational levels, and the poverty population grew. The American people were aware of these rhythms. They responded by emigrating from low-income peripheries, and population declined in these peripheries. If the new migrant was poorly educated or a member of a minority group, his move placed him in a central-city ghetto abandoned both by whites and, increasingly, by employment. The flight of white city dwellers into the expanding peripheries of metropolitan regions is a phenomenon that is accelerating as minorities move toward majority status, and all evidence points to industry following population into the suburbs at an accelerating rate. The exurban fringes of the largest of the nation's daily urban systems have now pushed 100 mi and more from the traditional city centers. More important, the core orientation implied in use of the terms "central city" and "central county" is fast on the wane. Today's daily urban systems appear to be multinodal and multiconnected social systems in action.

The essence of any such urban system is its linkages and interactions, which are changed by changing modes of communication. Both places of residence and places of work are responding to the social dynamics implied thereby. At the same time, new communications media, notably television, have contributed, regardless of what local conditions actually may be, to the universal image of decaying central cities, the new home of the former residents of the now-emptied periphery: the immediate on-the-spot experience of their riots; the careful documentation of their frustrations; and acute awareness of emerging separatist feelings. It is no accident that the suburbanization of white city dwellers has increased, supported by rising real incomes, increased leisure time, and the acquired realization of what the central city is said to be. I have shown elsewhere that gradients of distance-accretion are now beginning to replace those of core-centered distance-decay within the larger megalopolitan complexes, as persons of greater wealth and leisure seek homes and work among the more-remote environments of hills, water, and forest; most aspire to "Marlboro Country" as an ideal. In consequence, core-dominated concentration in on the wane; the multi-node multiconnection system is becoming the rule. The spontaneous creation of new communities, the flows that respond to new transportation arteries, the waves emanating from growth centers, the mutually repulsive interactions of antagonistic social groups, the reverse commuting resulting from increasing segregation along city boundary lines as employment decentralizes, and all the other facets of social dynamics today combine to constitute the daily urban systems that far transcend the Census Bureau's narrowly defined SMSA's.

With processes of concentration and decentralization operating simultaneously, those who are interested in future trends are, of course in their element.

Kahn and Wiener (1967) conclude that major sprawl will meet major sprawl, so that

. . . the United States of the year 2000 will see at least three gargantuan metropolises, Boswash, Chipitts, and Sansan, which should contain more than half the U.S. population, including an overwhelming proportion of the most prosperous and creative elements of society.

On the other hand, Friedmann and Miller (1965) say

Looking ahead to the next generation, we foresee a new scale of urban living that will extend far beyond existing metropolitan cores and penetrate deeply into the periphery. Relations of dominance and dependency will be transcended. The older established centers, together with the inter-metropolitan peripheries that develop them, will constitute the new ecological unit of America's post-industrial society that will replace traditional concepts of the city and metropolis. This basic element of the emerging spatial order we shall call the *urban field*.

The urban field may be viewed as an enlargement of the space for urban living that extends far beyond the boundaries of existing metropolitan areas . . . into the open landscape of the periphery. This change to a larger scale of urban life is already underway, encouraged by changes in technology, economics, and preferred social behavior.

What are the underlying social preferences? When President Nixon recently extolled the work ethic, he was focusing on the idea articulated by McClelland (1961) that the drive for achievement is a variable of key importance within the American culture, a culture in which status and self respect come from what a person does in the material world, rather than from his ancestry of his holiness (McClelland, 1961).

Social and spatial mobility are one key, built into and interrelated within a person's nervous system as a result of the attitudes and pressures of the culture. Children must "get ahead" and "improve themselves" through education. Workers must ascent the job hierarchy. Earnings must be spent on the best possible homes and material possessions in the best possible neighborhoods. Any increase in job or financial status must be matched by a move to a better neighborhood. "Downgrading" of the neighborhood through entry of those of lower status must be fought, and if it cannot be contained, one must flee to avoid the inevitable resulting loss of status. To do otherwise would be to abandon the aggressive pursuit and the outward display of success; one must always fight to win.

When a family seeks a home they look also for other things. The prime decision relates to the home, its price and type, determined by achieved status and by the family's needs at the stage in life cycle that the choice is made. Because a large number of homes qualify within these first bounds for all but the poor, neighborhood considerations then come into play. The scale of urban regions has brought complexity, and the rapidity of urban change produces uncertainty and insecurity. The whole is too large for the individual to comprehend. In the search for self-identity in a mass society, he seeks to minimize disorder by living in a neighborhood in which life is comprehensible and social relations predictable. Indeed, he moves out of his neighborhood when he can no longer predict the consequences of a particular pattern of behavior. He seeks an enclave of relative homogeneity, a territory free from status competition because his neighbors are just like him, a turf compatible in outlook because his neighbors are at similar stages in the life cycle. He looks for a safe area, free from status-challenging ethnic or racial minorities; a haven away from complexity, to be protected and safeguarded by any means: legal, extralegal, institutional, and illegal violence. In Chicago, Father Lawlor's block clubs are matched by the baseball bats and billy clubs of Cicero and Back of the Yards, each a symptom of defensive territoriality protecting that which has been achieved.

The resulting homogeneous niches are exquisitely reticulated in geographic space. High-status neighborhoods seek out zones of superior residential amenity near water, trees, and higher ground, free from the risk of floods, away from smoke and factories, and increasingly in the furthest accessible peripheries. Middle-status neighborhoods press as close to the high status as feasible. To the low-status resident least able to afford costs of commuting are relinquished the least desirable areas adjacent to industrial zones, radiating from the center of the city along railroads and rivers, the zones of highest pollution, and the oldest, most deteriorated homes. In the cores of the ghettos, widespread abandonment of properties marks the extremes and neglect.

The whole is more a Balkanization than a melting pot. Individuals, and ethnic and racial groups are everywhere asserting their identity, and many see deepening schisms resulting (Mulvihill and others, 1969).

If present trends are not positively redirected by creative new action, we can expect further social fragmentation of the urban environment, formation of excessively parochial communities, greater segregation of different racial groups and economic classes . . . and polarization of attitudes on a variety of issues. It is logical to expect the establishment of the "defensive city," the modern counterpart of the fortified medieval city, consisting of an economically declining central business district in the inner city, protected by people shopping or working in buildings during daylight hours and "sealed off" by police during nighttime hours. High-rise apartment buildings and residential "compounds" will be fortified "cells" for upper-, middle-, and high-income populations living at prime locations in the inner city. Suburban neighborhoods, geographically removed from the central city, will be "safe areas," protected mainly by racial and economic homogeneity and by distance from population groups with the highest propensities to commit crime. Many parts of central cities will witness frequent and widespread crime, perhaps out of police control.

The most pervasive feature of urbanization today, and the principal source of internal dynamics of the nation's daily urban systems, is segregation—of land uses and activity systems, of income groups, family types, and ethnic and racial minorities—and the action space within which the interactions of opposing forces are being played out is the larger reality of the daily urban system.

THE FEDERAL ROLE IN DAILY URBAN SYSTEMS' GROWTH

What of the growth dynamics of the systems themselves? Again there are surprises. I have just submitted a report to the Commission on Population Growth and the American Future in which I examined these dynamics (Berry, 1971). First, I used the Office of Business Economics' approximations of the Daily Urban Systems (DUS) of the nation—173 in all, based on my research following the 1960 census (U.S. Bureau of the Census, 1969; Berry, 1971)—and calculated the 1960–1970 growth rate of each. I plotted this information in a graph against DUS size in 1960 (Figure 7), and found the following:

- The median population growth rate of successive size classes of DUS's increased progressively with size to a population of 1,000,000 and stabilized thereafter at about the national growth rate. This is consistent with ideas of the relation of size to self-generative growth. The median growth rates by size-class are as follows (U.S. rate 13.3 percent):

1. 100,000–225,000 = −0.9
2. 225,001–500,000 = 3.5
3. 500,001–1,000,000 = 10.1
4. 1,000,001–2,250,000 = 13.6
5. 2,250,001–5,000,000 = 13.7
6. 5,000,001–10,000,000 = 12.7

- The interquartile range was stable for size classes of less than 1,000,000, and above that point it was also stable for the lower quartile. The upper quartile was, however, markedly greater than elsewhere in the size class 1,000,000–2,225,000, indicating an accelerated take-off of many economic areas of this size range in particular.
- The median growth rate was negative in the smallest size class, as was the lower quartile in the size range 225,000–500,000, indicating that declining DUS's are disproportionately the smaller ones (compare Figures 5

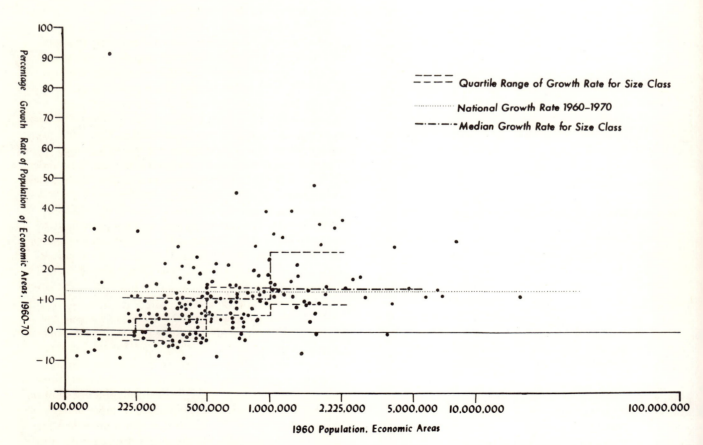

FIGURE 7 Relation of the population growth rate of Daily Urban Systems, 1960–1970, to their size in 1960.

and 6 again), focusing on lower-status wholesale–retail centers.

What are the factors associated with deviations from the size-related growth trends? We have already suggested that the hierarchical status of the DUS centers (metropolitan or otherwise) might be so correlated. What of differences in the economic base? As a result of a variety of experiments, we found useful ways of subdividing variables and of cross-classifying the data, and these are shown in Table 2.

The table indicates that either the federal government or residentiary (nonbasic) activities, or a combination of the two, were the principal source of earnings in the rapid-growth economic areas of the 1960–1970 decade. Together, the unplanned consequences of haphazard concentration of federal expenditures in particular places, and the rise to ascendency of the service sector, provided the propulsive sources of regional growth at rates greater than the nation in smaller DUS's in the decade. No longer was accelerated growth directly attributable to the emergence of new export industries or to successful competitive performance in basic industries in the classic sense. Whereas the major daily urban systems grew at about the national growth rate—itself fluctuating as a result of national fortunes and policies—the wider variations in growth performance of the smaller DUS's were the result, on the negative side, of a combination of increasing agricultural efficiency or resource depletion, and, on the positive side, of service-sector growth and the fall-where-they-may consequences of the federal dollar. What might then have been achieved, if governmental expenditures had been more judiciously planned? The pattern we see was the consequence of political pluralism and *de facto* laissez faire in public expenditure allocations.

GEOGRAPHICAL PERSPECTIVES ON URBAN POLICY

Charles F. Kettering, inventor of the first successful electric automobile self-starter, once described a "paradigm of progress." First, he said, they tell you you're wrong and they can prove it; then they tell you you're right but it's not important; then they tell you it's important but they've known it for years. All too frequently, society decides that something is important when it is no longer relevant. With these possibilities in mind, we should consider several propositions about contemporary urbanization.

- Urbanization today is to be thought of in the framework of a new geographic unit, The Daily Urban System, which is increasingly a product of communications-facilitated, racially driven decentralization; and preferences for open space associated with upward mobility in an achievement-oriented society. These Daily Urban Systems are multimodal phenomena joined by complex and varied links that are undergoing rapid and continuous change.
nomena joined by complex and varied links that are undergoing rapid and continuous change.

- Realization of scale and agglomeration economies no longer produces a greater-than-average growth rate of the largest Daily Urban Systems. Instead, the larger sizes converge on the growth rate of the nation.

- From a population of 1,000,000 downwards, there is a progressive decline in the growth rate with decreasing size and, presumably, lessening urban economies. Deviations from this declining growth rate are associated with increasing productivity and resource depletion in the primary industries on the one hand, and with the rise of the service sector and the haphazard pattern of fallout governmental expenditures on the other hand.

The impact of federal activity appears primary, not only affecting the national growth rate, and therefore the overall performance of the urban system, but also accelerating the growth of a variety of smaller places up to the point at which their size becomes commensurate with the performance at the national growth rate.

In the previous papers of this symposium, it has been pointed out that geographers have not only played important roles in the formulation of urban policy in the past, but that the spatial viewpoint offers a particularly salient perspective from which to view urban problems and to identify alternative solutions to those customarily advanced by advocates from other professions. John Borchert and Frank Horton have emphasized that in Minnesota, geographers, by means of their specialized research, helped to change perceptions so that concerted action could be undertaken at radically different new regional scales. These scales were responsible to revolutionary urbanization in the Midwest, moving progressively toward the level of the Daily Urban System. The result may well be an unprecedented ability to unravel the snarled and ineffective decision making that characterized the fragmented systems of local government. Minnesota is not unique. The Daily Urban Systems are now realities of life, but the spatial units we use to govern ourselves lag far behind.

Peter Gould reemphasizes the value of the spatial viewpoint and stresses that the perceptual maps that people carry with them may be more important to their actions than more objective assessments of the realities confronting them. A general example would be the idea that structure influences behavior through the mediation of cognition and that structure is, in turn, composed of those bundles of repetitive or sequential behavior that return processes. Perceptual bias affects not only the man in the street but also the public official and the elected representative. Many of

TABLE 2 Median Growth Rates of Various Types of Economic Areas, 1960–1970[a]

Population Size Class of Economic Area in 1970 (in thousands)	Median Growth Rate If Focus of Area Is a Center of Metropolitan Status (percent)				Median Growth Rate If Focus of Area Is a Center of Less Than Metropolitan Status (percent)					
	Source of Earnings in 1967									
	>12.5% Federal Government	>60% Residentiary	Federal and Residentiary	Diversified Sources	>12.5% Federal Government	>60% Residentiary	Federal and Residentiary	Diversified Sources	>25% Agriculture	Federal and Agriculture	>12.5% Mining
100–225	b	b	b	b	15.3	−2.05	c	8.6	−8.05	c	c
225–500	c	1.7	23.7	−3.0	9.7	4.9	c	4.0	−4.0	−2.5	−4.6
500–1,000	7.2	11.0	18.2	15.5	10.7	12.0	c	9.6	c	c	c
1,000–2,250	27.2	18.9	15.4	11.8	9.6	c	11.7	9.0	c	c	c
2,250–5,000	35.9	14.9	c	11.5	b	b	b	b	b	b	b
5,000–10,000	c	12.7	c	c	b	b	b	b	b	b	b
10,000 and over	c	11.1	c	c	b	b	b	b	b	b	b

[a]National Growth Rate 1960–1970 was 13.3 percent.
[b]No centers of this level.
[c]No centers of this type.

us have a biased view of contemporary urbanization, related to definition made according to late-nineteenth-century processes. Times have changed, and along with them the phenomenal nature of urban reality. Somehow the perceptual biases related to urbanization processes must be changed if we are to produce more satisfactory and more just urban lives.

The capacity to effect desired changes is within our grasp. The national growth rate can to some degree be modified by federal policy, and if the levels of governmental expenditures of the 1960's were sufficient to produce the most significant positive deviations of regional growth rates from the growth performance of the nation. What, then, can geographers contribute to an understanding of the desirable living patterns that might be achieved by alternative allocations of the federal dollar? On one scale, Julian Wolpert and his colleagues review his pioneering work on strategies for, and assessment of, community goal achievement. M. Gordon Wolman looks at environmental issues, relating attributes of the urbanizing physical landscape to the planner's art. Leslie King suggests the relation of stability to the diversification produced by increasing scale, and Richard Morrill considers the spatial aspects of following national equity goals rather than efficiency objectives and ends with discussion of growth-center strategies. I believe, however, that recent behavioral shifts are now actually producing the changes that Morrill calls for.

These contributions admit in common that today's societal problems are thorny ones and respond to them in a policy-oriented manner. They emphasize that although other scholars and professionals have much to offer to the cause, the spatial perspective of the geographer, with its focus on locational and environmental decision making, must become an essential part of the simultaneous and interactive efforts of a wide spectrum of talented professionals. The geographer's talent must be used in the truly interdisciplinary research enterprises that will be necessary if broader and better solutions to urban problems are to be achieved. And if there is a final message it is this: Cast aside your traditional perceptions of geography. It is now a refashioned, revitalized discipline, an increasingly policy-oriented social and environmental science.

REFERENCES

Berry, Brian J. L., 1971. Population growth in the daily urban systems of the United States, 1980–2000. Washington, D.C.: Commission on Population Growth and the American Future.

Current Population Reports, 1971. Series P-25, No. 461, June 28, 1971. U.S. Bureau of the Census. Washington, D.C.: U.S. Government Printing Office.

Friedmann, John, and John Miller, 1965. The urban field. Journal of the American Institute of Planners, 31 (1965), 312–319.

Hoover, E. M., and R. Vernon, 1959. Anatomy of a metropolis. Cambridge: Harvard University Press.

Kahn, Herman, and Anthony Wiener, 1967. The next thirty-three years: a framework for speculation. Daedalus, 96 (1967), 705–732.

McClelland, David C., 1961. The achieving society. Princeton: D. Van Nostrand and Co.

Mulvihill, D. J., M. M. Tumin, and L. A. Curtis, 1969. Crimes of violence. Staff report to the National Commission on the Causes and Prevention of Violence. Washington, D.C.: U.S. Government Printing Office.

Tisdale, Hope, 1941–1942. The process of urbanization. Social Forces, 20 (1941–1942), 312.

U.S. Department of Agriculture, 1970. Focus for area development analysis: Urban orientation of counties, Agricultural Economic Report 183. Washington, D.C.: U.S. Government Printing Office.

U.S. Bureau of the Census, 1969 (revised). Metropolitan area definition: A re-evaluation of concept and statistical practice, Bureau of the Census Working Paper 28, Washington, D.C.: U.S. Department of Commerce.

Weber, Adna Ferrin, 1967. The Growth of Cities in the Nineteenth-Century: A Study in Statistics. Originally published in 1899 for Columbia University by the Macmillan Company, New York, as Volume 11 of Studies of History, Economics, and Public Law. Ithaca: Cornell University Press.

Wirth, Louis, 1938. Urbanism as a way of life. American Journal of Sociology, 44 (1938).